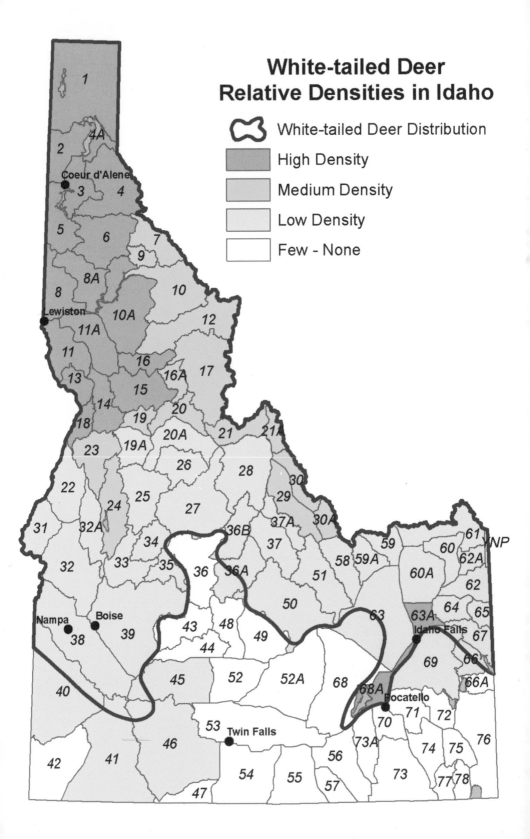

"One does not hunt in order to kill; on the contrary, one kills in order to have hunted. If one were to present the sportsman with the death of the animal as a gift, he would refuse it. What he is after is having to win it, to conquer the surly brute through his own effort and skill with all the extras that this carries with it: the immersion in the countryside, the healthfulness of the exercise, the distraction from his job."

Jose Ortega y Gasset, *Meditations on Hunting*

Books by this author:

Idaho's Greatest Mule Deer
Idaho's Greatest Elk
Idaho's Greatest Whitetails

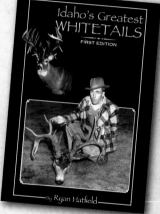

Coming soon:

Idaho's Greatest Mule Deer, 2nd Edition
Idaho's Greatest Trophy Game

# Dedication

To my grandma and grandpa - Rosie and Norman Kilborn. Thank
you for giving us such a wonderful family.

Also, to the Sniders (Paul, Sr., Paul, Jr., and Jack) –
Great people, great hunters, great friends.

Paul Snider, Sr. and a very young Jack Snider take a moment to celebrate a successful
Idaho whitetail hunt in the 1970s.

# WANTED

WE ARE ALWAYS LOOKING TO ADD TO OUR EVER-GROWING BASE OF HISTORICAL HUNTING PHOTOS OF ANY SORT, ESPECIALLY TRULY VINTAGE MATERIAL. WHETHER IT IS AN OLD-TIME RABBIT OR COYOTE HUNT, A HUGE ELK, OLD TRAPPING PHOTOS, BIRD HUNTS, OR HORSEBACK HUNTING AND CAMPING EXPEDITIONS, SEND IT ON IN! WE'RE ALSO GATHERING HISTORICAL IDAHO HUNTING MEMORABILIA SUCH AS OLD FISH & GAME LITERATURE, HUNTING EQUIPMENT, ANTLERS, AND OTHER MISCELLANEOUS ITEMS.

LASTLY, WE ARE BEGINNING WORK ON THE SECOND EDITION OF IDAHO'S GREATEST MULE DEER, AS WELL AS IDAHO'S GREATEST TROPHY GAME (INCLUDING SHEEP, MOOSE, MOUNTAIN GOAT, AND ANTELOPE.) IF YOU HAVE MATERIAL OR KNOW OF A LEAD WE SHOULD FOLLOW, PLEASE CONTACT US. PLEASE SEND FIELD PHOTOS, SHOULDER MOUNT PHOTOS, SCORE SHEETS, STORIES, HISTORICAL JOURNALS, AND/OR OTHER INFORMATION TO THE ADDRESS BELOW FOR CONSIDERATION TO BE INCLUDED IN UPCOMING EDITIONS.

SEND ALL INFORMATION TO:

## Idaho's Greatest Big Game
P.O. Box 2
Council, Idaho 83612
idahohunting@hotmail.com
www.idahobiggame.com
(208) 253-0002

Jess    Bonnie    Clarence    Patty    Donna

# Idaho Recluses

## Special whitetail print is the second limited print in the Idaho's Greatest Big Game Series

Herman Lunders
267-4/8 B&C Non-Typical
Idaho County 1955
State Record Non-Typical Whitetail

Ronald M. McLamb
186-7/8 B&C Typical
Bonner County 2001
State Record Typical Whitetail

John D. Powers, Jr.
257-6/8 B&C Non-Typical
Nez Perce County, 1983
Idaho # 2 Non-Typical

Alan Budleski
235-7/8 B&C Non-Typical
Kootenai County 2001
Idaho # 3 Non-Typical
(unofficial)

Idaho's Greatest Big Game
Collector's Series
IDAHO RECLUSES
by
Dallen Lambson

©2010 Dallen Lambson
and Ryan Hatfield

his fantastic drawing, titled "Idaho Recluses", was commissioned by Idaho's Greatest Big Game and drawn by nationally renowned artist Dallen Lambson of Pocatello. Dallen is the son of Hayden Lambson, one of the West's finest artists. As you can see, Dallen has come into his own as a top-quality professional.

This fine 16x20 work pays tribute to four of Idaho's greatest whitetails, allowing them to be together in their finest form. Featured are Idaho's top two non-typicals, a giant "unicorn" non-typical, and the state's top typical. It is limited to 25 signed and numbered artist proofs ($80 each) and 225 signed and numbered prints ($50 each). This is the second piece of a limited series that will accompany future releases of books chronicling Idaho's hunting heritage. We will reserve rights for customers wishing to collect identical numbers throughout the series, which will feature Idaho's greatest mule deer, elk, whitetails, and trophy game. Please call (208) 253-0002 or email us at idahohunting@hotmail.com to order.

# Acknowledgements

A book of this scale cannot be accomplished on one person's efforts. Without the willingness of the hunters and their families to share their stories and photos, we would not have this piece of history. For everyone that gave time, resources, memories, photos, and stories, I am truly grateful.

Thank you to the Boone and Crockett Club for permission to use their copyrighted scoring system and records. Some trophy listings in this book were compiled with the permission and assistance of Boone and Crockett Club. To learn more about the Club and its activities, log onto www.booneandcrockettclub.com. Thanks as well to the Pope and Young Club and to Idaho Department of Fish & Game for access to files and other information.

Special thanks to Dana Hollinger, Cabela's, Bass Pro Shops, John Stein, Michael Damery, Denny Diaz, Bill Lancaster, and others for access to their beautiful collections, photos, and information.

Many other organizations and individuals also provided photos, leads, information, or footwork: Thank you to Idaho Department of Fish and Game, Roger Selner of Trophy Show Productions, Eastmans' Hunting Journal, Steve Hornbeck, Sam McNeill, Jack Reneau, Mark Dowse, Lars Eidnes, Larry Carey, the Sniders (Paul, Jack, and Paul, Sr.), The Bonner County Sportsman's Association, Nick Clark, Mike Rainey, Brad Compton, Ralph Pehrson, Phil Cooper, Pete Gardner, Dan Hislop, Justin Webb, Brian Farley, Tracy Bennett, Craig Knott, Donald Vickaryous, Heath Hartwig, Russell and Karen Hatfield, Kylee Hatfield, and numerous others.

Special thanks also to Reflective Art, Inc. (www.reflectiveartinc.com) for use of many of Dallen Lambson's drawings, and to Dallen for providing beautiful work.

Last but not least, a very special thank you to all of the hunters mentioned in this book who were gracious enough to share their personal pictures and stories. The hunters that were able to participate in Idaho's Golden Era of hunting are the foundation and inspiration for this book and will always have my respect and adoration. Over the course of writing this book I had the opportunity to meet many great people and storytellers. It's a pleasure to be able to share their stories.

# Author's Note

To put together a book of this magnitude, the author has relied on hundreds of supposedly reliable sources of information. To help ensure its accuracy, all information was scrutinized, all leads followed, and all efforts made wherever possible to find the truth and the complete story. While every piece of information listed in these pages cannot be completely guaranteed, we believe its accuracy is as good as humanly possible.

If you are aware of any inaccuracies presented herein, have any additional information on listed trophies, have any information on trophy-class animals to be included in future editions, or know of old hunting stories and photos, please contact:

Idaho's Greatest Big Game
Box 2
Council, Idaho 83612
idahohunting@hotmail.com
www.idahobiggame.com

# Idaho's Greatest Whitetails

ISBN Number: 97809749766-2-4
Library of Congress Control Number: 2010900948

Published in the USA by:
Ryan Hatfield
Idaho's Greatest Big Game
Box 2, Council, Idaho 83612
(208) 253-0002
idahohunting@hotmail.com
www.idahobiggame.com

Cover and design by Chas Arthur www.chazmatic.com
and Ryan Hatfield.
Artwork by Dallen Lambson
Photography by author unless otherwise noted.
Printed in Canada by Friesens.

Cover photo: Herman Lunders and his 267-4/8 B&C
Idaho State Record Non-Typical whitetail.

Photo on inside title page: Rodney Thurlow's
jaw-dropping 238 B&C gross, 213-5/8 B&C net
trophy buck, taken in Bonner County in 1968.

**Find us on Facebook**

Just search for Idaho's Greatest Big Game

The purpose of this book, as well as the entire series, is to preserve a very important part of Idaho's history, and to pay tribute to some of the more amazing animals ever encountered in Idaho's mountains. It is not to promote or sensationalize the trend toward bigger is always better or more important. There's more to hunting than big antlers. It's all about memories and heritage.

# Idaho's Greatest

# Whitetails

By
Ryan Hatfield

Drawings by
Dallen Lambson

# About the Author

 yan Hatfield was born in Council, Idaho in 1972. He attended Council High School and has a Bachelor of Science in Forest Resources from University of Idaho.

Ryan is Managing Editor *for Eastmans' Hunting Journal* and *Eastmans' Bowhunting Journal*, the West's largest and most respected hunting magazines. He has also worked as Assistant Director of Big Game Records for Boone and Crockett Club. Previously, he spent time in the commercial fishing industry in Alaska and the forest resources industry in Idaho.

Being fascinated with hunting and Idaho history, it seemed a natural fit for Ryan to try and do something to preserve Idaho's hunting heritage. In 1998, he embarked on a journey still in progress – the attempt to preserve all possible stories, photos, and memorabilia associated with Idaho's hunting past. The first product of this was *Idaho's Greatest Mule Deer*, which was released in 2004. *Idaho's Greatest Elk* followed in 2006. *Idaho's Greatest Whitetails* now represents the third step in the series, which will continue on with more books in the future.

Whether chasing elk, deer, or a scenic mountain view, he is completely fascinated with Idaho's limitless beauty, rugged and diverse landscape, and storied history. He hails from a hunting and outdoor family who has roots in western Idaho since at least 1870.

When not working, writing books, exploring the outdoors, or spending time with his family, Ryan competes on the professional lumberjack circuit. He has been a member of the U.S. National Team many times and competes all over the United States, Canada, and Australia.

He and his wonderful wife, Kylee, have two awesome little boys, Owen and Wyatt. They hope to introduce both of them to a lifelong love of wildlife and wild places.

# Table of Contents

# Introduction

'll never forget my first "real" whitetail hunt. I was lucky enough to be tagging along with my friends, Jack and Paul Snider, two brothers from northern Idaho who, as you'll see later on in this book, are right up there with the best whitetail hunters in the state. Being a lifelong mule deer hunter, I was very excited to take a crack at something new, see some new scenery, and hang out with some great company. I had hunted whitetails before, but never even halfway seriously.

We made our way up some old logging roads and skid trails in very typical north-central Idaho whitetail habitat, and even more typical weather. It was November, of course, so the late fall rains were rolling through. This made for something that all Idaho whitetail hunters can relate to – the squishy sound of walking through that squeaky northern Idaho mud.

We reached our chosen starting point and Jack and Paul started strategizing how they were going to hunt this football field-sized sloped opening - completely within view - only 100 yards away. Me being the newbie, I "played along", thinking that they were pulling my leg. Any hunter worth his salt could easily see there wasn't anything up there but cheatgrass, rosebrush, and a little bit of blackberry. After a while, when the "joke" ran too long, it occurred to me – they weren't kidding. I listened as they plotted how they were going to hunt this miniscule little patch of nothing, and I began to have what maybe should have been a quicker and more obvious revelation - we weren't hunting mule deer; we were hunting whitetails. Yes, that was an obvious point, but I soon learned that the entire way they viewed their quarry and its habitats was different from what had made me effective as a mule deer hunter.

After a week of constant frustration (clothes ripped from star thistle, rosebrush, and blackberry; getting soaked from daily rains; and constantly getting my heart broken from getting busted by whitetail bucks before I could "bust" them), I had a profound new respect not only for whitetails, but also for dedicated Western whitetail hunters.

Hunters will argue which prey, mule deer or whitetail, are tougher to hunt for as long as hunting exists. Are whitetails more worthy adversaries than mule deer? I would contend that the answer is no. Not better, just different. Each animal has adapted to survive the best way possible in its habitats and from its natural predators. To take a big mule deer is no less difficult than to take a big whitetail. The routes to get there, though, are markedly different.

Whereas during a mule deer hunt you may get very few opportunities, the chances are that when it does happen, it will be a decent shot opportunity. During the course of a whitetail hunt, you can pretty well count on getting your heart broken several times, and seeing many bucks, with all of those chances being dismally poor. I suppose, in the end, they balance out about the same. Keep your betting cash in your pocket.

When even a knowledgeable hunter thinks about Idaho, whitetails are not usually the first thing that comes to mind. Big mule deer, great elk hunting – now that's Idaho. And the truth is Idaho's whitetail history is much more comparably young. Ask the old-timers in northern Idaho about hunting whitetails, and even they will tell you that it used to be that you usually only found whitetails in the valley bottoms, in farming ground, and closer to town. Mule deer were much more common in all the mountains around Sandpoint, up on Moscow Mountain, and many northern Idaho places that are now dominated by whitetails. Even while researching this book, coming across vintage whitetail information was tough.

Idaho's whitetail history, on average, is really only about 50 years old. It's been in these last few decades that whitetails have seriously taken over the north half of the state. Not only that, but they also have made serious pushes south, past the Salmon River and into hardcore mule deer ranges and habitats. It's now not uncommon to see them in the Salmon River Mountains, south clear into Boise, along the Snake River in eastern Idaho, in all sorts of agricultural areas, and in southern Idaho's sprawling suburbia. They have simply adapted better to human encroachment.

Another item that had gone in the whitetail's favor for many decades was that natural selection (or lack thereof due to absence of the wolf), had allowed whitetails to thrive in mule-deer-like terrain. Normally, their escape style would not do well in mountainous country, but since their main predation was now human, they began to thrive.

It's no secret that whitetails are among North America's most adaptable animals. From southern Yukon to Florida, and from Nova Scotia to Mexico, whitetails can fit in anywhere. Idaho is no different. Within Idaho's borders, whitetails can be found at 800 feet elevation along the lower Snake/Salmon/Clearwater Rivers to 7000 feet plus. They can just as easily fit in tall grass alongside an old hay barn as they can in dog-hair cedar patches in Idaho's darkest recesses. From Lolo Pass to Lewiston and from the Selkirks to Swan Valley, Idaho's whitetails have become a fixture, with no plans to vacate anytime soon.

After spending the majority of my life in and around Idaho, one of the things that amazes me the most is that Idaho's whitetail hunting continues to be one of the best kept secrets in the entire hunting world. Sure, occasional articles come out touting the Gem State's whitetail opportunities, but they come and go at about the same rate.

The truth is the hunter of average means likely has more of a legitimate chance of taking a mature whitetail in Idaho than perhaps anywhere else on Earth. When weighing public land percentage, private land access, mature buck ratios, ease of obtaining a tag, and trophy quality and potential, Idaho (along with Montana) may be the best "bang for the buck" whitetail hunting anywhere in the U.S.

While Idaho's mule deer population continues to struggle, and its most storied days of big mule deer are many years gone, Idaho's whitetail are doing well. It's not the boom of the '80s, but it's not that far off, either. Each year, I attend a few antler scoring events or "gun and horn shows", and it continues to amaze me the whitetail buck racks that come through the door. Take a look at the records book and you'll quickly see that the majority of those entries have come in the last three decades.

Idaho's whitetail history is comparably younger and perhaps a bit smaller than the mule deer and elk history in Idaho, but it's absolutely as important. Capturing that history, in words and photos, is a crucial part of keeping all those memories and that heritage alive. For that reason alone, this book was worth every ounce of effort put into it.

In very similar fashion to its two predecessors, *Idaho's Greatest Mule Deer* and *Idaho's Greatest Elk*, I became more shocked by the day at what I was able to turn up while researching and compiling this book. As you make your way through these pages, I'm sure you will be equally awed that Idaho could possibly have produced so phenomenally many truly giant, world-class whitetail bucks. I mean, come on; this is Idaho. But you can't argue with fact, and here it is, in full color.

As you read along, I'd like each of you to pay close attention to a common theme represented here. Story after story will show a high school kid killing a big deer on an after school hunt; or college buddies taking the big one on a whim hunt in the middle of the afternoon on a Saturday; or a teenage girl taking a huge buck within a rifle shot of her house on a ten-minute hunt before she had to go to school. What does it all mean? To me, it means that in a day in age where much of hunting is about money, big hunting leases locking up private access, Governor's tags, and catering to the rich, that Idaho is one of the few states whose history is built around everyday hunters with no special privileges just out hunting and getting lucky. Keeping "Joe Lunchpail" hunting and keeping hunting's base support (the masses) strong, vested, and interested is the key to ensuring the continued success of our hunting heritage. Teddy Roosevelt once said, "Those who are content to buy what they have, not the skill to get by their own exertions…these are the real enemies of game." American hunting was founded on the concept that every man, woman and child have access to similar opportunity, and I believe it's extremely important for all Idahoans to stand up to this trend and keep Idaho accessible to all.

Please note that some photos in this book are a bit questionable by today's print standards. It's generally not seen as acceptable to show hunters sitting on game, or posing with animals in pickup truck beds. However, this book is a history book, and while some of these photos aren't the most politically appropriate, they do represent the truth. They also help the viewer to paint a picture of that day that words cannot tell. As such, unless they were "over the top", they were included.

I hope you will truly enjoy looking at all of these tremendous historical trophies and fully appreciate the history each one represents. Collectively, they represent the finest results of millions of total days spent in Idaho's great mountains and prairies pursuing one of nature's most worthy adversaries. Individually, each one of these bucks might represent the dreams of a thousand hunters who spent hundreds of days each hiking to the tops of mountains in knee-deep snow; hopping in a Willys Jeep with old lever-action .30-30s, staking out scrapes in tree stands during a pouring rain; dragging a buck for hours down an old skid road; pushing the thickest brush patches, thickets, and dog-hair pines for buddies waiting "on stand"; playing sniper while waiting for a buck to come in to that old apple tree; untold numbers of shared campfires; and countless other days gone.

# Whitetails and EHD

## Periodic die-offs due to this indiscriminate gnat-spread pathogen are here to stay

A sizeable whitetail die-off in the lower Clearwater River region in 2003 prompted a bit of a panic for hunters and others concerned with wildlife. Suddenly, dead deer carcasses started dotting the landscape, and no one knew why. Deer from Lewiston to Riggins and Elk River to Kooskia all started turning up dead. A subsequent outbreak also killed a number of deer in Unit 8, east of Moscow.

After extensive research, it was determined that the easily noticeable result was caused by a nearly unnoticeable pest – a gnat. The disease killing these whitetails was Epizootic Hemorrhagic Disease, better known as EHD. It is spread by gnats, and can be fairly lethal in the right conditions.

This viral disease is normally confined to the deer family, but can occur in conjunction with a similar disease called Blue Tongue that affects domestic sheep and cattle. In human terms, the disease acts much like a flu bug, and is fairly common, but when combinations of conditions occur (i.e. a perfect storm), the disease can become much more widespread and deadly. Luckily, the disease does not affect humans.

Summer seems to be the prime time for EHD to rear its ugly head, coinciding with the height of the gnat population. After the first significant frost, it all but disappears. However, during its wrath, mortality rates can range from 20-80% of entire deer herds, meaning that while not common, the potential for disaster is always there. A high percentage of deer that survive in the affected areas will have immunity.

Following are some Questions and Answers prepared by Idaho Department of Fish and Game in regard to EHD. Please note that this is from around 2004.

1. **What is killing the deer?** The cause of death was confirmed as Epizootic Hemorrhagic Disease Serotype 2. EHD is a virus found in deer that is related to the Blue Tongue virus commonly found in domestic livestock. Visible symptoms of

EHD include loss of their natural fear of humans, loss of appetite, loss of activity and coordination, labored breathing, excessive salivation, unconsciousness, and ultimately, death.

2. **How did they get the disease?** EHD resides in a small portion of the deer population. It is spread from deer to deer by Culicoides spp. (gnats). There are three major driving forces in EHD outbreaks: 1) deer population and density; 2) level of immunity of deer to EHD; and 3) gnat population. In Idaho, about 10-15% of the deer sampled around the state have antibodies to EHD and thus are likely

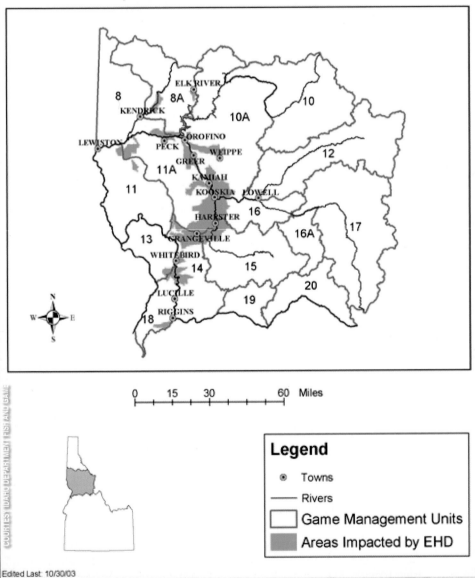

**Areas Impacted by EHD in the Clearwater Region (Confirmed or Suspected)**

Legend
- ⊙ Towns
- — Rivers
- ☐ Game Management Units
- ▨ Areas Impacted by EHD

Edited Last: 10/30/03

immune. However, conversely, about 80% of the deer in Idaho have no immunity to EHD. Gnat populations expand greatly during times of warm to hot weather that result in lots of wet areas due to receding water lines in ponds, streams, wet meadows, pastures, etc. Deer also tend to concentrate around water and shaded areas in hot weather. Since the majority of deer are not immune to EHD and the virus is in the population, and given high deer populations and deer densities, virus transmission via gnats is relatively efficient and results in many deer getting sick in a short time period and usually in a small geographic area.

3. **How many deer have died from this disease?** Estimates of deer mortality are limited. Personnel have removed several hundred carcasses from the Kamiah area. It is reasonable to estimate that carcass recovery is less than actual mortality. The actual death losses will never be known with certainty, but it is likely that as many as 2000 deer have died. Within affected areas, losses from the disease range from 20% to 80%. However, over the entire Clearwater Region, less than 10% of the entire whitetail deer population has been lost. Deer counts this winter will provide a much better picture of the remaining deer population.

4. **How long will the outbreak last?** Since virus transmission is dependent on gnats, anything that decreases gnat population, such as cool weather, will slow the rate of transmission. Gnats are not cold tolerant and frost will end the gnat life cycle. Reports indicate that infection rates slow considerably in the last two weeks in September.

5. **How common is the disease?** EHD is very common in deer in the U.S., especially in the southeastern and lower central parts of the U.S. The Midwest and Northeast are affected sporadically, with relatively large-scale outbreaks. In the West, outbreaks are known in most states, but the size and scale varies widely. In Idaho, EHD has occurred before and will likely occur again. Small outbreaks are known to have occurred in the Weiser and Peck areas recently. EHD outbreaks also occur in eastern Washington every three to five years. In 1996-97, 1000-1500 deer were lost in the Palouse area.

6. **Why don't we spray pesticides?** The gnat is widespread across the landscape. Appropriate breeding habitat is moist soil around shallow, stagnant water, including ponds, creeks, seeps, springs, flooded pastures, hoof prints that collect water, puddles, sprinkler overflow, water trough overflow, etc. The gnats can also fly up to a mile from their breeding sites. Spraying for gnat control is difficult. In addition, broadcast insecticide could potentially harm beneficial insects that are important for many species of wildlife and fish in the area.

7. **Will we have another outbreak in the future?** There is a good possibility that this disease could reappear in the future. The EHD virus is present in deer in Idaho. Deer density, population levels, immunity, and gnat populations drive the cycle. When these factors coincide, deer mortality will occur. Although up to 80% of local deer populations may die, the remaining deer usually have immunity, which will also be passed off to their offspring.

# A Brief Synopsis of
# Record Book Whitetails in Idaho

**W**hen most hunters think about Idaho, they think about big mule deer and lots of elk. In Idaho, whitetails have always been the neglected child of mainstream big game. However, the fact is that there are more quality whitetails taken in Idaho right now than just about any other big game animal.

The areas and options for looking for big bucks can be incredibly diverse. There are dense forests of predominately public land in the Panhandle all the way down through some of the wilderness areas, Palouse farm ground and canyon country that has limited access and much private land, river bottoms in southeast Idaho, and out-of-the-way nooks and crannies in non-traditional areas where whitetails may die of old age without even being hunted.

In stark contrast to mule deer and elk in Idaho, whose glory days have long come and gone, Idaho's heyday for whitetails was the decade of the 1980s. That being said, though, many big whitetails have been taken right up until a few years ago. Two horrific winters in a row in the Coeur d'Alene area, coupled with EHD disease losses in the Clearwater, have put somewhat of a screeching halt to those big bucks, though. The next few years will tell if we are just currently

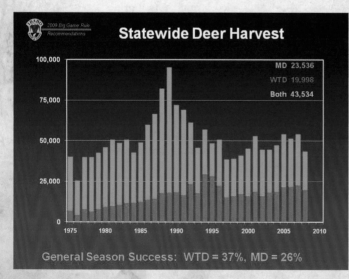

in a lull, or whether the faucet has been turned off.

Idaho has some excellent genetics for turning out non-typical whitetails and other freakish trophies. With lower typical minimums, those numbers for those trophies are much higher (as expected), but nonetheless, some of Mother Nature's creations here in Idaho can be pretty awe-inspiring.

While traditional hotspots throughout northern Idaho still reign king and always will, the ever-adaptable and opportunistic whitetails continue to spread to new areas and increase their numbers in fringe areas. The Swan Valley area on the South Fork of the Snake River, far southeastern Idaho, Lemhi County, Long Valley, Horseshoe Bend, and even clear down pushing into farm ground near the Owyhees, are just some examples of where whitetails are thriving at the expense of other big game, particularly mule deer.

The information in the following charts was compiled primarily through Boone and Crockett Club, Pope and Young Club, and Idaho Department of Fish and Game listings. While these numbers represent a decent portion of the picture, there are two variables out there that will always make it impossible to know the whole story. First, and more fixable, is that many hunters whose trophies would qualify at either the 160 typical or 185 non-typical minimums simply never have them scored. Secondly, the exceptionally keen and wily whitetail, with his wit and choice of dense habitat, is hard to kill. Many giant bucks are never killed or even found dead, and their history fades into the forest duff without so much as an acknowledgement. Just look at the shed antler section of this book for proof of that.

When looking at the data, the 1980s are far and away the best decade for big whitetails in Idaho. In the 1990s, it fell to nearly half of the overall numbers of B&C-class bucks. It has plateaued since then, although the 2000s potentially could see a very slight increase once stragglers come in later.

| Entries By Decade | |
|---|---|
| 1920s | 1 |
| 1930s | 2 |
| 1940s | 1 |
| 1950s | 6 |
| 1960s | 24 |
| 1970s | 31 |
| 1980s | 74 |
| 1990s | 40 |
| 2000s | 38 |
| Unknown | 5 |
| | 222 |

| Idaho's Boone and Crockett-Class Whitetails by County – All-Time | | | | |
|---|---|---|---|---|
| Rank | County | Typical | Non-Typical | Total Entries |
| 1 | Bonner | 20 | 19 | 39 |
| 2 | Kootenai | 18 | 16 | 34 |
| 3 | Nez Perce | 16 | 13 | 29 |
| 4 | Clearwater | 17 | 6 | 23 |
| 5 | Latah | 14 | 8 | 22 |
| 6 | Boundary | 11 | 6 | 17 |
| 7 | Idaho | 9 | 4 | 13 |
| 8 | Benewah | 5 | 6 | 11 |
| 9 | Lewis | 5 | 2 | 7 |
| 9 | Shoshone | 6 | 1 | 7 |
| 11 | Boise | 1 | 0 | 1 |
| 11 | Bonneville | 1 | 0 | 1 |
| 11 | Jefferson | 1 | 0 | 1 |
| 11 | Lemhi | 0 | 1 | 1 |
| 11 | Teton | 1 | 0 | 1 |
| | Unknown | 12 | 3 | 15 |
| | | 137 | 85 | 222 |

# Distribution of Idaho's
# Boone and Crockett Class Whitetails

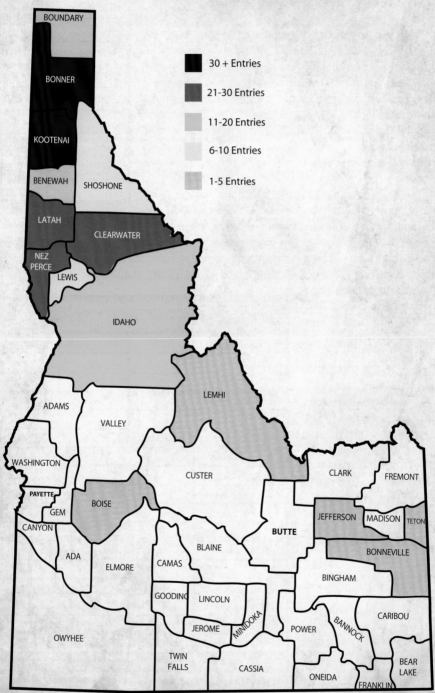

30 + Entries

21-30 Entries

11-20 Entries

6-10 Entries

1-5 Entries

# Idaho's Greatest Non-Typical Whitetails

## Idaho's Greatest All-Time
## Non-Typical Whitetails
## (Boone and Crockett Club Scoring System)

*Indicates that it has been officially scored but not submitted to B&C

| Rank | Score | Hunter | Location | Year | Main Beams R | Main Beams L | Inside Spread | Widest Spread | Bases R | Bases L | Points R | Points L | Abnormal Points |
|------|-------|--------|----------|------|---|---|---|---|---|---|---|---|---|
| 1 | 267-4/8 | Herman Lunders | Idaho County | 1955 | 26-6/8 | 27-6/8 | 29-1/8 | 35-5/8 | 5-1/8 | 5-1/8 | 16 | 23 | 94-4/8 |
| 2 | 257-6/8 | John D. Powers, Jr. | Nez Perce County | 1983 | 24-3/8 | 22-1/8 | 22-1/8 | 28-1/8 | 5-0/8 | 6-3/8 | 9 | 17 | 104-5/8 |
| 3* | 235-7/8** | Alan Budleski | Kootenai County | 2001 | 27-3/8 | 28-0/8 | 19-6/8 | 22-4/8 | 5-1/8 | 4-7/8 | 15 | 12 | 53-1/8 |
| 4* | 228-4/8 | Andy Cook | Nez Perce County | 1968 | - | - | - | - | - | - | - | - | - |
| 5* | 227-2/8 | Ron Morgan | Nez Perce County | 1992 | 26-2/8 | 26-3/8 | 18-6/8 | 23-5/8 | 4-4/8 | 4-4/8 | 11 | 13 | 34-4/8 |
| 6 | 226-3/8 | Hazel Bond | Nez Perce County | 1964 | 25-7/8 | 27-3/8 | 18-2/8 | 20-2/8 | 5-5/8 | 5-3/8 | 10 | 8 | 22-3/8 |
| 7 | 222-1/8 | Randy L. Clemenhagen | Latah County | 1995 | 26-5/8 | 26-1/8 | 22-2/8 | 27-2/8 | 5-4/8 | 5-1/8 | 11 | 11 | 47-5/8 |
| 8 | 220-2/8 | Steavon C. Hornbeck | Lewis County | 2000 | 26-6/8 | 27-5/8 | 20-2/8 | 26-7/8 | 4-7/8 | 4-6/8 | 9 | 9 | 28-6/8 |
| 9 | 219-7/8 | Kipling D. Manfull | Clearwater County | 1989 | 25-4/8 | 25-7/8 | 20-4/8 | 24-7/8 | 5-3/8 | 5-3/8 | 11 | 10 | 30-1/8 |
| 10 | 217-2/8 | Daniel V. Dodd | Benewah County | 1996 | 19-0/8 | 24-4/8 | 16-5/8 | 23-0/8 | 7-4/8 | 6-2/8 | 16 | 10 | 72-5/8 |
| 11 | 216-3/8 | Joseph S. LaPlante | Kootenai County | 2005 | 23-6/8 | 20-2/8 | 17-7/8 | 20-0/8 | 6-6/8 | 7-5/8 | 15 | 14 | 64-6/8 |
| 12 | 216-2/8 | Fred C. Colby | Bonner County | 2006 | 22-6/8 | 25-2/8 | 22-2/8 | 24-3/8 | 5-1/8 | 4-7/8 | 11 | 12 | 48-6/8 |
| 13 | 215-6/8 | Leroy Shaffer | Idaho | 1968 | 25-1/8 | 25-3/8 | 21-0/8 | 24-4/8 | 4-4/8 | 5-4/8 | 12 | 10 | 55-6/8 |
| 14* | 215-3/8 | Michael E. Young | Boundary County | 1986 | 25-0/8 | 24-6/8 | 15-3/8 | 19-1/8 | 5-2/8 | 5-3/8 | 9 | 10 | 32-6/8 |
| 15 | 214-4/8 | Don L. Twito | Idaho County | 1975 | 25-4/8 | 25-4/8 | 22-2/8 | 28-5/8 | 5-0/8 | 5-0/8 | 12 | 9 | 27-6/8 |
| 16 | 213-7/8 | Fred B. Post | Bonner County | 1978 | 29-1/8 | 29-2/8 | 19-3/8 | 23-6/8 | 5-3/8 | 5-5/8 | 8 | 9 | 20-6/8 |
| 17* | 213-6/8 | Scott Cook | Kootenai County | 1988 | 26-2/8 | 26-7/8 | 20-2/8 | 24-6/8 | 4-2/8 | 4-3/8 | 11 | 9 | 27-0/8 |
| 18 | 213-5/8 | Rodney Thurlow | Bonner County | 1968 | 27-1/8 | 24-6/8 | 23-6/8 | 27-5/8 | 5-4/8 | 7-0/8 | 9 | 9 | 52-1/8 |
| 19* | 208-6/8 | Toby Schnuerle | Boundary County | 1992 | 24-5/8 | 23-4/8 | 17-7/8 | 26-0/8 | 5-0/8 | 5-0/8 | 12 | 12 | 48-7/8 |
| 19 | 208-6/8 | Unknown | Idaho | PR1975 | 24-4/8 | 25-0/8 | 21-5/8 | 29-5/8 | 4-2/8 | 4-3/8 | 7 | 6 | 32-1/8 |
| 21 | 206-0/8 | Marion G. Macaluso | Shoshone County | 1993 | 24-1/8 | 25-1/8 | 17-5/8 | 22-0/8 | 5-3/8 | 5-3/8 | 8 | 11 | 32-3/8 |
| 22 | 205-1/8 | Clinton M. Hackney | Bonner County | 1990 | 21-0/8 | 22-2/8 | 14-6/8 | 25-6/8 | 5-0/8 | 5-0/8 | 12 | 13 | 57-5/8 |
| 23 | 205-0/8 | Lee Mahler | Boundary County | 1961 | 21-0/8 | 24-6/8 | 18-0/8 | 25-1/8 | 4-1/8 | 4-4/8 | 15 | 6 | 76-6/8 |
| 24* | 204-7/8 | George Hawkins | Idaho County | 1984 | 23-6/8 | 23-5/8 | 19-2/8 | 21-4/8 | 5-3/8 | 5-3/8 | 9 | 9 | 25-1/8 |
| 25* | 204-1/8 | Alfred Marshall | Latah County | 1990 | 24-0/8 | 22-3/8 | 21-4/8 | 23-7/8 | 4-6/8 | 5-2/8 | 10 | 9 | 37-5/8 |
| 25* | 204-1/8 | Aaron K. Penney | Nez Perce County | 2004 | 22-5/8 | 23-4/8 | 18-2/8 | - | 5-5/8 | 5-6/8 | 7 | 9 | 40-1/8 |
| 27 | 203-4/8 | Alfred P. Hegge | Kootenai County | 1929 | 24-4/8 | 25-2/8 | 16-4/8 | 19-3/8 | 5-6/8 | 5-5/8 | 9 | 13 | 54-6/8 |
| 28 | 203-1/8 | William M. Ziegler | Kootenai County | 1965 | 23-7/8 | 24-3/8 | 17-6/8 | 20-5/8 | 4-4/8 | 4-6/8 | 13 | 9 | 44-1/8 |
| 29 | 202-7/8 | Eric R. Steigers | Nez Perce County | 1973 | 25-1/8 | 25-4/8 | 18-2/8 | 21-0/8 | 4-7/8 | 4-6/8 | 10 | 10 | 36-7/8 |
| 30 | 202-4/8 | Picked Up | Boundary County | 1990 | 22-4/8 | 25-4/8 | 19-4/8 | 23-3/8 | 6-3/8 | 5-2/8 | 11 | 9 | 34-2/8 |

| Rank | Score | Hunter | Location | Year | Main Beams R | Main Beams L | Inside Spread | Widest Spread | Bases R | Bases L | Points R | Points L | Abnormal Points |
|------|-------|--------|----------|------|------|------|------|------|------|------|------|------|------|
| 31* | 201-4/8 | Picked Up by J. & M. Anderson | Clearwater County | 1987 | 23-3/8 | 24-2/8 | 20-4/8 | 23-0/8 | 5-3/8 | 5-3/8 | 10 | 11 | 38-2/8 |
| 32 | 201-3/8 | Leroy Coleman | Bonner County | 1960 | 21-1/8 | 21-6/8 | 21-3/8 | 23-4/8 | 5-2/8 | 4-6/8 | 16 | 11 | 33-0/8 |
| 32* | 201-3/8 | Monty Ewing | Lewis County | 1974 | 26-6/8 | 25-4/8 | 20-0/8 | 26-1/8 | 4-2/8 | 4-2/8 | 12 | 8 | 31-5/8 |
| 34 | 200-3/8 | Tim C. Baldwin | Nez Perce County | 1987 | 25-0/8 | 26-2/8 | 17-4/8 | 25-1/8 | 4-6/8 | 4-7/8 | 11 | 10 | 21-1/8 |
| 35* | 200-0/8 | Steve Myers | Latah County | 1981 | 23-0/8 | 21-1/8 | 20-2/8 | 24-0/8 | 4-5/8 | 4-7/8 | 8 | 11 | 44-4/8 |
| 36 | 198-3/8 | Milton R. Wilson | Nez Perce County | 1983 | 20-7/8 | 22-2/8 | 17-5/8 | 19-5/8 | 4-4/8 | 4-7/8 | 10 | 10 | 33-6/8 |
| 37 | 198-1/8 | Frank J. Cheyney | Kootenai County | 1967 | 24-6/8 | 24-3/8 | 19-6/8 | 23-3/8 | 5-5/8 | 5-4/8 | 10 | 9 | 23-1/8 |
| 37 | 198-1/8 | Luke D. Finney | Kootenai County | 1998 | 25-1/8 | 25-2/8 | 19-1/8 | 22-6/8 | 4-2/8 | 4-2/8 | 11 | 8 | 20-0/8 |
| 39 | 197-7/8 | Dean C. Weyen | Latah County | 1992 | 22-2/8 | 23-0/8 | 19-2/8 | 24-5/8 | 5-1/8 | 5-1/8 | 8 | 12 | 30-5/8 |
| 40 | 197-3/8 | Robert Zdenek Borysek | Bonner County | 2005 | 23-4/8 | 25-7/8 | 20-6/8 | 23-2/8 | 5-2/8 | 5-0/8 | 9 | 7 | 25-3/8 |
| 41 | 197-0/8 | D.L. Whatcott & R.C. Carlson | Kootenai County | 1980 | 24-2/8 | 26-4/8 | 25-3/8 | 28-7/8 | 5-0/8 | 5-1/8 | 8 | 9 | 18-3/8 |
| 42 | 196-6/8 | Jack S. Snider | Nez Perce County | 2004 | 25-2/8 | 24-6/8 | 19-5/8 | 23-2/8 | 4-5/8 | 4-4/8 | 8 | 8 | 29-3/8 |
| 43* | 196-0/8 | Picked Up by Sean Litteral | Benewah County | 1990 | 25-0/8 | 25-4/8 | 21-5/8 | 25-6/8 | 4-2/8 | 4-4/8 | 11 | 8 | 37-3/8 |
| 44 | 195-7/8 | Cecil H. Cameron | Latah County | 1989 | 23-1/8 | 23-4/8 | 19-0/8 | 21-4/8 | 4-7/8 | 4-5/8 | 9 | 9 | 26-1/8 |
| 45 | 195-6/8 | Picked Up by Brian T. Farley | Bonner County | 1994 | 23-0/8 | 23-0/8 | 17-0/8 | 18-4/8 | 4-4/8 | 4-1/8 | 9 | 8 | 28-2/8 |
| 46 | 195-5/8 | Paul S. Snider | Nez Perce County | 1989 | 24-6/8 | 24-7/8 | 19-2/8 | 22-1/8 | 5-2/8 | 5-0/8 | 10 | 9 | 19-3/8 |
| 46• | 195-5/8 | Kenny Charles | Benewah County | 1989 | 21-5/8 | 20-3/8 | 17-5/8 | 26-4/8 | 4-3/8 | 4-0/8 | 12 | 10 | 53-2/8 |
| 48* | 195-2/8 | Dave Steinbach, Jr. | Bonner County | 1988 | 25-3/8 | 24-7/8 | 20-4/8 | 23-6/8 | 4-5/8 | 4-3/8 | 8 | 10 | 26-6/8 |
| 49 | 195-1/8 | George B. Hatley | Bonner County | 1939 | 25-5/8 | 23-4/8 | 18-0/8 | 23-6/8 | 4-3/8 | 4-4/8 | 15 | 13 | 34-1/8 |
| 49* | 195-1/8 | Harold G. Larson | Latah County | 1982 | 23-2/8 | 25-5/8 | 21-5/8 | 24-0/8 | 4-2/8 | 4-3/8 | 7 | 9 | 17-2/8 |
| 51* | 194-5/8 | Unknown | Boundary County | 1989 | 24-4/8 | 24-4/8 | 19-5/8 | 22-7/8 | 4-7/8 | 4-7/8 | 11 | 9 | 37-4/8 |
| 52 | 194-4/8 | Jacob D. Lott | Clearwater County | 2005 | 25-7/8 | 27-0/8 | 21-7/8 | 26-6/8 | 4-5/8 | 4-5/8 | 8 | 7 | 16-5/8 |
| 53* | 194-0/8 | Jerry Gillispie | Clearwater County | 1981 | 20-4/8 | 23-6/8 | 23-3/8 | 27-0/8 | 4-7/8 | 4-5/8 | 15 | 6 | 43-7/8 |
| 54* | 193-7/8 | Gerald Madsen | Benewah County | 1986 | 27-2/8 | 26-7/8 | 20-2/8 | 22-4/8 | 5-0/8 | 4-7/8 | 8 | 7 | 13-1/8 |
| 55* | 193-2/8 | Marvin Hanson | Boundary County | 1984 | 20-6/8 | 22-7/8 | 19-3/8 | 23-1/8 | 5-0/8 | 5-0/8 | 10 | 9 | 32-1/8 |
| 56* | 192-4/8 | Deanna M. Dixon | Bonner County | 1992 | 24-3/8 | 24-0/8 | 18-2/8 | 23-6/8 | 4-4/8 | 4-3/8 | 9 | 7 | 23-6/8 |
| 57* | 192-2/8 | Gilbert Smith | Bonner County | 1973 | 25-1/8 | 27-0/8 | 21-7/8 | 25-1/8 | 5-0/8 | 4-7/8 | 9 | 7 | 40-5/8 |
| 58* | 191-7/8 | Gaylord R. Colvin, Jr. | Idaho County | 1957 | 21-6/8 | 22-7/8 | 19-2/8 | 23-0/8 | 5-3/8 | 5-2/8 | 11 | 11 | 19-1/8 |
| 59* | 191-6/8 | Rocky Mattison | Cook Creek | 1987 | 28-1/8 | 23-4/8 | 23-3/8 | 27-4/8 | 4-7/8 | 4-7/8 | 11 | 7 | 20-3/8 |
| 60 | 191-3/8 | Unknown | Lemhi County | PR1930 | 26-5/8 | 26-0/8 | 22-2/8 | 27-1/8 | 4-5/8 | 4-7/8 | 9 | 9 | 28-1/8 |
| 61 | 191-2/8 | Michael S. Emerson | Bonner County | 2005 | 23-3/8 | 23-1/8 | 18-1/8 | 21-0/8 | 5-5/8 | 5-6/8 | 9 | 8 | 29-5/8 |
| 61 | 191-2/8 | Picked Up by Luke D. Finney | Kootenai County | 2005 | 25-6/8 | 25-2/8 | 18-4/8 | 20-5/8 | 4-7/8 | 4-4/8 | 9 | 9 | 25-0/8 |
| 63 | 190-6/8 | Michael L. Albright | Nez Perce County | 2009 | 26-6/8 | 26-5/8 | 19-5/8 | 21-7/8 | 4-6/8 | 4-6/8 | 8 | 8 | 12-1/8 |

| Rank | Score | Hunter | Location | Year | Main Beams | | Inside Spread | Widest Spread | Bases | | Points | | Abnormal Points |
|------|-------|--------|----------|------|-----|-----|------|------|-----|-----|-----|-----|------|
| | | | | | R | L | | | R | L | R | L | |
| 64* | 190-4/8 | Donald S. Kline | Bonner County | 1980 | 23-5/8 | 22-0/8 | 17-5/8 | 21-2/8 | 5-0/8 | 5-3/8 | 10 | 10 | 29-7/8 |
| 64* | 190-4/8 | Mike White | Kootenai County | 1994 | 19-4/8 | 20-0/8 | 17-6/8 | 22-6/8 | 4-1/8 | 4-2/8 | 11 | 9 | 34-2/8 |
| 66 | 190-1/8 | Fred H. Muhs | Kootenai County | 1956 | 22-7/8 | 22-6/8 | 26-5/8 | 28-6/8 | 5-1/8 | 5-1/8 | 9 | 8 | 35-4/8 |
| 67* | 189-5/8 | Miranda Ross | Benewah County | 1990 | 26-1/8 | 27-5/8 | 19-1/8 | 21-6/8 | 4-7/8 | 5-2/8 | 8 | 7 | 15-0/8 |
| 68 | 188-6/8 | David W. Carver | Clearwater County | 1978 | 24-0/8 | 25-3/8 | 22-2/8 | 28-1/8 | 4-4/8 | 4-4/8 | 7 | 7 | 15-4/8 |
| 69* | 188-4/8 | Jason E. Gomes | Nez Perce County | 2002 | 25-3/8 | 27-0/8 | 21-5/8 | 24-1/8 | 5-0/8 | 5-4/8 | 6 | 7 | 11-7/8 |
| 70* | 188-0/8 | Leonard Butler | Bonner County | 1971 | 22-6/8 | 21-4/8 | 17-1/8 | 23-3/8 | 5-4/8 | 5-2/8 | 10 | 6 | 44-1/8 |
| 71* | 187-5/8 | Mike Rudeen | Latah County | 1952 | 22-3/8 | 25-3/8 | 23-3/8 | 25-4/8 | 5-3/8 | 5-3/8 | 7 | 6 | 13-4/8 |
| 71* | 187-5/8 | Lloyd Campbell | Bonner County | 1958 | 25-5/8 | 25-1/8 | 19-2/8 | 23-5/8 | 4-3/8 | 4-3/8 | 11 | 9 | 19-5/8 |
| 73 | 187-1/8 | Brad Corkill | Kootenai County | 1990 | 24-1/8 | 24-5/8 | 20-5/8 | 30-0/8 | 4-7/8 | 5-0/8 | 9 | 10 | 38-4/8 |
| 74 | 186-7/8 | Tami M. Van Ness | Latah County | 1990 | 24-0/8 | 24-3/8 | 17-5/8 | 21-0/8 | 4-2/8 | 4-1/8 | 8 | 6 | 20-6/8 |
| 75* | 186-6/8 | Kenneth R. Brown | Bonner County | 1977 | 19-6/8 | 20-0/8 | 16-7/8 | 21-1/8 | 5-0/8 | 5-4/8 | 15 | 12 | 42-3/8 |
| 75* | 186-6/8 | Johnny L. McReynolds | Kootenai County | 1983 | 24-5/8 | 25-0/8 | 18-1/8 | 20-2/8 | 4-3/8 | 4-3/8 | 9 | 8 | 26-3/8 |
| 77* | 186-4/8 | Lloyd Jones | Kootenai County | 1958 | 24-0/8 | 25-5/8 | 17-6/8 | 20-4/8 | 5-0/8 | 4-7/8 | 7 | 7 | 16-0/8 |
| 78* | 186-3/8 | Melvin Russell | Bonner County | 1939 | 20-2/8 | 20-3/8 | 16-4/8 | 22-2/8 | 5-3/8 | 5-2/8 | 9 | 8 | 32-7/8 |
| 79* | 186-1/8 | Ernie Andrews | Kootenai County | 1963 | 23-0/8 | 23-4/8 | 16-3/8 | 19-0/8 | 5-0/8 | 4-4/8 | 8 | 7 | 35-0/8 |
| 79* | 186-1/8 | Earl Nelson | Kootenai County | 2005 | 25-3/8 | 25-2/8 | 19-3/8 | 24-3/8 | 4-6/8 | 4-5/8 | 8 | 9 | 30-6/8 |
| 81* | 185-6/8 | Adrian Lane | Bonner County | 1961 | 21-6/8 | 25-1/8 | 21-2/8 | 25-2/8 | 5-0/8 | 4-6/8 | 10 | 7 | 33-2/8 |
| 82* | 185-4/8 | Nik Galloway | Clearwater County | 1992 | 24-7/8 | 24-2/8 | 17-7/8 | 20-5/8 | 4-7/8 | 5-0/8 | 9 | 9 | 15-7/8 |
| 83* | 185-1/8 | Darrell Tonn | Benewah County | 1975 | 24-4/8 | 26-4/8 | 17-0/8 | 19-1/8 | 4-7/8 | 4-6/8 | 8 | 9 | 14-7/8 |
| 83 | 185-1/8 | Nick Roberson | Nez Perce County | 1977 | 24-1/8 | 24-0/8 | 21-1/8 | 24-1/8 | 5-2/8 | 5-4/8 | 8 | 8 | 15-2/8 |
| 85 | 185-0/8 | Steve D. Spletstoser | Bonner County | 2004 | 23-0/8 | 25-0/8 | 23-5/8 | 25-6/8 | 5-3/8 | 5-1/8 | 11 | 7 | 33-5/8 |

## Highest Abnormal Point Total — Non-Typical Whitetail

| Rank | Hunter | Total | County |
|---|---|---|---|
| 1 | John D. Powers, Jr. | 104-5/8 | Nez Perce |
| 2 | Herman Lunders | 94-4/8 | Idaho |
| 3 | Lee Mahler | 76-6/8 | Boundary |
| 4 | Daniel V. Dodd | 72-5/8 | Benewah |
| 5 | Joseph S. LaPlante | 64-6/8 | Kootenai |
| 6 | Clinton M. Hackney | 57-5/8 | Bonner |
| 7 | Leroy Shaffer | 55-6/8 | Unknown |
| 8 | Alfred P. Hegge | 54-6/8 | Kootenai |
| 9 | Kenny Charles | 53-2/8 | Benewah |
| 10 | Alan Budleski | 53-1/8 | Kootenai |

## Most Points (Total of Both Antlers) — Non-Typical Whitetail

| Rank | Hunter | Total | County |
|---|---|---|---|
| 1 | Herman Lunders | 39 | Idaho |
| 2 | Joseph S. LaPlante | 29 | Kootenai |
| 3 | George B. Hatley | 28 | Bonner |
| 4 | Alan Budleski | 27 | Kootenai |
| 4 | Leroy Coleman | 27 | Bonner |
| 4 | Kenneth R. Brown | 27 | Bonner |
| 7 | John D. Powers, Jr. | 26 | Nez Perce |
| 7 | Daniel V. Dodd | 26 | Benewah |
| 9 | Clinton M. Hackney | 25 | Bonner |
| 10 | Ron Morgan | 24 | Nez Perce |
| 10 | Toby Schnuerle | 24 | Boundary |

## Widest Spread — Non-Typical Whitetail

| Rank | Hunter | Widest Spread | County |
|---|---|---|---|
| 1 | Herman Lunders | 35-5/8 | Idaho |
| 2 | Brad Corkill | 30-0/8 | Kootenai |
| 3 | Unknown | 29-5/8 | Unknown |
| 4 | D.L. Whatcott & R.C. Carlson | 28-7/8 | Kootenai |
| 5 | Fred H. Muhs | 28-6/8 | Kootenai |
| 6 | Don L. Twito | 28-5/8 | Idaho |
| 7 | David W. Carver | 28-1/8 | Clearwater |
| 7 | John D. Powers | 28-1/8 | Nez Perce |
| 9 | Rodney Thurlow | 27-5/8 | Bonner |
| 10 | Rocky Mattison | 27-4/8 | Unknown |

## Longest Main Beam — Non-Typical Whitetail

| Rank | Hunter | Long Beam | Other Beam | County |
|---|---|---|---|---|
| 1 | Fred B. Post | 29-2/8 | 29-1/8 | Bonner |
| 2 | Rocky Mattison | 28-1/8 | 23-4/8 | Unknown |
| 3 | Alan Budleski | 28-0/8 | 27-3/8 | Kootenai |
| 4 | Herman Lunders | 27-6/8 | 26-6/8 | Idaho |
| 5 | Steve Hornbeck | 27-5/8 | 26-6/8 | Lewis |
| 6 | Miranda Ross | 27-5/8 | 26-4/8 | Benewah |
| 7 | Hazel Bond | 27-3/8 | 25-7/8 | Nez Perce |
| 8 | Rodney Thurlow | 27-1/8 | 24-6/8 | Bonner |
| 9 | Jacob Lott | 27-0/8 | 25-7/8 | Clearwater |
| 9 | Jason Gomes | 27-0/8 | 25-3/8 | Nez Perce |
| 9 | Gilbert Smith | 27-0/8 | 25-1/8 | Bonner |

## Largest Base Circumference — Typical Whitetail

| Rank | Hunter | Largest Base Circumference | Other Base Circumference | County |
|---|---|---|---|---|
| 1 | Joseph S. LaPlante | 7-5/8 | 6-6/8 | Kootenai |
| 2 | Daniel V. Dodd | 7-4/8 | 6-2/8 | Benewah |
| 3 | Rodney Thurlow | 7-0/8 | 5-4/8 | Bonner |
| 4 | Picked Up | 6-3/8 | 5-2/8 | Boundary |
| 4 | John D. Powers, Jr. | 6-3/8 | 5-0/8 | Nez Perce |
| 6 | Alfred P. Hegge | 5-6/8 | 5-5/8 | Kootenai |
| 7 | Michael S. Emerson | 5-6/8 | 5-5/8 | Bonner |
| 7 | Aaron K. Penney | 5-6/8 | 5-5/8 | Nez Perce |
| 9 | Frank J. Cheyney | 5-5/8 | 5-4/8 | Kootenai |
| 9 | Hazel Bond | 5-5/8 | 5-3/8 | Nez Perce |
| 9 | Fred B. Post | 5-5/8 | 5-3/8 | Bonner |

# Herman Lunders
## 267-4/8 B&C Non-Typical
### Idaho County, 1955
*Idaho State Record Non-Typical Whitetail*

JOHN STEIN

| | | |
|---|---|---|
| **Idaho Non-typical Rank: 1** | **Abnormal Points: 94-4/8** | **Points (R,L): 16,23** |
| **Inside Spread: 29-1/8** | | **Widest Spread: 35-5/8** |
| **Main Beams (R,L): 26-6/8, 27-6/8** | | **Bases (R, L): 5-1/8, 5-6/8** |

**H**erman Lunders was born in 1910, and was one of eight children raised by his parents near Reubens, Idaho, in the fertile Palouse country farm ground. He spent 42 years working for the Camas Prairie Railroad as a section foreman.

He and his wife, Frankie, had 11 children between them, nine from previous marriages and two more together. He was 59 when the youngest was born.

He loved the outdoors and respected what a gift it was for all to enjoy. He hunted and fished to feed his family and for enjoyment; he was never a trophy hunter. One of his children, Betty, says she can remember having a wall tent and an old over-the-cab camper, trips to Red River Hot Springs, Lolo Campground, and elk camp at O'Hara Creek. He hunted most of his life with the same group of guys. Just like Herman, most all of them have passed away now.

As near as the family can tell, the buck was taken right around 1955, give or take a year. Herman was born in 1910, so he would have been about 45 years old. It was taken between Kamiah and Greer, on the north side of the Clearwater River.

Keith Lunders, a nephew, remembers what Herman told him about the buck. "Being a section foreman for the railroad, he was at work, but had his gun with him, which was not abnormal in that day and age. He and the crew were eating lunch on the tracks when a big buck and a few does swam the river, headed north.

"The story goes that when they reached the other side, Herman was going to shoot the biggest doe for meat, but his workmates convinced him to shoot the big buck instead."

Herman's gun of choice was a Remington .30-06 pump with a Leupold scope. He was very good with it. In fact, his son Butch said, "Knowing Dad, it would have been a neck shot so as to not waste any meat. Usually it would have been the head, but it was obvious with a scope he would have recognized it was special."

Butch went on to say, "Since Dad didn't have the money nor would he have spent it on mounting the head, he gave it to the Kamiah Gun Club. They agreed to have it mounted and displayed at the club, giving him credit for killing it. They did, it was, and it later disappeared."

**This photo, taken by the author along Highway 12 between Orofino and Kamiah, is believed to be within a mile or two of where Herman Lunders shot his historic state record whitetail. If you look close, you can even see the railroad track where Herman worked every day as a section foreman for the Camas Prairie Railroad.**

**Herman Lunders, still outfitted in his pinstripe work overalls, takes a moment to pose with his big whitetail. He never knew the significance of what happened that day, but in the typical mentality of people in that era, he probably wouldn't have cared much. After all, he wanted to shoot a doe.**

The history from there is a little bit clouded and convoluted, but it went through many hands after that. Being sold several times over and ending up in Texas, it became very difficult to track backward. At a bare minimum, it went from Johnny Nickel (a Kamiah resident involved with the gun club) to Jerry Rodriguez (an antler buyer) to John Stein (a collector) to Jack Brittingham to Aaron Koznetski, who is believed to own it now.

Some notes of interest on Herman's buck: At 35-5/8 inches wide, it's the fourth-widest whitetail in history. It's also the 24th-largest whitetail ever measured by B&C. Considering whitetails are the most hunted and most populous big game animal in North

America (by a good margin) and that there have been literally billions of them taken by hunters, that is an amazing statistic.

*A note from the author: Over 50 years ago, Herman Lunders did the unimaginable; he unknowingly killed the biggest whitetail in Idaho history. And nearly just as quickly, it all faded into obscurity.*

*For decades now the name, story, date, and other specifics surrounding this incredibly historic deer were simply listed as "unknown" in the B&C record book. Such entries are often circumspect, and particularly since it was our state record, it was really lacking in credibility. Regardless, for the people of Idaho, the family of the hunter, and other people who have interest in such things, it was a huge void.*

*As I began to research this book, this was the one glaring hole that bothered me the most and it's the one that I gave the most effort in researching. Following a lot of links in a chain and taking more than a few stabs in the dark, I kept trying.*

*Finally, I was led to Betty Cloninger, who was the step-daughter of a man named Herman Lunders, who I'd heard might possibly have been the man who killed it. It was an interesting phone call for both of us, but when she said that, yes, he was the one who killed it and that they actually had a photo of him with the buck from that day, I about hit the floor.*

*For days I waited with anticipation, until finally I received it over email (something Herman wouldn't have thought possible in 1955). As you can see, the photo is unbelievable, both from a classic, vintage photo perspective as well as a historical perspective. It gives everyone a chance to "know" Herman; it's conclusive proof that he was in fact the hunter; and it helps to paint a picture that no one else could possibly paint. The classic old-style hat, simple overalls, and handsome man holding his big deer all help to make it a fantastic photo.*

*Finding this information in time for this book was easily the most rewarding thing that happened in putting the book together. It also is the perfect example of why gathering this history and preserving it is so important. It may have never happened otherwise.*

*I owe a special thanks to Herman's family for helping with this. I know they were as excited as I was.*

Another view of Herman's deer, showing the crazy structure of the frame, the gnarly growth all over the lower main beams, and the enormous skull. The man holding the rack is believed to be Jerry Rodriguez, an antler dealer who at one time owned the rack and who may have purchased it from Johnny Nickel.

# John D. Powers, Jr.
### 257-6/8 B&C Non-Typical
### Nez Perce County, 1983

TROPHY SHOW PRODUCTIONS

**Idaho Non-typical Rank: 2**     **Abnormal Points: 104-5/8**     **Points (R,L): 9,17**
**Inside Spread: 22-1/8**     **Widest Spread: 28-1/8**
**Main Beams (R,L): 24-3/8,22-1/8**     **Bases (R, L): 5-0/8,6-3/8**

irst light crept over the eastern horizon, slowly unveiling the rugged, folded canyons and draws of north-central Idaho. Shapes began to appear; first trees, then rocks and smaller brush. Suddenly a black object appeared, backlit by the rising sun. At 1000 yards, the hunter filed it away in the back of his mind and went back to scanning his surroundings, hoping to find a good mule deer buck…

It was opening day of the 1983 deer season. John "David" Powers, Jr., 21, grabbed his .22-250, jumped into is blue Subaru Brat, and headed off alone for a day of hunting. He had seen a huge mule deer buck a couple of weeks earlier and had the buck ingrained in his memory, hoping for another chance.

David set up on a trail leading to an apple orchard where he had seen the big mulie. Some draws funneled together there and this location helped to cover a few good areas.

It was then, at first light, that he had seen the dark object moving toward him at over half a mile away. He gazed through his scope, but still couldn't tell what it was. He figured it was probably a black bear. Regardless, it was coming his way and light was improving, so he'd find out soon enough.

A couple of hours later, the "spot" showed up on the last ridge between them. At this point, David took another look through his Weaver scope and about died. It was a giant buck, but not the mule deer he was hoping for; it was an even bigger whitetail. The buck then disappeared in a draw between them and David got up and made time toward a spot he thought might get him within range.

Just as he was getting in position, a shot echoed from below. David was sick; he just knew that someone had beaten him to that huge buck. He stood still for a moment and then decided he might as well go down and see it up close and personal.

He wasn't being stealthy nor focused on hunting when he was suddenly brought back to reality. The big buck, still perfectly alive, jumped up 200 yards away! David quickly shot all five rounds before the buck disappeared.

David sprinted up to where he could look over the drainage and reloaded his rifle. He saw the buck again, which was now over 400 yards away. He shot until his rifle was empty again, and the buck went out of sight.

He hustled up to the last place he had seen the deer, and found blood. He followed until he found his buck, lying there in all its glory. A hunter just doesn't see a set of antlers like that very often, and he was overwhelmed.

After finally getting over staring at the antlers, he looked the buck over and found that he'd actually hit the buck with six of his ten shots. It was probably for the best; the buck had little left for teeth, and even though its body was very large, it was a little on the gaunt side. The carcass would later weigh in at 220 lbs.

TROPHY SHOW PRODUCTIONS

# Alan Budleski

235-7/8 or (243-7/8**) B&C Non-Typical
Kootenai County, 2001
**Including third antler

TROPHY SHOW PRODUCTIONS

**Idaho Typical Rank: 3\* Abnormal Points: 53-1/8 (61-1/8\*\*) Points (R,L): 15,12(14\*\*)**
**Inside Spread: 19-6/8** **Widest Spread: 22-4/8**
**Main Beams (R,L): 27-3/8,28-0/8** **Bases (R, L): 5-1/8,4-7/8**

 **I** was born in Wausau, Wisconsin and grew up on a dairy farm. Hunting was a big part of my life and whitetails were plentiful. When the leaves of the trees would brighten the skies with their multi-colored beauty, you could feel the deer hunting fever all over the area.

In mid November, the nine-day deer season (or holiday as most called it) would begin, bringing out young and old to try their skills at getting the big one. I have enjoyed hunting since I was twelve years old, and have spent a good amount of time studying various animals and their habits.

In October of 2000, I was offered a position with the Federal Railroad Administration as a Hazardous Materials Inspector. I took the job, and had to move my family across the country to our new home in Post Falls, Idaho. We had the good fortune to have many different animals visit us on the ten acres we called home, including whitetails, moose, bobcats, coyotes, and grouse. In the harsh winter months, we had the chance to see elk come down the mountain to find food.

I started to learn this new area as soon as we moved, and spent hours scouting out good hunting land. As I sat out on my deck in the evenings, I realized that there were some phenomenal animals very nearby. I noticed an 8-pointer (4x4) in the area and, with the pattern of deer movement, I felt the results could be promising.

When the season began, I found myself getting more and more worried. Where was that buck I had seen? Later into the season, as I walked into the kitchen, my wife looked at me and asked, "When are we going to get some venison?"

With only two days to go, I decided my priority would be to get meat and not worry about antlers. The next day I missed the early morning hunt due to my alarm clock not going off. Early afternoon would be my next chance to hunt.

As I stepped out of the door, snow began to fall. After setting up my stand, the flurries turned into a winter storm. Snowflakes were falling so hard that visibility diminished and every tree limb was covered with new fallen snow.

I decided it would be a better idea to try again tomorrow and started to pack up my stuff when I saw a deer walking at a fast pace. Her deep brown color stood out with everything covered in white. The way she was acting told me that there was something going on. I was right! Behind the doe was a 4x4, 90 yards away from me.

I waited and a buck finally stopped, put his nose to the ground, and raised his head toward the doe. I aimed for his neck, squeezed the trigger on my .270 Weatherby, and the buck dropped.

As I started walking closer, my heart began to race; something was definitely different about this buck. This was not the four-point I had seen moments before; he was the most beautiful animal I had ever laid my eyes on, and he was huge.

*Note: This buck is not currently eligible for B&C due to the third antler. If that rule were to ever change, the author feels the most logical thing to do would be to ignore the third antler in the score. Otherwise, the system would unfairly reward freak occurrences and put "normal" deer at an unfair disadvantage. If that happened, it is likely this buck would be entered into the book at its 235-7/8 score.*

**Alan Budleski poses alongside one of Idaho's most breathtaking whitetails.**

# Andy Cook

228-4/8 B&C Non-Typical
Nez Perce County, 1968

**Idaho Non-typical Rank: 4\***

ndy Cook set out at first light, hunting some feeder draws of a main tributary on the south side of the lower Clearwater River. He heard a shot some distance away, and only a few minutes later a commotion of crashing brush and hooves on rock came his way. He soon saw the perpetrator – a massive buck with a monstrous rack.

Andy fired a few rounds, but couldn't tell if he had hit the buck or not. With only one round left, he shot and dropped the buck.

When Andy's buck was officially measured, it won the annual competition of the Idaho State Trophy Club (a now defunct organization that was based out of Lewiston) and was big enough to be the state record. However, it has never been officially entered into B&C. Even now, over 40 years later, it still rates as one of the top whitetails ever taken in Idaho.

**Andy Cook's ultra-heavy whitetail is perhaps the single most massive buck in Idaho.**

*Note: Andy Cook's colossal buck from 1968 is one of the most impressive deer ever taken in Idaho. The mass is simply off the charts. Unfortunately, while this buck is listed in the IDFG listings, it is one of the only deer listed in this book for which no official score chart could be found. Therefore, there was no way to include any measurement data. It sure would be interesting to see what some of those circumference measurements looked like. A very special thanks to John Stein for going out of his way to dig up these old photos of this magnificent buck, and in turn providing a way for all Idahoans to be able to enjoy it.*

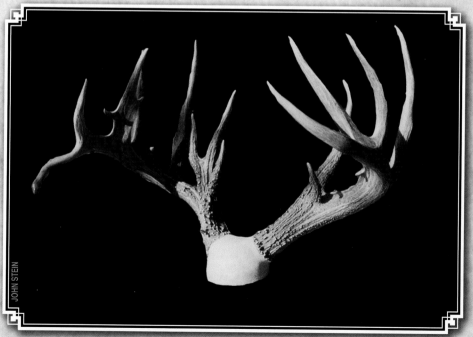

**Another view of Andy Cook's mega buck from 1968. Special thanks to John Stein for going the extra mile to dig up these photos, so that all Idaho hunters can see and appreciate this special buck.**

# Ron Morgan

## 227-2/8 B&C Non-Typical
## Nez Perce County, 1992

**Idaho Non-typical Rank: 5***     **Abnormal Points: 34-4/8**     **Points (R,L): 11,13**
**Inside Spread: 18-6/8**                                      **Widest Spread: 23-5/8**
**Main Beams (R,L): 26-2/8,26-3/8**                 **Bases (R, L): 4-4/8,4-4/8**

I grew up near Kendrick on my great-grandmother's 200-acre farm. From a young age, my younger brother Mike and I found ourselves riding motorcycles and shooting squirrels to pass the time. What a great way to grow up. Once I turned 12, my favorite pastime was hunting!

In October of 1992, I was attending college at Lewis-Clark State College and working part-time at the Lewiston Post Office. I was supporting myself and had gotten rid of a lot of my possessions to help pay for college.

One Sunday afternoon I had the day off and wanted to go hunting. It was a nasty, rainy day and I had tried calling a few friends to come along, but couldn't find any takers. I decided to go alone; what a day it turned out to be.

I left Lewiston in my 1980 Plymouth Volare Station Wagon (I had purchased it for $500 when I could no longer afford my Toyota 4x4), with my JC Higgins .30-06 my grandpa Boyd Eberhardt had given to me when I turned 12. I was headed for some of my old stomping grounds.

I decided to hunt at an area where I knew there should be some big deer. It was one of those spots where you frequently saw does, smaller bucks, turkeys, bear, elk - you name it. I had been there many times and always thought I should see a nice buck, but

never encountered one. This trip started out revealing the same results, but ended much differently.

It had been pouring rain all afternoon and I had worked my way down into the bottom of a canyon. I had seen a few does and some turkeys, but nothing that piqued my interest. Evening was fast approaching and I decided to start hiking out and working my way back to my car, since I had school the next morning.

I was about a third of the way out of the canyon when I stopped on the steep trail to catch my breath. While I stood there, I just happened to look over my shoulder at a small, flat, brush-covered bench 75 yard below me. That's when I saw a huge buck standing broadside and looking at me. I slowly raised my aught six topped with a Weaver 4x scope and couldn't believe my eyes. I had strange thoughts, like the rack was so enormous it must be a mulie or a small elk.

When I quit doubting, I had the crosshairs zeroed on the buck's head. I had shot some deer in the head, so as to not ruin any meat, but had missed as many more by doing this as well. I kept thinking, "I can't miss; I can't miss; no one would ever believe me!" I pulled the crosshairs back down on the vitals at the front shoulders and squeezed.

My heart sank when the buck lurched and took off. Had I missed? I couldn't believe it; I couldn't have missed! I watched as the buck ran into thicker brush and appeared to drop 25 yards from where it had been standing! Excitement overwhelmed me.

I started down the straight-up-and-down open hillside to the brushy flat the buck had dropped on. The rain had slowed earlier, but was now pouring again. Going down the hill, I was rushing but trying not to fall flat on my face. I'd take a step down and slide a couple of feet in the grass and mud because it was so wet and steep.

Once off the steep face, I started trying to work my way through the brush to where I thought the buck had dropped. Darkness was coming fast and it was starting to get difficult to see. I found where the buck had originally been hit, and found some blood and hair. I worked back and forth through the brush… and there he was!

By the time I got to the buck, it was nearly dark. He was lying in a thick patch of thorny bushes of some sort, but I reached in and started counting points. I counted 11 on one side and 13 on the other and thought, "That can't be right." I counted over and over again.

Once the initial shock wore off, I realized it was dark, raining, I was still by myself near the bottom of the canyon, and I needed to get this thing cleaned and out of there. I quickly field-dressed the buck and then started back up out of the canyon. While I walked out, I kept thinking to myself what an awesome animal I had just taken, and how upset the guys I had invited would be for not going. I was also hoping my dad, Dave Morgan, would be home. He had a Honda four-wheeler that would come in very handy for getting the buck out of the canyon.

Heading out of the canyon and nearing my car, it was raining so hard and was so dark that I walked into a barbwire gate across the road. I hadn't expected to be out so late and didn't have a flashlight on me. I knew the gate was there, but just couldn't see.

When I got back to my parents' house, I told my dad about the humungous buck I had shot and asked if he would help me get it out. I think the only reason he went was because he didn't believe me!

I went back in the way I had come out, straight down over the canyon face, so that I could easily get back to where I had left the buck. Dad rode the four-wheeler on an old logging road down to the area I had described. It took us awhile to locate each other in the bottom, but eventually we met up and got to the buck. When my dad finally saw the buck, he couldn't believe it either.

Though I've always regretted it, I sold the antlers to pay for my last year of college. I had enough leftover that I also purchased a new Ruger M77 .300 Win.-mag. with a 3-9 Leupold scope. I still have that rifle. Since then, Cabela's has acquired the antlers and has them on display at their Post Falls, Idaho store on a full body mount. I was able to get a replica of the antlers made and have a shoulder mount of them in my home.

**Ron Morgan's giant whitetail, taken on a solo hunt in the rain, is one of Idaho's best. It's also one of very few deer ever to sport a 7x7 typical frame.**

# Mrs. Ralph (Hazel) Bond

### 226-3/8 B&C Non-Typical
### Nez Perce County, 1964

**Idaho Non-typical Rank: 6**      **Abnormal Points: 22-3/8**      **Points (R,L): 10,8**

**Inside Spread: 18-2/8**                                                        **Widest Spread: 20-2/8**

**Main Beams (R,L): 25-7/8, 27-3/8**                                  **Bases (R, L): 5-5/8,5-3/8**

**W**hen Hazel Bond fired the shot that dropped her big whitetail in 1964, it was historic on many levels. First, at that time, it was the Idaho state record – the biggest Idaho whitetail of any kind ever entered into B&C. Second, it was taken by a woman. Few women hunted in that day, and for a woman to outdo the boys at that level was not without notice. Third, the buck was so big in an era where big whitetails were not the norm that this buck received the 3rd Award at Boone and Crockett Club's 13th Big Game Competition.

      Hazel Bond wasn't your typical woman. She enjoyed hunting as much as the men, and didn't need anyone to show her around or hold her hand. She knew how to shoot a gun – her husband Ralph had taken her target shooting for a long time before she got interested in hunting – and bagged a few elk, several deer, and much small game over her time. In an interview way back when, she said, "I love to hunt. The only thing I mind is that I didn't really get started at it sooner."

Hazel was hunting some mid elevation country a ways from Lewiston on November 1, 1964. She first saw this giant buck when he was coming off of a wooded ridge. The buck trotted into some thick brush and hesitated briefly before turning around and running right by her.

The buck was very close, and she had little time to think. With only time for one shot, she fired her .32-caliber Remington Model 141 with open sights and made it count. It would be the only shot she'd need.

*Note: Hazel Bond's great whitetail has a 204 net typical frame - one of the largest frames of any buck ever recorded anywhere in the western United States.*

**Hazel Bond loved hunting as much as any hunter, man or woman. Here she poses with a smaller buck, but her 1964 whitetail will always be one of Idaho's finest.**

# Randy L. Clemenhagen

## 222-1/8 B&C Non-Typical
### Latah County, 1995

**Idaho Non-typical Rank: 7**　　**Abnormal Points: 47-5/8**　　　**Points (R,L): 11,11**
**Inside Spread: 22-2/8**　　　　　　　　　　　　　　　　　**Widest Spread: 27-2/8**
**Main Beams (R,L): 26-5/8, 26-1/8**　　　　　　　　　**Bases (R, L): 5-4/8, 5-1/8**

**E**very year hunters venture into the woods with high hopes of taking a trophy such as this one, but very few will ever get the opportunity. I believe a mature whitetail buck is the craftiest big game animal in North America. He can quickly adapt to any situation. He's a survivalist, with a bag of tricks so deep the human mind may never find the bottom. I have no doubt that if it weren't for the rut, there would only be a handful of bucks of this caliber ever taken. Of the five years I hunted him, I would never have known he existed if it weren't for the rut.

　　It all started in late fall of 1990. I was hunting a small tract of private land and the season was winding down, but the rut was heating up. There was excitement in the air. It was a cool morning as I made my way up a ridge to a vantage point I liked, where I could see a few finger ridges and brushy draws.

　　As I scanned the area, I noticed movement above me. Although the deer were 700 yards away and moving at a slow jog, I had no problem seeing that the trailing deer was a buck - and what a buck he was! My heart automatically kicked into overdrive. When I pulled my gun up, I could feel my pulse pounding. This was a buck every hunter dreams of taking.

As the massive buck followed the doe across the ridge, I nervously waited for them to come into range. At 400 yards, they stopped. Without a rest, I knew I didn't stand a chance. I'd be wasting bullets and schooling him. From his size, I'd say he had a few years of schooling and didn't need me to further educate him with a foolish shot.

There was a small pine behind me, and I tried to get to it for a solid rest, but when I tried to slip back, the deer caught my movement. Within seconds, all my hopes had turned into a sick stomach.

After collecting myself, I headed up the ridge. When I came across their tracks, it looked like an elk and deer were traveling together. I followed them into a draw, but

it wasn't until I got into the thick of it before he broke away from me. With too much brush for a clear shot, I was left with nothing but a great and haunting picture in my mind.

The following year new hope was sparked when my brother found one of his sheds. He was every bit as impressive as I thought he was. When the rut hit full swing, I began seeing those elk-like tracks in the scrapes, and huge rubs were showing up everywhere. Though I devoted all of my hunting time to this area and tried many tricks and techniques, I couldn't catch him out in daylight hours.

The next year would prove to be an interesting one. When I noticed he had started to work the area, I decided to get there before light and set up by a scrape. Before shooting light I noticed a deer making its way down the trail. I could tell it was big, and through my scope I was sure I saw antlers. If he kept coming slowly, it would be light enough to shoot when he hit the scrape. As he came closer, he had to drop into a shallow dip barely deep enough to hide him, but that's all it took. Once again I was left sitting there in disbelief while he vanished before my eyes.

When it got light, I made my way over to where he disappeared, only to be assured by the huge track that it was him. For the next week, I never saw a sign of him. I don't know if he sensed I was there and was avoiding the area or what.

A week or so later, I caught a really nice typical checking a scrape but somehow managed to miss him. And so passed another season.

In the spring, I was overwhelmed with joy with the discovery of a set of sheds from the big non-typical. My day was shot; all I could do was look at those sheds. I lost all focus on what I was doing and finally had to go home.

In 1993, it was the rut before I saw any sign of him. He didn't seem to be working the area nearly as much as before. Time was running out, so I decided to try something different - devoting my attention to the does. I noticed smaller bucks were starting to check them, so I knew it wouldn't be long before the big guy showed up.

On Thanksgiving a big guy did show, but it was the huge typical I'd missed the year before. I didn't hesitate much before pulling up and dropping him. He was a beautiful 6x6 that grossed in the upper 170s.

The following season was filled with a great deal of sadness. I heard a rumor that someone had taken a massive buck near where I hunt. Fear became even more real when the season ended without a sign of him. I just knew he was dead.

When the 1995 season came, my hope of him being alive dimmed. However, this season held new life; it was the first year my son Malcolm could pack a gun. I was so excited! We didn't concentrate on one area, and only periodically checked the area where the big buck had been. It was hard to let that flicker of hope die.

Then one day while checking the old scrape line, we found one of those unmistakably huge tracks. I couldn't believe it; I was sure it was him. We started working the scrapes and adding scent to them, and noticed an increase of his presence in the area. I knew we couldn't afford to blow it this time, so we went with the safest plan - the old "sit and watch the ladies and wait" trick.

At first light on Thanksgiving Day, we noticed deer feeding along the ridge. We sat and watched as it got lighter. Soon there were a few deer, and one was noticeably larger than the others. When I put the glasses up, I knew it was "him".

They were well out of range, 800 yards away. With a lot of open space and the wind not in our favor, I knew we had a lot of ground to cover quickly. We would have to make a wide sweeping circle around the ridge and come in underneath them.

We hadn't gone far when my son whispered, "Dad, there's a buck!" To my surprise, there stood a great 4x4 75 yards away. I could tell by the excitement in his voice that he wanted to shoot. Many thoughts raced through my mind. Although the other deer were around the ridge, a shot would surely spook them. If he didn't shoot, the buck would likely

**Randy Clemenhagen invested several years and some major physical and mental effort into harvesting this all-time great whitetail.**

run to the other deer and spook them anyway. I also thought of how exciting it would be to watch my son take such a nice buck for his first deer.

He knelt down and shot, and the buck whirled and headed into the brush, not appearing to be hit. After a thorough check, it was clear he had shot over the buck.

We quickly went around the ridge and noticed movement. It was a doe feeding. When she put her head down, I got my grunt call out and blew it. Her head popped right up. She looked in our direction and then took a few steps toward us.

Another doe stepped up behind her and kept looking over her shoulder. I knew there was another deer, so I blew a few grunts. Within seconds, a huge rack appeared over the ridge. Trust me; words can't describe the adrenaline rush that overtook me.

He only gave me a head shot, and shooting offhand at 150 yards with a severe case of buck fever wasn't looking good. I tried to adjust, but nothing helped. Once again, I softly blew the call and he stepped forward. That's all I needed.

I slowly raised my rifle and touched it off. He dropped from sight, and I was sure he went down. I heard my son say, "Yes! You got him, Dad!"

I took off with all I had up through the brushy, steep slope. What should have taken me ten minutes took just a few seconds. When I got up to him, he was on his back with his antlers buried in the mud and grunting. As I tried to get around him, he started thrashing until he got loose. When he flopped over, I was only a few feet from him. My blood ran cold when I realized I'd only broken his back and he could still move his front end. As he partially got up with those wild eyes, flared nostrils, and rack full of mud and brush, my life passed before my eyes. I thought for sure I was dead, but he turned and lunged downhill, rolling and kicking his way down to a big brush pile. He got hung up and I put the final shot in him.

My son had caught up with me by then and we walked over to the big buck together. I'll bet we just sat there and stared at him for half an hour. Malcolm congratulated me about 20 times with handshakes, high fives, and hugs. I told someone later, "He darn near shook my hand off."

It couldn't have been better. My son is a wonderful friend and one heck of a hunting partner. I was so blessed to have him be a part of this hunt. I rode an emotional rollercoaster as we took pictures. I was overwhelmed with joy, yet waves of sadness swept over me when I realized the hunt had reached an end. What an incredible animal and an unforgettable hunt. Thank you, Jesus.

**Here are two sets of shed antlers from Randy's buck, mounted on real skulls.**

# Steavon C. Hornbeck

### 220-2/8 B&C Non-Typical
### Lewis County, 2000

| | | |
|---|---|---|
| **Idaho Non-typical Rank: 8** | **Abnormal Points: 28-6/8** | **Points (R,L): 9,9** |
| **Inside Spread: 20-2/8** | | **Widest Spread: 26-7/8** |
| **Main Beams (R,L): 26-6/8, 27-5/8** | | **Bases (R, L): 4-7/8,4-6/8** |

**M**ost of us define ourselves in terms of the passions that consume our thoughts and energies. For me, those passions long have centered on big whitetails in the Northern Rockies. My health has been enhanced by countless miles walked, with an occasional loaded pack after a successful hunt. I'd never have met my wife if not for a brief relocation to Montana, inspired by prior shed hunting results. My life is filled with friendships built around whitetails.

Interestingly, the circumstances of the kill contradicted a couple of the highest values I hold in whitetail hunting. First, I had quit hunting early that day. I had made my way to an isolated timbered bench, made my hunt and come up empty. After checking other spots, I had decided to head home. This hardly fit with my usual daylight-to-dark approach. Also, when I saw the deer, I was motorized, which is hardly my idea of a classic hunt. That morning, I'd borrowed my wife's Honda 90 to reach the bottom of a deep canyon before light. I've cursed the intrusions of "guys out for a ride" who have foiled my hunts and created no opportunity for themselves in doing so. But in this case, the bike likely was pivotal to my success.

I'd idled down the road at dawn, apparently less than 100 yards from this buck. The fact that I'd motored past him in half-light might have made him feel secure in staying bedded when I rode out that afternoon. Had I walked the road that morning, my footsteps on the frozen road surely would have alerted him, and he'd have buried himself in the brush.

Shortly before spotting this buck in his bed that afternoon, I'd been watching a very respectable mule deer that also was bedded. As I slowly road out of the canyon, I glanced into visible pockets as I passed the roadside brush.

As soon as I spotted my buck in his bed, I looked away and motored up to a point where brush again obscured my line of sight. I then rocked the bike back onto its kickstand and left it idling as I slipped my .270 over my head and off my shoulder and began slowly side-stepping down the road with my scope near my eye.

**One of Idaho's greatest-ever whitetails, in a tasteful "as it lay" photo.**

STEVE HORNBECK

**Idaho whitetail have adapted to steep terrain. This buck lived in picturesque country, where he no doubt spent many days surveying his kingdom.**

In the instant I'd seen him, my brain had registered "huge whitetail." As I side-stepped, I told myself, "Confirm whitetail, then kill him." I made eye contact with him through my scope and he turned his head, readying for a quick exit. This opened his shoulder for a clean shot, and in an instant it was over. It was 4:10 p.m.

As I watched the deer in his death throes, I was overwhelmed by the absence of adrenaline throughout the entire event. Awe and reverence best describe what I felt during the ensuing moments.

As I contemplated the work ahead of me, I met Colby and Brian Thomason, two 15-year-old cousins who quickly identified the buck as "the one we videoed this summer." They were congratulatory without a hint of jealousy, disappointment, or anger as we admired the deer and shared a Pepsi and coffee in celebration before heading home. I hope they each have their days of killing big bucks as well.

Perhaps the most interesting part of my buck's story concerns his shed antlers. Before I shot him, I'd heard a 200-inch-gross buck in the area had dropped his rack the previous year, but I hadn't known much more than that. Right after I got the deer, I received the first details from Nick Clark, an outstanding taxidermist who operates Clark's Taxidermy in Lewiston. Nick told me that a former employee, Doug Smith, had been turkey hunting when he'd found an exceptional set of sheds in the spring of 1999. Nick ended up acquiring them from him. When Nick and his nephew, Trever Yochum, saw my deer, they immediately said, "It's the Smitty buck."

In talking with Doug, I learned the sheds had been picked up four miles from where I'd shot the buck. Interestingly, the antlers had been shed at a higher elevation in midwinter than where the deer had been shot in late October.

Now armed with knowledge of where my buck's 1998 rack had been found and where he'd been killed, the question of his 1999 rack became prominent. We began to discuss making an all-out assault on the area between those locations.

Given the distance and difficult terrain, the odds were against us. Nonetheless, plans were made to comb the mostly north-facing slope as soon as the snow receded.

Snow held on abnormally long that spring, and it was March before Nick, Trever, and I started looking. We started the morning of March 11 by revisiting the kill site. We then worked the canyon in the snow but came up empty.

Early afternoon found us climbing out of the canyon separately and meeting up later. As the three of us sat there enjoying the day and pondering the impossibility of our mission, I casually scanned the snowy, timbered slope. "Bingo!" I shouted almost by reflex as a ribcage-sized left antler filled my view.

It's him! It's him!" Trever yelled when he saw the distinctive flyer point coming off the G-2, which was visible through binoculars.

Emotions made boys out of men for several minutes. We then went back to dissecting the hillside. After a position change to expose a different viewing angle, I spotted the other antler.

Comparing the sheds to the actual rack was fascinating. The 1998 sheds had a gross typical score of 194 and 15 inches of extras. The 1999 rack had a gross typical score of 182-7/8 and 16-3/8 inches of extras. The buck's rack from 2000 had a gross typical frame of 201-3/8 and 28-6/8 inches of extras – a massive jump.

A buck of this magnitude is rare, and to take him was a blessing. Every kill is the result of some blend of luck and skill. Dedication, effort and time spent in good areas are critical, but they can't guarantee the amazing rewards I enjoyed in 2000.

**This regal buck has one of the largest typical frames of any buck in the West, grossing over 200 inches. Three sets of his shed antlers grace the ground underneath him in this photo, taken by the author in 2004.**

# Kipling D. Manfull
### 219-7/8 B&C Non-Typical
### Clearwater County, 1989

**Idaho Non-typical Rank: 9**  **Abnormal Points: 30-1/8**  **Points (R,L): 11,10**
**Inside Spread: 20-4/8**  **Widest Spread: 24-7/8**
**Main Beams (R,L): 25-4/8,25-7/8**  **Bases (R, L): 5-3/8, 5-3/8**

hree years of chasing one particular animal is a long time, but when it's a giant record book non-typical, it can seem like eternity. Such was the case for Kip Manfull, whose dreams were haunted by such a buck during the late 1980s.

His fateful and final encounter with the buck to which he will be eternally linked actually happened upon returning from an elk hunt on October 22, 1989. He had killed a spike bull and was in the process of bringing it home when he happened to look out and see the buck out in a field. His two hunting partners for the day, his brother Chris and Joe Austin, dropped Kip off and left, leaving it up to Kip to go after the buck.

Kip managed to get himself to within 200 yards, but had only a neck shot since the buck was facing away. He shouldered his .25-06 and dropped the buck with one shot.

He was just starting to feel that overwhelming sense of joy and relief a hunter gets when he knows he's just dropped the buck of his life, when the buck jumped up and took off. Kip decided to back off and give the deer time to settle down before pursuing.

When he came back, he started trailing the buck, up to the point where the buck had jumped a fence onto some adjoining private property. Just then, a man came up to Kip. It wasn't the property owner, but another man who was keeping an eye on the place. He told Kip that he wouldn't let Kip come and get the deer until the next day. Kip tried to explain and negotiate, but the man insisted that he wait until the next morning. Kip had no choice but to acquiesce to the man's wishes, even though he had a bad feeling about it.

The next morning, Kip did as instructed and returned to the property. When he got there, he was met by the same man, who now had a rifle. At this point, Kip knew he had better go get the Sheriff. Sometime later, he returned with the Sheriff, Randy Pomerinke, and the man finally gave in and told them that Kip could go after the deer, but that he could only take a pistol – no rifle.

Kip returned with his brother to claim the deer, which turned out to be no easy task. It had rained during the night, eliminating most of the sign and all of the blood. Kip spent most of his search looking under trees, figuring the buck would have tried to keep dry during the rainstorm.

After quite a search, he looked up and saw a big fir tree. He walked up to it and saw a fresh deer bed that was still warm! He looked up, and there the buck stood, only 20 yards away! Kip had no chance at a shot before the buck took off and jumped another fence, this time off of the property. For the second time in about a day, Kip was devastated.

They continued to trail the buck for another half an hour, when Kip finally jumped him again. This time he was able to connect on two shots with a .44 magnum and finally brought the buck down for good. Coincidentally, the buck died only 100 yards from Kip's house!

KIP MANFULL

**This majestic and wily whitetail survived to a ripe old age fairly close to human habitation. Kip actually encountered this buck fairly close to home on the way back from an elk hunt.**

# Daniel V. Dodd

217-2/8 B&C Non-Typical
Benewah County, 1996

| | | |
|---|---|---|
| **Idaho Non-typical Rank: 10** | **Abnormal Points: 72-5/8** | **Points (R,L): 16,10** |
| **Inside Spread: 16-5/8** | | **Widest Spread: 23-0/8** |
| **Main Beams (R,L): 19-0/8,24-4/8** | | **Bases (R, L): 7-4/8, 6-2/8** |

F riendly brotherly rivalry has inspired many remarkable feats over the history of mankind. Whether small or monumental, seeing a sibling do something special can be a strong motivator for the sibling left holding the bag.

Such was the motivation for 29-year-old Daniel Dodd when he saw his twin brother, David, take a big whitetail buck. They had just parked the truck and were getting out when David spotted a buck and anchored it with his .270. Dan was more than a little bit surprised at the shot, and both were equally surprised when David pulled a great set of antlers out of a foot of snow.

Later, Dan found out that David was winning a big buck contest in the area. With family pride on the line, Dan figured he had better go out and see if he couldn't find a better one.

Dan went out with a co-worker, Brian Johnson, to the exact same area where David had just taken his big buck. At 6:30 a.m., they pulled up on top of a ridge north of

Tensed. Dan was greeted by a light snow, a decent wind, and the news that Brian was a little more interested in catching a few more winks than getting out in the cold.

Dan told him he'd work his way down the ridge and be back later. He then traced his way down the ridge, which just so happened to be the same ridge where his brother had taken his big buck. It was a travel route from some agricultural areas up to some more natural forest and brush cover, and they had been having luck hunting it from the top in the morning and intercepting bucks heading up to bed.

He was halfway down the ridge when he sensed something. He looked to his left and saw a buck running full speed downhill and quartering away. His first impression from the rack was that it reminded him of a caribou.

He shouldered his lever-action .35 Remington, picked a spot ahead of the buck's direction of travel, and as soon as hair entered his scope, he fired. It was a miracle shot that made contact before the buck disappeared. Then all was quiet.

He ran down and found plenty of blood in the freshly fallen snow. He followed it and found the buck piled up in a tree 20 yards away. It had died fairly instantly, because at that speed, just the momentum would have taken him that far.

He ran back up and got Brian, who was more than a little amazed and disgusted, all at the same time. They were able to drag it whole back to the pickup.

Dan's 1996 trophy buck is easily one of the most amazing bucks in the state. Its right main beam, split three times over, is as wild as it gets. Fish and Game later aged the buck at over ten years old.

**David Dodd took this big 160-class buck in the same spot only days before his twin brother Daniel encountered his historic non-typical.**

# Joseph S. LaPlante
## 216-3/8 B&C Non-Typical
### Kootenai County, 2005

**Idaho Non-typical Rank: 11**    **Abnormal Points: 64-6/8**    **Points (R,L): 15,14**

**Inside Spread: 17-7/8**    **Widest Spread: 20-0/8**

**Main Beams (R,L): 23-6/8,20-2/8**    **Bases (R, L): 6-6/8, 7-5/8**

**M**issing a big buck earlier in the season, Joe LaPlante had good reason to be a little disappointed. Being a senior in high school and busy with activities didn't help much with getting out to hunt more, either. Thanksgiving weekend was coming, though, and he'd have a few days to hunt rutting bucks.

The family was building a house, and hadn't moved in yet, but Joe and his dad, Mike, decided to hunt close to their new home. They left before first light, heading out into fresh snow and that feeling of anticipation you get when the first blast of cold air hits you.

They split up, with Joe following his normal hunting route, but it was hard to be quiet walking in crunchy and compacting snow. It was just getting toward first light and Joe made his way along a skid road.

He was 50 yards away from a property fence when he looked up and saw a buck. The light wasn't great, and he had trouble making out specifics. They stared at each other only 50 yards apart, with the buck out in the open. The intense stare-down lasted a full minute. Joe tried not to panic and hoped for the buck to look away so he could move.

Feeling as though he had no choice, Joe decided to risk it. He raised up and shot his .257 Roberts with open sights as fast as he made his target acquisition. The buck ran off, and Joe was convinced he had missed. It was 6:30 a.m.

He looked for blood and found some. He then went and got his dad to help. They came back and followed the trail, eventually finding the buck tangled up in the branches of a downed tree. It was only then that either hunter had a chance to see what kind of headgear the buck was packing. Suffice it to say that it was one huge, welcome surprise. Joe's big buck had 29 total points, and each one seemed to go a different direction than the last.

Joe has great respect for his dad and is very conscious about how important their time together is. For him, this will always be one of their most special days.

**Joe's jaw-dropping non-typical has some of the biggest bases of any whitetail in Idaho history. Beyond that, the buck has an unbelievable amount of character. So does Joe, who last time the author heard, was attending West Point.**

# Fred C. Colby
### 216-2/8 B&C Non-Typical
### Bonner County, 2006

**Idaho Non-typical Rank: 12**  **Abnormal Points: 48-6/8**  **Points (R,L): 11,12**
**Inside Spread: 22-2/8**  **Widest Spread: 24-3/8**
**Main Beams (R,L): 22-6/8,25-2/8**  **Bases (R, L): 5-1/8, 4-7/8**

O n a warm fall day in 2005, I was helping a friend clear brush around his property when I saw what appeared to be a nice looking shed antler. Even though it was chewed and weathered, it looked very promising.

I asked if it would be possible to put up a couple of trail cameras to see if I could catch a picture him and see what exactly he was wearing for headgear. Permission was granted, so I borrowed two cameras from a buddy and set them up in different locations, hoping the buck would still be crossing through.

For the first few weeks, nothing much was captured other than a few does and small bucks. Then it happened; I got one good shot of him. When I saw the photo, I about died. There in the photo was the largest buck I had ever seen.

In late summer of 2006, I set the cameras out again and started seeing the same buck. I started patterning him, but little did I know that about 30 other hunters were after him as well.

Now came the hard part - getting permission from the landowner to actually hunt the buck. He was a good friend and was fine with it, but his wife was not. I talked to her and explained that this was a once-in-a-lifetime buck and that many other hunters were after him. She finally said I could hunt the buck under the conditions: If I got him, she got to hang the mount up in the high ceiling area of her house. Also, I could not shoot any deer other than this one.

I started building two ground blinds in the river bottom 75 yards from the trails I had seen him using. I used natural vegetation and a couple of dead trees, and had a small but effective setup. For about a week, I would head out and be in the blind by 8 a.m. It was a bit late, but he was showing up at closer to 10 a.m. anyway, and I had to get the crew running at the brewery before leaving for a few hours.

**This is a live photo of Fred's trophy buck from November 14, 2005, a year before Fred finally took him.**

On a sunny and slightly warm day, I debated which rifle to take. I settled on my Savage Model 110G. I called my buddy and let him know I would be out again that morning, but would probably take a couple of days off after that and start again the following week.

As I arrived and walked out to the blind, Dan said he would come out with me and sit to watch and see what was passing though his place. As we walked down into the river bottom, a few does ran off. I kicked myself for not circling into the second blind, but by then it was too late, so I settled in to the blind I had been using the previous two days.

Two hours later a small four-point followed a doe about 200 yards away. Other than that it was very quiet.

Later, two does came up out of a small depression near the river. I hadn't even seen them cross the swampy area. As they crossed, I noticed antlers on a third deer. As he stepped up, I was breathless. It was him, and he was only 80 yards away!

I eased the rifle into position and tried to line up a shot, but he was straight on to me. I kept holding on his chest, hoping he would turn even just a tiny bit.

**Taken only days before their fateful encounter, this live photo may be the single most significant photo ever taken of a live whitetail in Idaho.**

As he started to turn, I was actually startled by the sound of my own gun going off! Instinct had kicked in and I had taken a shot. The buck had jumped up and turned, but immediately fell over. He had fallen victim to a perfect heart shot.

I would like to say I was overcome with elation, but in reality I felt humbled and somewhat sad. I field-dressed him in awe, and took great care to not cut too high, as I knew I was headed off to the taxidermist with this one.

The "Selle" or "Colburn" buck as he has been called, had been a ghost for many a hunter. I was simply the lucky one that fate decided to let meet him at 11:17 a.m. on November 17, 2006. I haven't harvested another whitetail since that day, choosing instead to let many pass by in hope that some other hunter may get their buck of a lifetime, as I did.

**Fred Colby holds up the antlers of one of Idaho's biggest whitetails. A shed antler tipped him off that a big buck was in the area.**

# Leroy Shaffer
## 215-6/8 B&C Non-Typical
## Idaho, 1968

**Idaho Non-typical Rank: 13**     **Abnormal Points:  55-6/8**     **Points (R,L): 12,10**
**Inside Spread: 21-0/8**     **Widest Spread: 24-4/8**
**Main Beams (R,L): 25-1/8, 25-3/8**     **Bases (R, L): 4-4/8,5-4/8**

**T**his is a huge buck that Dana Hollinger and Bob Howard bought in Idaho quite a few years ago. Unfortunately, they were unable to supply any history on this great-looking buck other than the name of the hunter. If you have any information on this buck, get in touch with us and maybe we can get it updated for a future edition of *Idaho's Greatest Whitetails*.

# Don L. Twito
## 214-4/8 B&C Non-Typical
### Idaho County, 1975

COURTESY OF BOONE AND CROCKETT CLUB

**Idaho Non-typical Rank: 15**      **Abnormal Points: 27-6/8**      **Points (R,L): 12,9**
**Inside Spread: 22-2/8**      **Widest Spread: 28-5/8**
**Main Beams (R,L): 25-4/8, 25-4/8**      **Bases (R, L): 5-0/8,5-0/8**

D on Twito was ranching in the Twin Falls area back in 1975. Fall is often a time when ranchers have a bit more time on their hands, so Don and his brother, Ken, loaded up four mules and two saddle horses and headed north for an October deer hunt on the Clearwater River.

They had been hunting for quite a few days and moved camp a time or two, taking their time and looking for a good buck. They ended up on the lower Selway, and had ridden up toward Fog Mountain for the day.

He and Don split up, and late that afternoon, Don looked up and saw a big buck out in the wide open. The massive deer took off, giving him the flag, but then stopped behind some trees 200 yards away.

Don could see the buck's head and neck, so he touched off a round from the old .30-06 and drilled the buck where the neck met its massive shoulders. With evening coming on, he made quick time field-dressing it and eventually packed it out on the mules. Ken was later able to tag a good buck of his own, as well. Of his huge trophy, Don said, "It was just one of those deals where you luck out."

Note: While there is no way to know for sure (short of DNA testing), several things about the antler conformation make you wonder if this buck could potentially be a crossbreed between a mule deer and a whitetail. With one G-2 measurement of 16-3/8, the deer has one of the longest points ever measured.

# Fred B. Post
## 213-7/8 B&C Non-Typical
### Bonner County, 1978

MICHAEL DAMERY

**Idaho Non-typical Rank: 16**    **Abnormal Points: 20-6/8**    **Points (R,L): 8,9**
**Inside Spread: 19-3/8**    **Widest Spread: 23-6/8**
**Main Beams (R,L): 29-1/8, 29-2/8**    **Bases (R, L): 5-3/8, 5-5/8**

*These are notes taken during a conversation with Fred Post in autumn of 2002, at his home in Coeur d'Alene. His wife Martha, Mike Damery, and Molly Rice were present.*

red Bartleson Post passed from this earthly realm he loved on January 1, 2003. Fred was the great-great-nephew of Fredrick Post, who visited the area in 1850, returned to Germany, and brought back his wife and three nephews; Fred's grandfather was one of the nephews. This great-great-uncle is remembered for founding Post Falls, Idaho. This is how Fred told us the story of his big whitetail:

Early on the morning of November 24, 1978, Fred ate a breakfast of bacon and eggs prepared by Martha before heading out the door for a winter's day of hunting. It had snowed about a foot the previous night. It was a partly sunny day on that first mountain west of Cocolalla Lake, right on the ridge parallel to the lake, leading up to that mountain. He carried his lunch in a fanny pack with all the equipment he would need.

Fred hunted through powder snow in semi-open timber. He had been hunting three or four hours before he spotted the deer. There was a large boulder in the area, and when Fred was about 25 yards away from it, the deer stood up by the boulder.

The deer never saw Fred. He fired his 180-grain bolt-action .30-06 Winchester Model 70 equipped with a 2-1/2 power scope. The shot hit the buck in the shoulder; he ran about 20 yards and then dropped.

Fred turned to Don LaVoie, his hunting partner for the day, and also the owner of the local Budweiser Distributing Co. and said, "I've got a job here."

The men took the antlers back to their rig, a new brown Suburban. Some other friends out hunting had a camper, so the antlers were placed in the camper, notifying them help would be needed. They then split the deer in half and each took one side and dragged it back, the snow making the task easier.

Fred and Don eventually took the meat down to the large cooler at the distributing company's warehouse. Fred made a call home at the first payphone they reached in Athol to share the exciting news with his wife. Martha commented that she thought Fred had been drinking. ~ Mike Damery

**Fred Post's deer tag from 1978.**

# Rodney Thurlow
### 213-5/8 B&C Non-Typical
### Bonner County, 1968

ROXANE JENSEN

| Idaho Non-typical Rank: 18 | Abnormal Points: 52-1/8 | Points (R,L): 9,9 |
|---|---|---|
| Inside Spread: 23-6/8 | | Widest Spread: 27-5/8 |
| Main Beams (R,L): 27-1/8,24-6/8 | | Bases (R, L): 5-4/8,7-0/8 |

uck, both good and bad, can be a real fleeting thing. No one knew that in the fall of 1968 better than Rod Thurlow. Right around the first of November, his business, "Vic and Rod's Tire", had burned right down to the ground. Scarcely two weeks later, Rod would finally see the pendulum swing his way, in the form of one of the most awe-inspiring whitetails Idaho has ever seen.

Rod, then 30 years old, loved to hunt. He also had a ten-year-old daughter that did not like to see her daddy go out into the woods alone. As such, whenever Rod didn't have a partner, little Roxane insisted that she go along – to keep him safe.

They woke up early and hopped into an old Willys jeep. It was new to them, however, and this would be their maiden voyage in it. Rod had shopped around for one with all the windows intact, and had finally found one that he wanted.

They were greeted by heavy snow, and the Willys gouged twin troughs as they pioneered a trail up toward Gold Creek. They parked, gathered their gear, and then headed up the hill, with the idea of stopping at some old stumps at the top of the hill where they could sit and watch an open pasture area.

They hadn't even made it out of sight of the Willys when a doe came across in front of them, followed by a mammoth-sized buck. They were on a dead run across the open space, heading for timber on the opposite side.

Rod took off after them while Roxane tried to fish the rifle clips for her dad's .30-06 out of her pack. Rod started shooting at the buck while heavy snow continued to fall, and exhausted more than one clip in the process. Finally, as the deer were nearly into the timber 400 yards away, Rod nailed the buck with a miracle shot.

Even though Roxane was only ten, she remembers that day vividly. She says the hardest part was the drag to the jeep, which was hard on both of them due to the deep snow. Even harder was loading it whole. Ironically, the buck's antlers were so big that by the time they got home, it had busted three windows out of Rod's new Willys; those same windows he'd tried so hard to find intact. He was pretty unhappy, but we can only hope that he found some solace every time he thought of the big buck that it took to break them.

**Rodney Thurlow's huge trophy whitetail actually gross scores a whopping 238 B&C, but due to major symmetry deductions only net scores 213-5/8. Still, it is easily one of the most stunning bucks Idaho has ever produced.**

# Marion G. Macaluso
## 206 B&C Non-Typical
### Shoshone County, 1993

**Idaho Non-typical Rank: 21**    **Abnormal Points: 32-3/8**    **Points (R,L): 8,11**
**Inside Spread: 17-5/8**    **Widest Spread: 22-0/8**
**Main Beams (R,L): 24-1/8,25-1/8**    **Bases (R, L): 5-3/8,5-3/8**

W hen Marion "Mac" Macaluso booked a guided hunt in Idaho with High Country Outfitters at a show in Erie, Pennsylvania, it was for elk, not whitetail. For a hunter from the East, whitetail was of little concern. However, when asked if he'd like to have a deer tag in his pocket as well, he said, "Sure; why not." He had no idea how important that decision would be in the outcome of his hunt.

They hunted hard for several days, and Mac was exhausted. It was rough, thick, cliffy country, and none of the ground he had encountered was sympathetic to his aches and pains.

On October 15, the final day of Mac's hunt, they were side-hilling through dense vegetation on a damp and misty day typical to the unfriendly confines of northern Idaho. They were still looking for elk, but the thing that kept running through Mac's mind was that the area they were in seemed like perfect whitetail habitat.

Just then, a big whitetail buck popped up to look at the commotion. The buck stared at them for only a split-second, and Mac had little time to think; he simply raised his .300 Win.-mag. and fired at the deer's neck. The 40-yard shot hit home, and the buck went tumbling down the hill. A tree stopped the freefall; otherwise, he would have gone way down into a hole.

Suddenly, Mac's tough and fruitless hunt had turned into a historic success story. They made their way down to the deer and were all stunned at the size. It wasn't an elk; it just looked like one.

The pack out would have been miserable, but luckily they had a pack train of horses and mules to get the job done. That was no sad news for an exhausted hunter from Pennsylvania.

By the way, Mac didn't get his elk. He seems to be okay with it, though.

**Mac Macaluso came all the way from Pennsylvania for a guided elk hunt, and bought a deer tag almost as an afterthought. It's a good thing he did. This buck is the largest ever to come from Shoshone County.**

# Clinton M. Hackney
## 205-1/8 B&C Non-Typical
### Bonner County, 1990

**Idaho Non-typical Rank: 22**    **Abnormal Points: 57-5/8**    **Points (R,L): 12,13**
**Inside Spread: 14-6/8**                                        **Widest Spread: 25-6/8**
**Main Beams (R,L): 21-0/8,22-2/8**                              **Bases (R, L): 5-0/8,5-0/8**

ourteen-year-old Clinton Hackney was about as excited for whitetail deer hunting as any kid growing up in the mountains of northern Idaho. He hunted hard, but hadn't had any luck yet. He'd seen the track of a big buck near his home, and had tried hard to find him, but the best he'd come up with so far was part of a big shed antler.

In mid November, he had an open day away from school, but after several days of already giving his all, he was more than just a little bit discouraged. His dad, Clifford, sensed it, and told Clinton, "You're not gonna kill anything by sitting in the house. You ought to at least go up to the field and sit and see if anything comes by at dusk. It's only an hour or two."

Clinton knew his dad was right, so he gathered up his things and headed out to do just that. He had his Russian 7.62x54 and enough clothes to keep him warm, so he went and staked out a big pasture opening.

He could scarcely believe his eyes when he looked up and saw what he first thought had to be an elk on the far side of the field 150 yards away. It didn't take him long to realize that this was no elk; it was the huge whitetail buck he'd been after!

Without hesitation, he raised his rifle, aimed, and fired. The buck didn't flinch. Clinton fired again with the same exact result. Panicked, he fired one more time and then watched his trophy buck walk into the timber.

He looked for blood, and found a small amount, but even using a flashlight long after light was gone, no buck surfaced. With visions of that big buck in his sights, that was one long night for a young hunter.

The next morning, Clinton headed back out to resume the blood trail, along with his dad, mom, and uncle. They tracked and ultimately found the buck, much to Clinton's delight and his family's amazement.

Clinton's buck was an exceptionally old deer. He had little left for teeth and may have been blind in one eye.

# Lee Mahler
## 205 B&C Non-Typical
### Boundary County, 1961

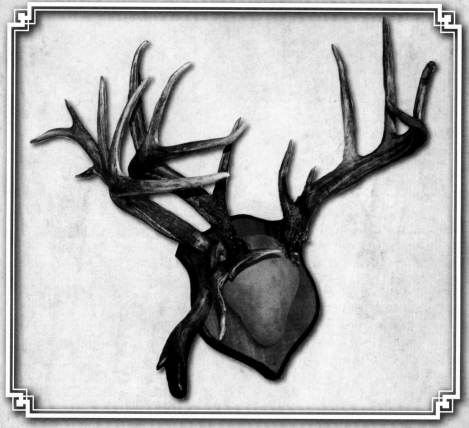

**Idaho Non-typical Rank: 23**        **Abnormal Points: 76-6/8**        **Points (R,L): 15,6**

**Inside Spread: 18-0/8**                                               **Widest Spread: 25-1/8**

**Main Beams (R,L): 21-0/8,25-1/8**                      **Bases (R, L): 4-1/8,4-4/8**

B ack in the '60s, the percentage of mule deer in northern Idaho was significantly higher than it is today. In fact, Lee Mahler, who has hunted for many years in the Sandpoint area, says that they only killed a whitetail once in awhile back in his younger days. Whitetails generally stuck to the valley bottoms.

In mid November of 1961, Lee, along with Bill Mackey, Harold McNally, and another hunter, decided to hunt those lower areas for whitetail. They were in the Copeland area, just south of the Canadian border. It had been a mild fall up to that point, with no snow for tracking.

Two hunters, including Lee, were on stand while the other two put on a drive. Lee had been in position and standing behind a tree for half an hour when he saw a deer come loping across a field. The buck stopped right behind an old apple tree.

Lee waited patiently until the wary old buck stepped out, and then he shot him right in the neck at 100 yards with his Browning semi-automatic .30-06. He had no idea until he walked up to his trophy how big it was, and says that the body was as big and impressive as the antlers. He didn't know what to think.

The men came over to see what Lee had shot, and he yelled out, "Hey, Bill; I think I'm in trouble."

"Why?" Bill replied.

"I think I just shot a caribou!" Lee joked.

The men all came over to investigate and were amazed at what they saw. Lee says they were all pretty excited about it, and with good reason. At that time, Lee's buck was the largest whitetail ever taken in the panhandle area.

Author's note: Lee's buck, with three "antlers" all coming out of the same base, is one of the more amazing and unique trophies you may ever see. This type of trait, where the main beam seemingly splits multiple times and forms separate and often fully developed antlers, seems to express itself most often in whitetails.

**This clipping was provided by Fred Scott, who killed the #3 non-typical elk in Idaho. The caption that went with the clipping said, "MANY-ANTLERED WHITETAIL – A very unusual whitetail buck boasting three sets of antlers on the right side of his head was killed recently by Lee Mahler, Bonners Ferry, Idaho. Two of the 'extra' racks show almost perfect conformation. Deer was shot near Bonners Ferry."**

# Alfred Marshall
## 204-1/8 B&C Non-Typical
### Latah County, 1990

| Idaho Non-typical Rank: 25* | Abnormal Points: 37-5/8 | Points (R,L): 10,9 |
| --- | --- | --- |
| Inside Spread: 21-4/8 | | Widest Spread: 23-7/8 |
| Main Beams (R,L): 24-0/8,22-3/8 | | Bases (R, L): 4-6/8,5-2/8 |

 nly a junior in high school, Alfred Marshall wasn't exactly a seasoned hunter yet. In fact, he'd taken a grand total of one deer at that point in his budding hunting career – a doe. His upbringing was as a meat hunter, so that was just fine with him.

He was still hoping for his first buck that November day in 1990 when he and his high school friend, Shane Anderson, went out on a quick after school hunt in northwest Latah County. There was only about a half-hour of light to really try anything, so Alfred quickly grabbed his Savage .30-06 and he and Shane took off from the house.

They were about half a mile from the house and on the four-wheeler when Shane said that he thought he saw something. They stopped and then scrambled for the top, which was an open, grassy field. Shane pulled up and took a shot, but evidently missed. That's when Alfred saw a buck and a doe running.

He pulled up and fired a round, and to both boys' disbelief, the buck dropped right there in sight. It was 150 yards or so, and somewhat of a miracle shot. The boys ran over there and were pretty excited.

Alfred thought it was a nice buck, but really didn't think much more about it. They dressed it out and then loaded it onto their four-wheeler and took it back to the house.

**Alfred's big whitetail, like many deer in this book, was taken on an after-school hunt.**

It was when they showed up there and Alfred's brother-in-law saw it and started freaking out that he had his first clue that he might have done something out of the ordinary. Many comments later from several different people and it really started to sink in that this buck was significant.

That spring, his big buck won the coveted buckle at the Big Horn Show in Spokane, an honor bestowed on just the most fortunate of hunters in the region.

# Aaron K. Penney
## 204-1/8 B&C Non-Typical
### Nez Perce County, 2004

**Idaho Non-typical Rank: 25\***  **Abnormal Points:  40-1/8**  **Points (R,L): 7,9**
**Inside Spread: 18-2/8**  **Widest Spread: N/A**
**Main Beams (R,L): 22-5/8,23-4/8**  **Bases (R, L): 5-5/8,5-6/8**

N ovember 18, 2004 came with two inches of fresh snow.  I spent the morning running errands in town, anticipating spending my afternoon buck hunting.  I knew the whitetail rut was gaining momentum, and soon bucks would be carelessly chasing does.

I returned home, loaded my gear, and grabbed my Marlin .30-30 lever action topped off with a 4x scope. Since I was planning on hiking, trailing buck tracks, and watching scrape lines, I decided a good brush gun would be my choice for the day.

I arrived at 2 p.m. near an area where two years earlier I had taken a nice 6x6 buck. My plan was to hike up several ridges where I could watch the shallow draws for deer. I parked the pickup in an area about 300 yards from where I thought I could set up and attempt to rattle in a buck off a small ridge.

As I walked through the snow, I saw only a few fresh tracks of smaller deer heading off to the north, away from where I was heading.  I set myself up under a small fir tree free from snow, and then rattled and grunted for 30 minutes.

As I sat there waiting and seeing nothing, I got bored and figured my chances would be better hoofing it. At least I might get a chance to chase some deer.

I hiked down the ridge to a large meadow and made a large loop back in the direction of where I parked my truck. I could see my truck 400 yards away, but a deer was standing between us. I looked through my scope and saw that it was just a small spike. As I got closer, he trotted off across the meadow and up into the trees.

I got into my truck and drove up the skid road to where it circled back toward the ridge I was just on. I found a nice spot to stop and decided that I would walk a couple more ridges. I was now back on the same ridge I had just walked a few minutes before, but on the opposite side.

As I started walking down the skid road, I saw four does take off through the brush to my left at 40 yards, heading toward the skid road I was walking on. I watched closely, because the chance was good for a buck to be following them.

Sure enough, I saw a buck running behind the does through the brush. I could see that his tines were tall as I took quick aim and followed him in my scope, leading him a little in front of the chest. I touched off a shot and then lost sight of him.

I took off running down the skid road, hoping to get a second shot. I saw the four does come bounding out of the brush and across the road in front of me, but no buck! I walked down the road anticipating the buck to come running out. When I came to the spot where he should have been, I didn't see any sign of him. I walked back up the hill 40 yards and found him lying down with a single shot in his right shoulder. He was done.

It wasn't until then that I realized how big this buck really was. I knew he was a good one from the split-second I saw him running through the brush, but now I was up close and personal. He was a beautiful 7x9. Then I realized that I was only about 100 yards from where I shot the 6x6 buck two years earlier.

**Aaron's 2004 non-typical has over 40 inches worth of abnormal points.**

# A.P. Hegge
## 203-4/8 B&C Non-Typical
### Kootenai County, 1929

KEVIN LUNDBLAD

**Idaho Non-typical Rank: 27**  **Abnormal Points: 54-6/8**  **Points (R,L): 9,13**
**Inside Spread: 16-4/8**  **Widest Spread: 19-3/8**
**Main Beams (R,L): 24-4/8,25-2/8**  **Bases (R, L): 5-6/8,5-5/8**

Alfred Hegge was a barber by trade, and had six children. When not working or parenting, though, his true passion was hunting. He spent a lot of time in the mountains, and his family can remember him driving around in his '39 Dodge while pulling a trailer full of gear for the hunt. He didn't just hunt deer around home; he also used to spend a lot of time down on the Lochsa on elk hunts.

Long before the '39 Dodge, though, Alfred killed this big old whitetail buck in 1929 near the head of Spirit Lake. A good 20 years before the advent of a modern scoring system, Alfred probably never knew the complete significance of his historic buck, which is one of the oldest trophy animals in all of Idaho. He just knew it was fairly big and certainly unique, so he held onto it. Even after more than 80 years, it remains one of Idaho's all-time greats.

Another fascinating item about this buck is that there is an actual field photo taken the day it was killed. Cameras were a true rarity in that day and age, and almost no one packed them around on casual hunts close to home. The fact that it exists at all is simply amazing and makes it one of the more precious and historic hunting photos in all of Idaho. Alfred is actually not in the photo – he's the photographer. However, to be able to look at that photo and sneak a peek back at that special day is priceless.

**This photo rates right as one of Idaho's most historic hunting photos. Pictured are Melvin Hegge (left) and Harry Hegge, Alfred P. Hegge's sons, posing with Alfred's record book non-typical in 1929.**

# William M. Ziegler
## 203-1/8 B&C Non-Typical
### Kootenai County, 1965

**Idaho Non-typical Rank: 28**   **Abnormal Points: 44-1/8**   **Points (R,L): 13,9**
**Inside Spread: 17-6/8**   **Widest Spread: 20-5/8**
**Main Beams (R,L): 23-7/8,24-3/8**   **Bases (R, L): 4-4/8,4-6/8**

 illiam "Bill" Ziegler, then a spry 20-year-old college student attending University of Idaho, embodied much of what life is like in that Moscow area – many small-town kids, heading to the college life in the middle of the Palouse, with hunting opportunities all around.

Bill was staying in the dorms on campus, and a friend of his there was a young man named Bob "Bird" Luchini. Bird's parents lived in Post Falls, and since he had some hunting spots up there, Bill decided to go hunting with him. While he had hunting experience, he'd never hunted whitetails before; not even once. This was a new experience in new terrain and he was really looking forward to it.

They left that morning from Bird's parents' house and drove about ten miles to an area near some wheat fields that had some timbered canyon bedding areas. They hadn't gotten out exceptionally early, so it was daylight when they started.

They split up, with Bird going down into the timber and Bill walking along an old skid road. It was a whole new experience for Bill, who was acquainting himself to a completely different hunting environment.

They hadn't been apart for more than a few minutes when Bill heard a fence squeak, like something had either passed through it or hit the top wire going over it. He started watching intently toward the direction of the sound, and spotted a big buck sneaking away from him. While Bill didn't have much experience with whitetails, he knew enough to know it was a big buck and that he wanted it. The buck was 50 yards off, and Bill let him have it from his antique 1894 Winchester, complete with octagon barrel. The shot was good, and Bill had his buck. He remembers not only being impressed by the antlers, but also the body, which was tremendously fat.

Bill Ziegler's first-ever whitetail hunt lasted all of a half hour, and it produced not only his first buck, but also an all-time record book non-typical. Now that's something worth remembering.

# Eric R. Steigers
## 202-7/8 B&C Non-Typical
### Nez Perce County, 1973

| Idaho Non-typical Rank: 29 | Abnormal Points: 36-7/8 | Points (R,L): 10,10 |
|---|---|---|
| Inside Spread: 18-2/8 | | Widest Spread: 21-0/8 |
| Main Beams (R,L): 25-1/8,25-4/8 | | Bases (R, L): 4-7/8,4-6/8 |

I n the fall of 1973, 18-year-old Eric Steigers was a freshman at University of Idaho in Moscow – the heart of the Palouse country and good whitetail hunting.

Being a poor college student, when the season rolled around he was using an old Winchester 7mm-mag. that his dad had paid $55 for at an estate auction.

Eric, along with his dad (Ralph), Uncle Leroy, and cousin, Shannon, took off for an early season deer hunt. It was warm and pleasant, and Leroy started off the day by filling his tag.

Eric hunted hard that day, and by afternoon had covered at least five good miles. He finally came out on an old logging road within sight of a paved highway. The hunting party approached a bottleneck of trees, with Shannon (accompanied by Leroy) on the left, Eric in the middle, and Ralph on the right.

As they pushed through, a buck jumped up between Eric and Leroy and ran back toward where the hunters had just come from. Eric fired four times at the buck as it ran straight away from him, with all bullets hitting everything but deer. He had one last chance and one last shot as the deer turned to the right to jump a fence 150 yards distant. He fired and had little indication he had hit it that time either, other than a slightly awkward flick of the tail from the buck as it vanished from sight.

Uncle Leroy was the first to get to the 10x10 buck, and he let loose with a healthy dose of whooping and hollering. Eric, who up to that point had very little time to get a good look at the buck, was equally excited, and more than a little bit shocked. It was one of those moments forever frozen in time that Eric will always look back on with the fondest of memories.

Note: Eric took the buck to legendary outdoor writer Jack O'Connor, who lived just half an hour away down in Lewiston. Jack was an official measurer for Boone and Crockett Club back in the day before the Club had rigorous training courses for measurers and detailed rules for difficult-to-measure whitetails. As such, when Jack measured it, he had it measured in the 163 range as a typical, which made it fall short of minimums needed to qualify for B&C. Almost 35 years later, I was able to measure this buck for Eric and get it officially recognized as an all-time record book non-typical.

# Picked Up
## 202-4/8 B&C Non-Typical
### Boundary County, 1990

COURTESY OF BOONE AND CROCKETT CLUB

**Idaho Typical Rank: 30**      **Abnormal Points: 34-2/8**      **Points (R,L): 11,9**
**Inside Spread: 19-4/8**                                        **Widest Spread: 23-3/8**
**Main Beams (R,L): 22-4/8,25-4/8**                **Bases (R, L): 6-3/8,5-2/8**

T his tremendous non-typical whitetail buck has some great mass to go along with a uniquely shaped frame. Along with plenty of abnormal points, long tines, and wild eyeguards, it would have made any hunter happy. However, that was not how fate would end this buck's life. The buck was found dead, leaving his earthly realm from unknown causes.

Steve Crossley, who was an antler collector, bought this rack many years ago and has since sold it. Sadly, no information on who found the buck is available. All that Steve knew was that it was reportedly picked up by a hunter in Boundary County in 1990.

If you recognize this tremendous buck, or know anything at all about it, please get in touch with us. It would be great to be able to tie some history to such an impressive trophy.

# Picked Up by Jason and Matt Anderson
## 201-4/8 B&C Non-Typical
## Clearwater County, 1987

| Idaho Typical Rank: 31* | Abnormal Points: 38-2/8 | Points (R,L): 10,11 |
| --- | --- | --- |
| Inside Spread: 20-4/8 | | Widest Spread: 23-0/8 |
| Main Beams (R,L): 23-3/8,24-2/8 | | Bases (R, L): 5-3/8,5-3/8 |

iving in the mountains of central Idaho, while having a few drawbacks, also has its exceptional privileges. The scenery is outstanding, and there are seemingly endless places to explore. Step right out your back door and the world is your playground. Whether it's fishing the Clearwater, hunting whitetail and elk, shed hunting in the spring, or hiking to scenic vistas, an outdoorsman would have a hard time finding a better place to be.

John Anderson and his boys, Jason and Matt, were out riding their trail bikes in the canyon country near their home on a nice February day in 1987. The boys, who were both in their teens, loved nothing more than to be in the mountains. It was also a nice break from school.

They had spent most of the trip cutting trail through the bottom of the canyon and were crossing the creek when they spotted what looked like a deer skull. They could only see the base of the antlers, a small amount of hide, and a few vertebrae above the water. Because it was so massive, they assumed it was a mule deer or maybe even a small elk. They made their way out into the water and retrieved it, and were all stunned when they pulled an absolutely huge whitetail rack out of the creek.

The Andersons spend quite a bit of time in the mountains near their home, and love to hunt whitetails. While there is no way to be sure, they believe they may have seen this buck once while he was alive. While it's unfortunate that no hunter got to enjoy tagging this wary old monarch, at least he was recovered in time for all to see what a great buck he was.

# Leroy Coleman
## 201-3/8 B&C Non-Typical
### Bonner County, 1960

BILL WOLTERING

| | | |
|---|---|---|
| **Idaho Non-typical Rank: 32** | **Abnormal Points: 33-0/8** | **Points (R,L): 16,11** |
| **Inside Spread: 21-3/8** | | **Widest Spread: 23-4/8** |
| **Main Beams (R,L): 21-1/8,21-6/8** | | **Bases (R, L): 5-2/8,4-6/8** |

*Special thanks to Bill Woltering for providing this story.*

**L**eroy Coleman was working for the Geaudreau (pronounced Goodrow) Lumber Company near Old Town, Idaho. The mill was at the base of Hoodoo Mountain. He was hunting up on Hoodoo that day in November of 1960. The buck appeared on the hillside above, chasing a doe at 200 yards. The shot from Leroy's Savage .30-06 was a hit, but it took a long tracking job and another well-placed shot to finish the great buck.

Leroy was a true old-time Idaho hunter, and didn't think much about antlers. He knew how much I admired and respected them, so he gave them to me.

We later heard about the Big Horn Show in Spokane. I believe it may have been the first one. I talked Leroy into entering the competition. We were first told that the rack wouldn't score as a non-typical, and that it would have too many deductions to score well as a typical. I wouldn't accept that and later had it scored by an official scorer. The rack went into the B&C record book with a score of 201-3/8. Years later, after I mounted the buck, I entered it in the Big Horn Show, where it won 1st Place in the non-typical category.

Leroy was injured in a logging accident in the spring of 1966. I packed him out of the woods on the blade of a skidder and loaded him into the bed of his 1957 Ford pickup, and then hauled him to the hospital in Newport, Washington. He was one of the toughest men I have ever known.

# Tim C. Baldwin
### 200-3/8 B&C Non-Typical
### Nez Perce County, 1987

**Idaho Non-typical Rank: 34**     **Abnormal Points: 21-1/8**     **Points (R,L): 11,10**
**Inside Spread: 17-4/8**                                         **Widest Spread: 25-1/8**
**Main Beams (R,L): 25-0/8, 26-2/8**                    **Bases (R, L): 4-6/8, 4-7/8**

One evening while driving back from a fishing trip, my dad, Mike, and brother, Scott, saw a dandy whitetail buck run across the road. We had hunted for whitetail in that general area, but never that particular drainage. That was about to change.

A few months later, during the whitetail season, we decided to give that area a try. I was hunting with my wife, Marie, and brothers, Toby and Scott. We left the truck before the sun came up to get a good start and get away from the road before shooting light. As the trees, brush, and meadows became visible with the first light, like so many sunrises in hunting country, the excitement was in full swing.

Marie and I hadn't made it far when I noticed two deer standing 50 yards away looking at us through the brush. I raised my .30-06 and looked through the scope, hoping to see antlers. What I saw I did not expect. For a split-second, I saw the bigger deer looking at me. Not only was he a buck, but I could also see incredible mass and some extra points just as he turned and bolted away.

He ran to my left and I could only see quick glimpses of him through the brush. I had no shot as he kept quartering away from me.

Panicked and calm all at the same time, I looked in the direction the deer was running and saw an opening around 100 yards away. I held on that spot and waited, hoping he would run through the opening. Just as I had hoped, the buck appeared in that clearing and he was running hard. With whitetail hunting, this is a pretty typical shot scenario, and one that we're used to dealing with. I took aim and fired, and my shot found its mark. I was stunned, relieved, and ecstatic. Walking up to this big trophy buck is something I'll never forget.

The buck is an 11x10 and scores 200-3/8 B&C. Amazingly, this big deer was not the nice 5x5 that ran across the road in front of my dad and brother a few months prior. But, thanks to that buck being spotted months before the hunt, we found a productive hunting spot that provided this buck as well as more nice whitetails for Scott and my dad in years to come.

TIM BALDWIN

# Steve Myers
## 200-0/8 B&C Non-Typical
## Latah County, 1981

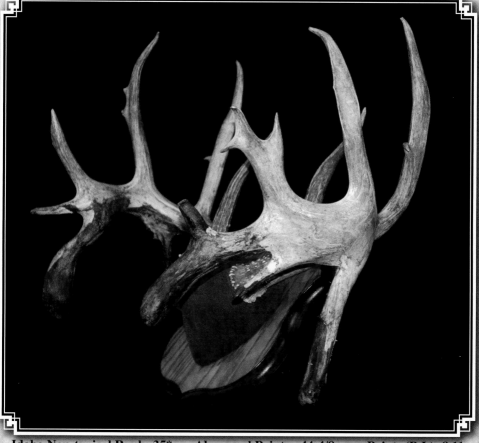

| Idaho Non-typical Rank: 35* | Abnormal Points: 44-4/8 | Points (R,L): 8,11 |
|---|---|---|
| Inside Spread: 20-2/8 | | Widest Spread: 24-0/8 |
| Main Beams (R,L): 23-0/8, 21-1/8 | | Bases (R, L): 4-5/8, 4-7/8 |

teve Myers, then 22 years old, had been farming at a place in Latah County. Being young and into hunting, he paid a lot of attention to the bucks he had seen and felt that he knew every deer on the place. Now, looking back on it and knowing more about the craftiness of these smart old bucks, Steve knows better. After all, he had never seen this buck until he had it in his sights.

It was a drizzly November day that had everything muddy. Steve wasn't overly excited about getting wet, but he'd been seeing a good buck or two and grabbed his pre-'64 .270 Winchester and headed up to a place he called "the bench", where bucks seemed to like to lay.

He walked up a trail and came to a spot where he often saw rattlesnakes, so his mind was somewhat preoccupied with that and his eyes were "looking small". He took another few steps up the trail when he looked over and saw a forked horn buck lying right by the trail, less than a rifle length away! He couldn't believe it. He and the buck stared at each other, each afraid to blink. Finally, Steve backed up a bit and started conversing with the deer. The little buck didn't offer much of a response, so Steve moved on.

He had taken just a few steps when he saw a coyote. He shot it and then looked back; the buck was still there, refusing to move. That must have been one comfortable bed.

Steve finally walked on, moving the coyote off the trail as he passed by it, and walked up to the top. He was only about 40 yards from the coyote when a huge buck jumped up. The wild-racked deer was in the buckbrush with two does, and Steve was stunned at the rack it was carrying; points seemed to be going everywhere.

He quickly leveled down on the buck's shoulder and knocked him down almost instantly. Rain continued to fall lightly as Steve approached, shocked at what had just taken place. After all, he hadn't ever seen this buck on the place before, and had really never seen anything like it anywhere else, either.

Steve's 8x11 non-typical, one of the more awe-inspiring deer ever grown in the Gem State, is truly one of a kind. With all those bulbous droptines, heavy mass, and great frame, not many bucks will ever match its unique character.

Steve said that being young and naïve, he almost sold it for $50. Good thing for him he thought better of it.

# Milton R. Wilson
## 198-3/8 B&C Non-Typical
## Nez Perce County, 1983

**Idaho Non-typical Rank: 36**   **Abnormal Points:  33-6/8**   **Points (R,L): 10,10**
**Inside Spread: 17-5/8**                                        **Widest Spread: 19-5/8**
**Main Beams (R,L): 20-7/8,22-2/8**                             **Bases (R, L): 4-4/8,4-7/8**

 ilton Wilson and Barb Goeckner had known each other for a long time. Their parents were friends, and Milton and Barb also worked together in a first aid station at Potlatch in Lewiston. She always saw him as a brother and they also hunted together.

Milt and Barb, along with her husband, Ted, met for breakfast that mid November morning and worked up a plan for the day. They decided to leave Milt's old blue Ford pickup at the bottom of a major drainage and drive the Goeckners' '74 Jeep Wagoneer to the top and hunt down.

The area they were hunting was mid to low elevation, with brushy and timbered draws, some grassy slopes, and agricultural and grazing ground. They split up, with Ted in the bottom of the draw, Barb in the middle, and Milt up top. Their hope was to push any deer in the area back and forth between them. Any deer would do, as they were more concerned with meat than antlers.

They had been hunting for a while, and considering it was mid November, it was fairly warm. To that point, no one had taken a shot.

Barb was still-hunting along and trying to remain some-what equidistant between her two partners when she jumped a deer. It came busting out of the draw quite a ways off, but Barb fired a borrowed Savage .350-3000 rifle and hit it in the leg. She didn't bother to even look for antlers, since any deer was legal.

Milt, who was about 300 yards up the hill, also saw the buck. It ran into the next draw, and then Barb heard Milt fire his Ruger M77 .30-06. "I got him!" she heard him shout.

Milt field-dressed the buck, but had emphysema, so Barb and Ted did most of the dragging. It was fairly warm that day, so they did their best to work hard and keep it as timely as possible.

They decided to split the deer, with Barb taking the meat and Milt taking the ant-lers. Milt has since passed on, but Barb and Ted still remember that special day, a special friend, and a special buck.

**(Left) Ted Goeckner poses with Milton Wilson's big non-typical way back in 1983. (Right) Barb Goeckner, with the trophy buck at the Lewiston Gun and Antler Show in 2008.**

# Frank J. Cheyney
## 198-1/8 B&C Non-Typical
### Kootenai County, 1967

**Idaho Non-typical Rank: 37**     **Abnormal Points: 23-1/8**     **Points (R,L): 10,9**

**Inside Spread: 19-6/8**     **Widest Spread: 23-3/8**

**Main Beams (R,L): 24-6/8, 24-3/8**     **Bases (R, L): 5-5/8,5-4/8**

On November 1, 1967, Frank Cheyney woke up early and climbed into his old 1948 Plymouth. He then headed from his home near Hayden Lake to an area near Rose Lake for a whitetail hunt.

By his recollection, he had hiked nearly six miles before he saw a buck that didn't take a whole lot of thinking to pull the trigger on. At somewhere around 375 yards, he saw a monster of a buck and was able to put it down with his .270. In the process, not only did he take one of Idaho's biggest bucks, but also one of its most breathtaking trophies.

*Note: This massive, regal buck hangs at Idaho Department of Fish and Game Headquarters in Boise, where it commands attention at the center of the conference room.*

# Luke D. Finney
## 198-1/8 B&C Non-Typical
### Kootenai County, 1998

**Idaho Non-typical Rank: 37**       **Abnormal Points: 20-0/8**       **Points (R,L): 11,8**
**Inside Spread: 19-1/8**                                        **Widest Spread: 22-6/8**
**Main Beams (R,L): 25-1/8,25-2/8**                   **Bases (R, L): 4-2/8, 4-2/8**

ixteen-year-old Luke Finney was born into a hardcore hunting family who spends as many or more days in the field as any family in the state. His dad, Jack, and uncle, Gary, are both very accomplished hunters and Luke, even at his tender age, was catching on quick.

On November 15, Luke, Jack, Gary, Josh Vogan, Dan Ratza, Eric Kacalek, and three other hunters all took to the woods, primed for the early stages of the whitetail rut. Luke had already passed up better than ten bucks so far that season, with his mind set on a wallhanger.

They set up for their first deer drive, with three deer drivers (Jack, Dan, and Eric) and the other five on stand. Luke knew the area well, and so he and Josh went to the far end of the drive. The majority of the hunt area was extremely thick, but the area where Luke set up was much more open and conducive for a shot.

Jack jumped a buck out of "the thick stuff", and the buck proceeded up an old skid trail. Luke was in perfect position to catch the action, and the buck crossed the skid trail heading straight up only 150 yards away.

Luke had only one opening and had to make it count. When the deer crossed into it, Luke fired his 7mm-mag. at the deer, which was on a dead run. Luke "got lucky" as he says, and the wounded buck turned around and staggered back down the hill, falling into the trail. Luke hurried down and finished off the buck, which had lost the use of his back end.

Admittedly, Luke was pretty excited. The buck was absolutely huge, with points going everywhere. To a 16-year-old, it must have seemed even bigger. He finally yelled down to his dad about how huge the deer was. Jack hollered back, "Who shot it?"

When Luke yelled back saying it was him, Jack's voice jumped up a couple of octaves, very excited for his son.

# Dean C. Weyen
## 197-7/8 B&C Non-Typical
### Latah County, 1992
*Idaho State Archery Record (Non-Typical)*

**Idaho Non-typical Rank: 39**     **Abnormal Points: 30-5/8**     **Points (R,L): 8,12**
**Inside Spread: 19-2/8**     **Widest Spread: 24-5/8**
**Main Beams (R,L): 22-2/8,23-0/8**     **Bases (R, L): 5-1/8, 5-1/8**

L ong-time bowhunter Dean Weyen wasn't looking to set a state record, or any kind of record for that matter. He was just out looking to punch his tag on a decent whitetail buck and fill the freezer.

As such, he got out of his rig long before light on a cold mid-November morning and headed to a tree stand he had hanging in a favorite spot on a ridge a little less than two miles away. He had taken two bucks in each of the last two years from the same location, and had confidence in this newfound honey hole.

He had planned on trying to rattle in a buck from his stand at first light, but loud, crunchy snow made him rethink his approach. He changed his plans and rattled as he walked instead, deciding to get to his stand during midday instead of first light. Rattling produced instant results, with a small 4x4 coming in to investigate. The buck soon winded Dean, though, and split.

Around noon, he made it to his stand. He climbed up, got in position, and took a good look around, taking time to enjoy just being outside.

He did a rattling sequence and then stopped to listen. Just like earlier that morning, a 4x4 came in to investigate. Dean thought the buck looked good enough, and likely would have taken him if a shot had presented itself, but the buck walked away without ever exposing himself enough for a shot.

Dean rattled again, trying to bring the buck back, when he suddenly heard a different deer crunching through the snow. He turned to look and was stunned; a great big non-typical buck was headed in toward his tree stand.

Dean dropped the rattling antlers and grabbed his bow, a High Country Sniper, just in time to send a 125-grain Thunderhead broadhead into the buck's chest from 30 yards. And just like that, Dean had taken the biggest whitetail any bowhunter has ever taken in Idaho.

**Dean Weyen has the claim to fame of taking Idaho's largest whitetail with a bow. He used a tree stand and rattling combination to lure this handsome buck into bow range.**

# Robert Zdenek Borysek

### 197-3/8 B&C Non-typical
### Bonner County, 2005

**Idaho Non-typical Rank: xx** **Length of Abnormal Points: 25-3/8** **Points (R,L): 9,7**
**Inside Spread: 20-6/8** **Widest Spread: 23-2/8**
**Main Beams (R,L): 23-4/8,25-7/8** **Bases (R, L): 5-2/8, 5-0/8**

**S**ome people lead more adventurous lives than others, but few have the tales to tell that Robert Zdenek Borysek does. Robert was born in Czechoslovakia in 1935. For the next two decades, Eastern Europe wasn't exactly the prime place to live out a carefree childhood. One refuge that he had was that his dad introduced him and his brother, Joseph, into shooting and hunting.

In September of 1951, when he was just 16, his parents were forced to leave the country due to the communist movement. They sneaked over the Austrian border during the night and stayed in Austria for a year. During that time, his dad became an American spy, and was shot on the Austria/Czechoslovakia border in June of 1952. He was taken prisoner and was killed there. To this day, Robert doesn't know where his father is buried.

Just a few months later, Robert, his mom, and his brother were relocated to Chicago. Robert did his best to adjust. He worked in a stove factory, studied English, and in 1955, joined the U.S. Air Force. He wanted to fly jets, but with his somewhat broken English, it was just not in the cards. He went on to become a jet mechanic instead. After his honorable discharge, he spent many years in real estate and financial services.

A long 55 years removed from the tumultuous times of his family, Robert was living in Idaho. It was the last day of the deer season, and he had hunted very hard with no luck. He was driving down the highway near Priest River when he saw a doe on the hillside, made much more visible because of snow. He parked his car and began ascending the hill, which was no easy task due to ice and steep slopes. He had to zigzag in order to make it all.

He was almost to the top when he saw two does running. Just in case a buck was going to follow, he raised his Browning 20-gauge over and under slug gun. As requested, a buck came sailing into the opening at 80 yards, but the rack was so big Robert admits being a bit confused. He whistled and the buck stopped in its tracks. It was just long enough for him to squeeze the trigger and hit the buck right through the ears, dropping it right in its tracks.

Robert says he was somewhat freaked out when he approached, because all of the buck's hairs were standing on end as it died. Spooked by the ordeal (including the unnaturally large antlers), he panicked a bit and ran down the hill and sat in his pickup, convinced he had made some sort of mistake.

After he settled down and had time to think, he decided that whatever he'd done, he had to go up and take care of it and face any consequences. Reaching the deer and being of a sound mind now, he examined the carcass and put his mind to ease that it was indeed a whitetail. That's when it hit him in regard to the size of the buck he had taken.

He field-dressed his trophy, dragged it down close to the highway, and then realizing he couldn't take it in his car, he hid it. He then got in his car and left to find cell reception. He made a phone call to a friend, Tom, who came out with his pickup and hauled it back to town for him.

The buck made quite a stir in town. Everyone that saw it wanted to come and take a closer look at the exceptionally large and massive antlers.

Robert has hunted his entire life, including as a youth in Czechoslovakia. His biggest regret about the hunt is that Joseph, his brother and hunting partner for 40 years, had passed away and couldn't be there for that special day.

Robert says, "At this point in my life, I am very much interested in people and their experiences. I also have very strong feelings about the suffering of people throughout the world and the stupidity of men." Considering his life experiences, who would disagree?

**Robert Borysek took his massive Bonner County buck with a 20-gauge slug gun, within earshot of a highway.**

# David L. Whatcott & Randy C. Carlson
## 197 B&C Non-Typical
### Kootenai County, 1980

**Idaho Non-typical Rank: 41**      **Abnormal Points: 18-3/8**      **Points (R,L): 8,9**

**Inside Spread: 25-3/8**                                          **Widest Spread: 28-7/8**

**Main Beams (R,L): 24-2/8,26-4/8**                           **Bases (R, L): 5-0/8,5-1/8**

A good portion of the quality whitetail hunting in Idaho is either on private land or controlled through private access. David Whatcott and his hunting partner, Randy Carlson, knew that well. They were from the Coeur d'Alene area, where private ground is plentiful and good hunting can be at a premium.

One day in November during the 1980 deer season, they were hunting when they came across a local rancher. They weren't on his property, but some of his comments left such a sour taste in their mouths that they decided to head in a different direction.

On short notice and a whim, they picked an area they had never even hunted before. They got into some deer that morning, including a big buck, and Randy got off a shot. It hit the buck, but when he went to investigate, he found only hair and no blood.

A week later, David and Randy jumped into the '72 Ford pickup and headed back to the same location, hoping to run into that big buck again. It was plenty cold that morning as they ascended the canyon from the bottom, with David heading up the open side and Randy pushing through the thick stuff on the other side.

They met back up later, and decided to sit on a bench area and have a cigarette. They were talking about the fact that they weren't seeing any deer sign when Randy suddenly jumped up and said, "There's a buck!"

Randy tried to shoot, but his gun dry-fired – the second time that it had done that in a week. David then jumped up and shot from 35 yards with his .30-06 as the buck ran by him. He connected behind the shoulder and the buck rolled down the hill. Randy then shot, successfully this time.

When they got to the deer, Randy was pretty positive it was the same deer he had shot at the previous weekend. As they began to field dress the trophy buck, they found a spot on the hindquarter where Randy had indeed grazed the buck.

**David Whatcott (left) and Randy Carlson pose with their great trophy buck from 1980. What a great vintage photo.**

# Jack S. Snider
## 196-6/8 B&C Non-Typical
## Nez Perce County, 2004

**Idaho Non-typical Rank: 42**  **Abnormal Points: 29-3/8**  **Points (R,L): 8,8**
**Inside Spread: 19-5/8**  **Widest Spread: 23-2/8**
**Main Beams (R,L): 25-2/8,24-6/8**  **Bases (R, L): 4-5/8,4-4/8**

It's amazing what a small chance encounter can do to set events in motion. An innocent glance down at the ground usually wouldn't occupy a guy's mind too long, unless that glance happened to bring you "eye to eye" with a big droptine whitetail shed. As Jack reached down and picked it up, he knew right then that he had just become committed to a new relationship. He was going to find that buck.

Nearly four years later, and still chasing the same buck off and on, he revisited the area in October of 2004. He still looked at that antler from time to time, and believed the buck was still running around. He had never found a carcass, and Lord knows he'd have heard about it if somebody had killed something like that.

Jack had been committed to helping his dad with a mule deer tag he had, but Paul Snider, Sr. had no desire to be out in the October rain that day. As such, Jack decided to run up and see what he might find. The rain had a real presence that day, and it didn't take long for Jack to get soaked.

He'd been out for quite awhile and was about ready to start back. He pushed his way across a star thistle hillside and started toward a brush patch. A year previous, he had kicked a buck out if it, so he had that in the back of his mind as he approached, also thinking about what the buck did when it bolted.

He got close, and as if it was instant replay, a deer flushed from cover. He couldn't see it, but knowing what had happened a year ago, he zeroed in on an opening where he thought it might go.

He missed his chance as the buck passed through the opening, but saw the droptine. As it passed through a second opening, Jack fired his .270. As soon as it had started, it was now quiet. The buck was out of sight, and Jack had no idea if he had hit the object of so many of his thoughts over the proceeding four years. He was sick thinking he may possibly have blown it.

He moved forward to look for some sign, which could disappear in a hurry in that rain. About a minute later, he spied the buck 150 yards away, walking slowly. He also spotted that trademark droptine. He sent another round behind the buck's shoulder and the buck again disappeared.

Jack had to trace and retrace the events, trying to get on a blood trail, and finally

**Jack Snider had this buck on his mind for four years, and did everything right in bad weather, earning his trophy the hard way.**

**A perfect 8x8 double-droptine buck, Jack's trophy is any hunter's dream buck.**

found blood. He looked and looked, but couldn't find the buck anywhere. He began to panic all over again.

He saw a big root wad below him and though he might try to climb it to survey the scene He ran down and took a running leap for the top of it, and as he was in mid air, he saw a buck lying in the crater left by the upheaval of the root system. He says it scared the holy heck out of him. A look down after he had once again touched earth revealed that it was his buck! The giant had literally found a final resting spot in a natural grave.

Jack looked down in disbelief. He then stared at it for several minutes, speechless and in awe, before he even approached it.

He halved the buck and packed it out in two trips. It was a real chore since the buck ended up weighing 262 lbs. field dressed.

Jack was overwhelmed with relief and satisfaction that day. He didn't have anyone to share it with on the mountain, but that would change soon. He says that taking that buck back to show his dad was one of the best and most enjoyable moments of his entire life.

**Jack found his buck hidden in a crater left by an uprooted Douglas-fir.**

# Cecil H. Cameron

## 195-7/8 B&C Non-Typical
### Latah County, 1989

CECIL CAMERON

**Idaho Non-typical Rank: 44**　　　**Abnormal Points: 26-1/8**　　　**Points (R,L): 9,9**
**Inside Spread: 19-0/8**　　　　　　　　　　　　　　　　　　　　**Widest Spread: 21-4/8**
**Main Beams (R,L): 23-1/8,23-4/8**　　　　　　　　　　　　　**Bases (R, L): 4-7/8,4-5/8**

H unting opportunities aren't the best in Washington, and it's fairly common for a lot of Evergreen State hunters to come to Idaho in search of greener pastures. Cecil Cameron worked in western Washington as a heavy equipment mechanic, and loved to hunt the more open country in Idaho. He had been to Idaho a few times on hunts, and had done some drop camp hunts, but had never been on a guided hunt. That changed in 1989 when he and his brother, David, booked a hunt in the Moscow area with Jack Skille.

The first day of the six-day hunt didn't start well. He had forgotten his license clear back in Washington, so he had to go to the regional office in Lewiston to get it all sorted out.

Over the next four days, they saw deer but nothing had come together yet. With one day left, things were looking a bit bleak.

On the last day, Cecil and David went separate directions with their guides. Cecil and his guide, Kelly Phillips, still-hunted up a brushy ridge in five inches of snow as a light snow fell.

They were a couple of hours into the hunt when they heard a buck grunt. They sat still and soon caught movement through the trees. Almost as if by a miracle, a big buck came traipsing through with his head low to the ground sniffing for a doe.

Without hesitating, Cecil hit the buck in the boiler room with his aught six at 75 yards. The buck got up, and Cecil tried to shoot again, but misfired. By the time that was sorted out, the buck had fallen back down and had already expired.

Being a first-time whitetail hunter, Cecil didn't really know what he had in front of him. His guide cleared that up for him right away. They went back for the pack boards, and rain into some of Jack's other clients from Minnesota. When they heard about the buck, they went all the way back with them, just to see it. Being veteran whitetail hunters, their excitement was as obvious as his guide's.

As they packed it out, they saw a pretty fair-sized buck right out in the open. It was an ironic end to what turned out to be a great hunt.

**Cecil Cameron shows the results from his 1989 guided hunt in the Moscow area. What a gorgeous photo.**

# Picked Up by Brian T. Farley
## 195-6/8 B&C Non-Typical
### Bonner County, 1994

**Idaho Non-typical Rank: 45**   **Abnormal Points: 28-2/8**   **Points (R,L): 9,8**
**Inside Spread: 17-0/8**   **Widest Spread: 18-4/8**
**Main Beams (R,L): 23-0/8,23-0/8**   **Bases (R, L): 4-0/8,4-1/8**

The loss of significant numbers of mule deer during winters of deep, long-lasting snows and severe cold temperatures are a sad fact of life across the Western states. Such was the case in the winter of 1992-1993, possibly the worst such loss on record. The huge die-off was a well documented disaster here in Idaho and across the Intermountain West. Mule deer numbers plummeted, and nearly 20 years hence, here in Idaho they have never recovered.

Less noticed and generally not reported was a similar loss of whitetail deer in the Panhandle of northern Idaho, where they make up approximately 80% of our deer population, and the bulk of our harvest.

That following spring (1993), there was on display at all of our local horn shows perhaps the greatest collection of large trophy whitetail deer antlers I had ever seen before or since. The vast majority of these great local bucks were not hunter harvested, but were "pick-ups", found with antlers intact, winterkilled.

These were of that "special " class of mature bucks that due to our heavily timbered steep mountainous habitat and their nocturnal nature not only are rarely ever hung on a meat pole, but also for the most part live out their lives undetected and unseen by human hunters. Such was the case with this buck.

I was cruising timber and locating property lines near Lake Pend O'Reille with a logging contractor friend on a piece of ground that I was interested in purchasing to build a new ranch. While pushing through a stand of particularly dark second-growth timber, I simply walked up on this great set of antlers. From the scene laid out before me, it was obvious that this buck simply found himself trapped in this inhospitable place by snow that came too hard, too fast, and piled up much too deep.

Tomb-like, there was literally no sunlight penetrating this dark, lonely place that was to be his final stand. There was nothing nutritious available for him to fill his paunch, with the exception of fir needles that he may have been able to reach.

I bent to pick up all that remained of this once proud, crafty buck and then held his crown in my hands. I thought not only of what his last days must have been like stuck here alone in this dismal place of killing snows, but also what life in his prime must have been like for him.

Did he and I cross paths? Almost assuredly so, since this was only a short drive from my home and I had hunted this area for years. However, neither I nor any family member ever hung a tag on a buck like this. I had seen mega non-typicals in the headlights near here with the same antler configuration. This of course kept me coming back, and back, and back. But not surprisingly, laying eyes on one of these brutes during shooting hours never happened.

How many times had this particular buck given me the slip? How close had I come to settling my sights on him? Was it his flag I had seen in the distance in the gloom of the November forest? Was it his hooves that made the soft yet unmistakable "chuck-chuck" in the damp duff of the forest floor, slipping away again, unseen in the heavy cover, always just one jump ahead?

I know the answer. It's one of those semi-tangible things that keeps me going.

The elation I felt at finding such a treasure was tempered at the same time by the sadness of his loss. I took comfort in knowing that a buck that lived long enough to produce such a great scoring crown certainly did his best at propagating his kind as he was perfectly designed to do.

I would hunt his sons again, someday, down the trail. Similar sentiments had been felt whenever I had been blessed to take home a mature or trophy critter.

His days were done. The troubles and challenges of his hectic life "on the edge" of continual escape and avoidance from all things desiring to reduce him to food, myself included, were now behind him.

In the end, my love for him and his kind, coupled with my DNA-programmed "drive to kill" relationship I had with him, found him as the ultimate victor. He lived freely, bred freely, and died freely, and no hunter had a hand in his demise.

It was truly a life well lived. For hunters, as lovers of wild things and wild places, it was a life to be envied. He came into the world as a defenseless wobbly-legged Bambi and is now gone. Long live the King.

# Kenny Charles
## 195-5/8 B&C Non-Typical
### Benewah County, 1989

**Idaho Non-typical Rank: 46**   **Abnormal Points: 53-2/8**   **Points (R,L): 12,10**
**Inside Spread: 17-5/8**                                       **Widest Spread: 26-4/8**
**Main Beams (R,L): 21-5/8,20-3/8**                             **Bases (R, L): 4-3/8,4-0/8**

hitetail are adaptable creatures that do much better around people than mule deer or elk. They don't need much room to roam; they don't usually migrate as far; and they can live in remarkably small areas, often completely undetected. As such, it's not uncommon to see a good buck now and then close to human habitation. It's also not uncommon for successful whitetail hunts to be less than arduous adventures. Sometimes a guy just gets lucky, and that's what Kenny was thinking, right up until that buck stabbed him in the leg with its antlers…

Kenny had just been laid off from his truck driving job and had some unexpected time on his hands to do a bit of whitetail hunting. He headed out to do just that, and was driving his old 1975 Chevy pickup down the road. Only about three miles outside of St. Maries, he had just passed the last house before the road he was on turned to timber and forest ground.

It was November, and the rut was on, so it was no surprise to him when he looked over and saw a whitetail take off for cover. Kenny pulled his pickup over and began pursuing. The season was still either-sex, so when he made out the body of a whitetail, he took the 75-yard shot with his aught six. He then moved forward and saw a flash; it was a big buck!

The buck had got hung up in a tree, but was still moving. Kenny moved in to try and finish off his deer, but when the buck caught the movement, he turned and stabbed his pursuer right below the knee with an antler tip. Kenny then grabbed his rifle and finished the job "up close and personal."

It was only then that he really had a chance to look at his buck. It was a real stunner; a non-typical buck with double droptines, and one of them looked more like a moose paddle than a deer tine. It was the trophy of a lifetime.

Sadly, Kenny was only 25 at the time and hard up for cash, and sold the rack, so all he has for proof are the photos you see here. He says, "If I had it to do over again, I wouldn't have done it. I'd rather starve to death first."

Kenny Charles' double droptine non-typical, with a massive paddle-like structure on the right main beam, is one of the more unique whitetails in the state.

# Paul S. Snider
### 195-5/8 B&C Non-Typical
### Nez Perce County, 1989

**Idaho Non-typical Rank: 46**    **Abnormal Points: 19-3/8**    **Points (R,L): 10,9**
**Inside Spread: 19-2/8**    **Widest Spread: 22-1/8**
**Main Beams (R,L): 24-6/8,24-7/8**    **Bases (R, L): 5-2/8,5-0/8**

 was almost feeling sorry for my brother Jack as he was flinging his body against the wall of brush. I quickly forgot all about it, though, when I saw a huge buck sneaking nonchalantly by him 30 yards away.

I was hunting with Jack and a hunting partner, Randy Olmstead. On an earlier hunt in the same area, Rich Earp and I had seen a herd of elk, and since Rich and family had elk tags, we decided to hunt the same area again that weekend. Rich and his wife, Pam, were going to hunt the bottom part of the draw over toward some benches where we had seen the elk. Jack, Randy, and I were going to hunt the brushy draws under the farm fields over to the same area.

I dropped Jack and Randy off on top of the hill, and then drove down a ways to park the truck. I then hunted toward them, and when I was nearly there, I spotted a nice buck on the move. A few minutes later, Jack and Randy arrived. We talked strategy, deciding to send one low, one high, and one through the middle, and then we drew straws for position. I drew the top straw.

We were sidehilling over to the brushiest draw in Nez Perce County when I heard a couple of shots. Knowing it could be pushing a buck around, I ran around to the top of the draw, hoping to see what all the fuss was about. Not seeing anything, I returned to a good-looking draw I had passed by in a hurry.

I set up where I could see the top of the draw, and here came Jack fighting his way down it. He was so deep in brush that he had to lunge and hope his body weight would push the brush down far enough for him to fall forward, just so he

**Paul Snider, Jr. holds up the massive rack of his 1989 trophy buck, which was taken in thick, brushy country.**

could have the privilege of doing it all over again.

I was starting to feel sorry for him when I saw movement 30 yards to his right. I looked over and about died. A huge buck was sneaking by Jack, but going the opposite direction. Jack was so covered up that he couldn't even see or hear the buck.

The buck looked tall and heavy, but I couldn't count points well because of the early morning sun being low on the horizon. Due to the steep slopes, I was also looking kind of down at him as he went uphill and away from me. I put the crosshairs of my .270 Winchester between his shoulder blades and squeezed the trigger, dropping the buck in his tracks. The angle was safe to shoot, even though the buck wasn't all that far from Jack, but not knowing what was going on, Jack yelled and asked what I was shooting at. "I just shot a monster buck!" I yelled back.

Randy and Jack went on around to see if they could catch up with that other buck and see if he was hit. In the meantime, I went on over to check out my buck.

A half-hour later, Jack returned to find me still staring at my buck, unable to do much else since I was pretty overwhelmed. He had points everywhere, and was the biggest buck either of us had taken at the time.

We dressed him out and then started dragging him down the draw. Big mistake; we got so brushed in that we were actually picking the carcass up and throwing him into the wild rose brush, and then jumping over it and doing it again, repeating the horrible process all the way down the hill. We all got scratched up pretty bad getting that buck out of there.

Years later, I look up on my wall and remember a great trophy and a great hunt. Jack only seems to remember the brush. Thanks, Jack, for being a great bird dog.

**Paul Snider, Jr.'s "wall of fame".**

# Dave Steinbach, Jr.
### 195-2/8 B&C Non-Typical
### Bonner County, 1988

| | | |
|---|---|---|
| **Idaho Non-typical Rank: 48*** | **Abnormal Points:  26-6/8** | **Points (R,L): 8,10** |
| **Inside Spread: 20-4/8** | | **Widest Spread: 23-6/8** |
| **Main Beams (R,L): 25-3/8,24-7/8** | | **Bases (R, L): 4-5/8,4-3/8** |

I n most places and with most people in the U.S., Thanksgiving is a time to spend with family. To a whitetail hunter, it means something if not more important, at least more urgent – the peak of the rut.

Thanksgiving morning of 1988 found Dave Steinbach, Calvin Rusho, Calvin's dad, Cliff Rusho, and Jeff Barker out on the prowl for a big whitetail buck. They piled into the rig and headed for a favorite spot. It was a prime day to be hunting – in addition to the rut, they also had eight inches of fresh snow on the ground.

The plan was to set Cliff on stand while the other three made a drive and tried to push deer his direction. Halfway through the hunt, though, Calvin shot a 3x4. They kept going and made it to Cliff without any other major events, so they all helped load Calvin's buck.

Everyone was a bit cold, so they decided to head to Calvin's grandma's house to warm up and get some hot chocolate. While they warmed up, they got to talking, and one thing that came up was all the fresh tracks they had seen. Ultimately, they decided to head back out and give the area another shot that afternoon.

They arrived back at the same area and found a lone, fresh track. It looked like a good buck, and they didn't think that track was there earlier. Dave started following it, but eventually lost it in a maze of other tracks.

He was out a ways when he heard footsteps coming. He looked and eventually saw a big buck, suddenly in full-tilt run mode. The shot was fast and close (not more than 30 yards). It was as much an instinctive shot as anything, but Dave's .30-06 bullet found its mark and the buck went down. It jumped up and Calvin shot again, and then the buck vanished.

Dave waited, and Calvin joined him. They started tracking, but it didn't take long. The buck was dead only yards ahead of the hunters. Both hunters were pretty overwhelmed with what they saw. The buck was a big one, and had more points than they could believe. Needless to say, Dave was pretty happy about their decision to come back to an area they had just been to hours before.

# George B. Hatley
## 195-1/8 B&C Non-Typical
### Bonner County, 1939

| | | |
|---|---|---|
| **Idaho Non-typical Rank: 49** | **Abnormal Points: 34-1/8** | **Points (R,L): 15,13** |
| **Inside Spread: 18-0/8** | | **Widest Spread: 23-6/8** |
| **Main Beams (R,L): 25-5/8,23-4/8** | | **Bases (R, L): 4-3/8,4-4/8** |

*When I first tried to track this story down, I must admit I was more than a little bit surprised when I discovered the hunter was still alive. After all, it was 2004, and the trophy was taken way back in 1939. Luckily for all of us, George Hatley was only 15 when he took the deer; he lived a good, long life, and had a great memory. Following is a story George wrote about his hunt, which took place over 70 years ago.*

y father, Ray Hatley, hunted in the Nordman area of Bonner County in the fall of 1936 and took me with him in '37 and '38, when I harvested my first deer. The next year, 1939, was a particularly good hunt for me as people who saw my buck's antlers "oohed and aahed" and made complimentary comments on it being an unusually good trophy.

We had transported our camp from Moscow to the end of the road leading toward Reeder Creek in dad's 1928 Chevrolet pickup. It was mid November, and there was around six inches of snow on the ground.

We cleared a swath big enough for our 8x10 wall tent and set up camp. We had a homemade wood-burning camp stove for cooking food and heating the tent. We made "mattresses" out of Douglas-fir branches. Our bed consisted of three thick quilts, two or three blankets, and a bed tarp. Years later, we would change to sleeping bags and thick foam pads.

We hunted afoot and walked Forest Service trails considerable distances. One day we were hunting a ridge called Brushy Ridge west of Reeder Creek. The ridge was covered with willow brush and an occasional Douglas-fir or pine tree. It was cold out and snow made for some good tracking. My dad had killed a small spike buck the day before, which was now hanging back at camp, so hopefully now it would be my turn.

It was mid morning and I was half a mile from camp when I saw a buck standing under a 15-foot-tall fir tree 100 yards away and facing me. He didn't move or show up as well as a deer standing broadside, but it was obviously a buck.

I squatted down almost to a sitting position and rested my left arm on my left knee to steady the rifle, which was a long, octagon-barreled Model 94 Winchester .30-30. My grandfather had purchased the rifle many years prior in Pullman, Washington for $16. The buck was uphill from me and the bullet struck him in the lower neck and he dropped.

For a 15-year-old boy, it was a momentous occasion. We dragged him to camp, with the snow helping to make dragging easier.

The horns were kept in the woodshed for many years. In the mid 1970s, when my son, Craig, was in high school, he felt the rack had been neglected and took it to a local taxidermist and had him mount them on a walnut plaque. Now they hang in the den of my home.

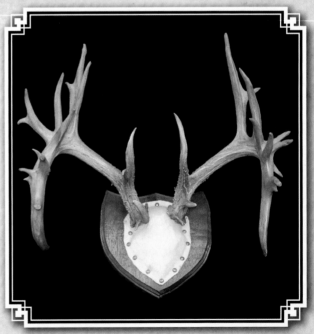

**One of Idaho's oldest trophy whitetails, George Hatley's 1939 Bonner County buck also has the third-most points of any buck in the state (28).**

# Harold G. Larson
### 195-1/8 B&C Non-Typical
### Latah County, 1982

**Non-typical Rank: 49***      **Abnormal Points: 17-2/8**      **Points (R,L): 7,9**
**Inside Spread: 21-5/8**      **Widest Spread: 24-0/8**
**Main Beams (R,L): 23-2/8,25-5/8**      **Bases (R, L): 4-2/8,4-3/8**

eing nearly 60 years old when he killed his big deer, Harold Larson had taken more than his share of whitetail bucks. Still, when he walked up to this buck, he says, "It kind of got to me." Decades worth of looking for a buck like this one will do that to a person.

That fall, Harold was mostly just looking to fill his tag. He and his hunting partners – cousin Eddie Galloway, and Harold's two sons-in-law, Jesse Ray Long and Mike Morey – were hunting close to home that day. They often hunted together and enjoyed each others' company.

Eddie took a 4x4 that morning, and that had been about the only thing of note for the morning. They met up around noon and were having lunch on the hill over an impromptu campfire, talking and joking. Mike and Jesse wanted to keep hunting, but Harold was more of a mind to call it a day. He grabbed his rifle and told them he was going to hunt back toward the truck.

Most of the area that surrounded him was fairly steep, but he was temporarily in a flatter pocket of real estate. He had gone about 200 yards and was topping over a knoll when he saw a buck 100 yards off, walking through the timber. He didn't key in too hard on the rack, other than that he noticed it was definitely a buck, and shot it with his .30-06 behind the shoulder. A follow-up shot just before it made it to the timber also connected.

Harold made his way over, slowly but surely, and the closer he got, the weaker his knees got. He says he got the shakes for a while, and just stared at the rack in disbelief.

Harold Larson's big-framed 7x9 non-typical, taken on a casual hunt close to home, has an impressive net typical frame of 177-7/8. It is also just big enough to qualify for the all-time records book.

**A seasoned hunter, Harold Larson still got the shakes when he walked up to this monster buck.**

# Jacob D. Lott
## 194-4/8 B&C Non-Typical
## Clearwater County, 2005

**Idaho Non-typical Rank: 52**     **Abnormal Points: 16-5/8**     **Points (R,L): 8,7**
**Inside Spread: 21-7/8**     **Widest Spread: 26-6/8**
**Main Beams (R,L): 25-7/8, 27-0/8**     **Bases (R, L): 4-5/8, 4-5/8**

I t began when Chad Burke, Charlie Stamper, and I were hunting in the early cow elk season. We saw this deer in the middle of a wheat field right before dark. Of course, each of us wanted him, but knew the rut would be our best chance.

That morning it was 20 degrees and clear. I woke up late, and it was 8 a.m. when I got out to where I wanted to hunt. I grabbed my 7mm and hurried down into a canyon, hoping to see the buck we had seen earlier in the year.

About 20 minutes into the hunt, I came upon a 130-inch 5x5, but decided to let him go. It was only five minutes later when I saw a buck headed up the ridge above me 130 yards away. I couldn't tell how big he was, so I sat and watched him through my binoculars. I finally got a good look and could tell as he walked away from me that his spread was wider then his hips and that he had good tine length.

Guessing it was a 160 buck, I decided to shoot. He would soon break over the ridge, so I set my pack down and took aim. I touched off a shot, but the buck just kept walking, seemingly unaffected. I was getting ready to shoot again when he fell.

Right then I started getting the shakes. I got closer and the buck was struggling, so I fired one more round and ended it. When I got a better look, I realized I had taken a much bigger buck than I had originally thought.

I need to thank Chad, Bert, Charlie and family for letting me stay at their place and hunt with them. If it wasn't for them, I never would've been able to take a deer like this.

# Jerry Gillispie
## 194 B&C Non-Typical
### Clearwater County, 1981

JERRY GILLISPIE

| | | |
|---|---|---|
| **Idaho Non-typical Rank: 53\*** | **Abnormal Points: 43-7/8** | **Points (R,L): 15,6** |
| **Inside Spread: 23-3/8** | | **Widest Spread: 27-0/8** |
| **Main Beams (R,L): 20-4/8, 23-6/8** | | **Bases (R, L): 4-7/8, 4-5/8** |

n only his second year of hunting, 22-year-old Jerry Gillispie had a goal: kill a buck. He had taken a doe in his first hunting season, but he now wanted a nice rack to put up on the wall.

His brother, Larry, and cousin, Monte Gillispie, accompanied Jerry on this hunt near the Dworshak Reservoir breaks. It was timbered and brushy country, fairly thick cover perfect for holding and hiding crafty whitetail bucks.

They departed the cab of the Toyota pickup and instantly wished they hadn't. The weather was raging – a terrible wind and torrential rain that had most all hunters staying under cover for a day of watching football. Jerry remembers hearing at least one tree get blown over and countless snapped branches.

They split up and Jerry began slowly still-hunting, half focused on the hunt and half on the storm. More than once, the ridiculousness of the whole idea came to mind.

He was picking his way along when he saw the body of a deer about 40 yards away. The head was hidden behind a tree, but as near as he could tell, it looked like a big doe or a small buck. Squinting through the driving rain, he watched until it moved and he could see antler. He didn't bother to look at much after that, so when he shouldered his Winchester .30-06 and fired, he didn't have much idea what size of buck it was.

Upon getting shot at, the buck wheeled and ran – right at Jerry! Jerry raised up again to shoot as the buck passed by a mere eight feet away, but could only see hair in the scope and never got the shot off. Twenty yards later the buck toppled over and crashed.

Jerry now had plenty of time to see the rack, which was stunning in size and shape. Just when he was beginning to think he had his buck, it suddenly kicked, got up, and took off down the hill.

Panicked, Jerry started trying to follow the blood trail, which was washing away fast in the hard rain. He frantically looked everywhere and then, in desperation, fired three shots to get Larry and Monte over to help him.

Hearing the shots, they ran over and got the pickup, which they promptly got stuck and almost blew the engine. When they finally got to Jerry, they began searching. They had looked just about everywhere and had about exhausted their options when Monte finally found the buck laying some distance up the mountainside. A quick drag of the whole-bodied buck to the pickup was a welcome end to an otherwise physically and mentally exhausting day.

**Everything about this photo "screams" 1981. Gotta love it.**

# Deanna M. Dixon
## 192-4/8 B&C Non-Typical
### Bonner County, 1992

| | | |
|---|---|---|
| **Idaho Non-typical Rank: 56*** | **Abnormal Points: 23-6/8** | **Points (R,L): 9,7** |
| **Inside Spread: 18-2/8** | | **Widest Spread: 23-6/8** |
| **Main Beams (R,L): 24-3/8, 24-0/8** | | **Bases (R, L): 4-4/8, 4-3/8** |

I almost didn't go hunting that frigid day of November 28, 1992, as I had a cold and wasn't feeling well. However, with the season almost over and my dad catching a glimpse of a big buck early that morning, I got motivated.

I was only 19 and grew up in the woods outside the small town of Priest River. My whole family has always enjoyed hunting and the meat it provides, but I had never shot a deer myself. I passed up quite a few deer that year, including smaller bucks that Dad had rattled in for me. I was determined to shoot a big buck.

That day, armed with lots of Kleenex and cough drops, we climbed in the Bronco and headed out. My dad and I got dropped off on one side of a mountain and he went farther down the ridge while I hiked up an old skid trail. I contemplated a spot near an opening, but decided since the big bucks stay in the brush, that was where I was going to go. I finally decided on a spot under a big tree with branches almost touching the ground, where I could look out and see a game trail in the ravine below.

While I was getting situated, my grandpa, Bill Dixon, and my brother, Billy Dixon, drove around to the other side of the mountain and hiked in to find a spot of their own.

After an hour, while I was sitting against the tree and sucking on a cough drop, I heard a loud crashing sound coming up the other side of the mountain behind me. I knew it wasn't human, as I could hear bounding and antlers plowing through branches, so I turned

DEANNA DIXON

**Deanna Dixon is all smiles after taking this big-framed non-typical in 1992.**

around to face uphill and got my rifle ready.

I was leaning against the tree and remembering everything my dad taught me when a huge buck appeared on top of the hill above me. I released my safety, aimed my grandpa's .308 Remington and calmly squeezed the trigger. I knew I had hit him, but the way he barely flinched and took off down the ridge, it didn't seem so.

My adrenaline kicked in and I ran to see if I could get another shot, but there was no sight of him; just big tracks and a blood trail in the snow. Hearing my shot, my dad and brother caught up to me. As we waited awhile before tracking him, I tried to convince them that he was the biggest buck I had ever seen!

It was almost dark when the blood trail ended at the river's edge. I was devastated that I wounded him and may never find him.

The next morning, my whole family joined in the search. My dad and I hiked in on the other side of the river from where his trail ended. As we neared the river, we heard crashing and one splash. It was brushy, and by the time we reached the edge of the river, he was gone up the other side. We were amazed at how he could leap to the middle of the river and up the other bank so quickly in his condition.

On the other side, my mom, Janet, caught a glimpse of him but wasn't able to get a shot. We caught up to him several times and could hear him bounding off, but could never see him. He was smart, circling and hiding in thick brush and watching his backtrail.

I was supposed to get back to college the next day, but instead I kept searching for him. We finally came across his big tracks, but no blood, and a line in the fresh snow where it looked like he was dragging a leg.

**Deanna, along with her dad (standing), look on as Gordon Whittington (then the Editor for *North American Whitetail* magazine) inspects the huge buck. Deanna had taken the buck to Priest River and entered it in the contest at Mac's, and Gordon, who just happened to be hunting in the area, got wind of it. It was an amazing coincidence.**

From up on the hill, we could see his trail lead down into a thicket, so we decided to try and outsmart him by sneaking way around behind him. It worked and I was finally able to finish him off. It turned out that my first shot hit his shoulder bone and veered down through his brisket, barely missing his vitals.

We later discovered that we had collected several of his sheds over the years, and that Vern Garland had named him "Old Joe". He had photographed the buck for years in an alfalfa field during the summer months, but said he always disappeared during hunting season. Old Joe was one super smart buck, and it took a lot of luck, perseverance and family effort to finally get him.

# Gaylord R. Colvin, Jr.
## 191-7/8 B&C Non-Typical
### Idaho County, 1957

RICHARD HENDERSON

**Idaho Non-typical Rank: 58***  **Abnormal Points: 19-1/8**  **Points (R,L): 11,11**
**Inside Spread: 19-2/8**  **Widest Spread: 23-0/8**
**Main Beams (R,L): 21-6/8, 22-7/8**  **Bases (R, L): 5-3/8, 5-2/8**

**G**ay Colvin was the Postmaster in Whitebird in 1957, but was riding for cattle in the Chapman Creek area on that fateful October day in 1957. He had seen a big buck up there a couple of times, and when he went back up again, he made sure and had his rifle with him.

He was lucky enough to cross paths with the big ol' buck one more time, and made him pay the price. He shot the huge whitetail either from the saddle or in real close proximity to his ride, and that was the end of it.

Dick Henderson, who is also in this book with a 171-3/8 typical, was a young teenager who stopped by to pick up the mail when he saw Gay's trophy buck. Enamored with it for many years, Dick now owns the buck, which was taken a few miles south in the same county six years later.

IDFG

# Michael S. Emerson
## 191-2/8 B&C Non-Typical
### Bonner County, 2005

MICHAEL EMERSON

**Idaho Non-typical Rank: 61**     **Abnormal Points:29-5/8**     **Points (R,L): 9,8**

**Inside Spread: 18-1/8**     **Widest Spread: 21-0/8**

**Main Beams (R,L): 23-3/8, 23-1/8**     **Bases (R, L): 5-5/8, 5-6/8**

I n early fall of 2005, after learning about a herd of elk that moved along a mountain range behind my home, I decided to hike a couple of miles and scout it out. After this early scouting trip and seeing plentiful elk sign, I decided to hunt the area.

A few weeks later, I left early one morning, took a compass reading, and began my upward climb. It was an unusually warm fall morning, so I walked in the shade of the fir trees for many hours.

I bugled and cow called every half-hour or so, but received no response. With evening closing in quickly, I chose a place to sleep for the night. As I lay there under the clear night sky, I began to hear a faint bugle in the distance, and the startling sound of a couple of owls screeching back and forth.

I awoke the next morning with high spirits, but this is where my elk hunt took a 180-degree turn. After some cold coffee and a light breakfast, I packed up camp and put on my hunting gear. I picked up my pack, and my doe bleat call rolled out of an unzipped pocket onto the ground. I'm not sure why, but I couldn't resist turning that can over a couple of times. After all, archery deer season was open also!

As soon as the sound of the second bleat ended, the sound of breaking branches and twigs became louder and louder! I searched my surroundings and the maker of all the racket – a huge buck – ran to within 20 yards of me. I drew my bow as he ran in and then he stopped behind several bushes, standing as still as a statue. He finally stepped forward and I grunted with my mouth, stopping him instantly.

**Michael Emerson nicked this buck with an arrow in September, and was extremely fortunate to find the buck again in November, when he took the buck with his lever-action .44 magnum.**

Releasing my arrow, I watched as it went right over his back. Focusing through the peep sight, I had not seen several small branches sticking out from a tree. I mentally kicked myself as the branch continued to bounce up and down. I followed up the shot looking for blood, but after some time, I found none. I hunted elk for the rest of that day, returning home that evening. For weeks afterward, not a day passed when that big buck wasn't in my thoughts, knowing I'd likely never get another chance at him.

As November came and my desire to hunt the rut grew, I was in the woods as much as possible. I replaced my bow with my Model 94 .44 magnum lever action, mostly to increase my odds of putting meat in the freezer. Spending many days in the woods closer to home, I saw several small bucks but never got any clear shots.

On another outing, I walked back into an area where three small ravines fed into one draw. Finding a good spot to sit, I was ready for a long day. After several rattling and grunting sequences, I just sat quiet.

Looking down the draw, I saw several does running. I took my estrous call and used it a couple of times, hoping to draw them in.

Half an hour later, I saw movement. Appearing in the bottom of the draw was a buck – a big one. I readied my rifle as he walked up from the bottom. Sixty, fifty, forty…I gave him a mouth grunt and stopped him. I could not believe the size of this buck! I squeezed the trigger and heard a good thud, and then watched as he ran up the hill and back down the draw. Then, it was deafeningly quiet.

After a few minutes, I gathered my gear and began tracking him but he only ran 80 yards. I stood there, stunned, and gazed in awe at the largest buck I had ever seen or taken!

After taking several pictures, I began to get ready to field dress my prize. Upon rolling the buck over, I noticed a small wound on his back where he had been cut. At that moment, I was amazed to realize that this was the same buck I thought I had missed during archery season. The cut had healed over quite well.

The following day, my dad accompanied me to pack the meat out and share in the excitement. I will always remember this buck and this hunt, and look forward to sharing future hunts with my dad. Thanks, Dad, for taking me and teaching me how to hunt, so I can always enjoy the outdoors.

MICHAEL EMERSON

# Picked Up by Luke D. Finney
## 191-2/8 B&C Non-Typical
### Kootenai County, 2005

LUKE FINNEY

| | | |
|---|---|---|
| **Idaho Non-typical Rank: 61*** | **Abnormal Points:25-0/8** | **Points (R,L): 9,9** |
| **Inside Spread: 18-4/8** | | **Widest Spread: 20-5/8** |
| **Main Beams (R,L): 25-6/8, 25-2/8** | | **Bases (R, L): 4-7/8, 4-4/8** |

I f you've read *Idaho's Greatest Mule Deer* or *Idaho's Greatest Elk*, you're probably getting well acquainted with the Finney family. There's a very good reason they keep "showing up"; they are some of the best and most knowledgeable hunters around. They also make it a priority, and aren't weekend warriors. They live it a couple hundred days a year.

That's why it's not much of a surprise to hear that Luke found this tremendous buck in December, after the season but still before shed antlers drop. Luke Finney and his uncle, Gary, had been out for several hours, and Luke was waiting for Gary at a meeting point. He had been hearing ravens off in the distance, but wasn't yet convinced he wanted to go down there to investigate.

When Gary showed up, Luke told him he was going to drop down there and check it out real quick. He proceeded to do just that, and when he did, he got a real shock. This buck lay there, only partially decomposed. It had been extremely cold, and the carcass had likely been frozen for a portion of that time. Luke figures it was the victim of a wounding loss, but there's no way to know for sure.

On a side note, Gary has this buck's shed antler from two years prior, and found it only a ridge away from the buck's final resting place.

# Michael L. Albright
## 190-6/8 B&C Non-Typical
### Nez Perce County, 2009

MICHAEL ALBRIGHT

**Idaho Non-typical Rank: 63\***  **Abnormal Points:12-1/8**  **Points (R,L): 8,8**

**Inside Spread: 19-5/8**  **Widest Spread: 21-7/8**

**Main Beams (R,L): 26-6/8, 26-5/8**  **Bases (R, L): 4-6/8, 4-6/8**

For 18 years I have hunted whitetails, consistently shooting average "basket" bucks that either looked bigger at a distance or came out of the brush so fast that I had no time to accurately judge them. I admit walking up and being a little on the disappointed side at times. In 2009, my luck would change.

That morning I left my house and picked up my friend, Chuck, and we then drove to meet my dad, Marvin. He jumped in with us and we made our way to a canyon. He had left his pickup at a place where we would end our hunt the next day.

We dropped down into the canyon hunted for five hours, steadily making our way to Dad's truck. No one had any luck, and we all eventually met and drove around to our starting point. When we got back to my pickup, Chuck and I decided we would probably just head back to town, since a storm was moving in.

On our way back to town, Chuck and I were following my dad when he called on the CB and said he knew a landowner who had a spot to hunt and it would only take a few hours. We decided to give it a try, even though it was in the middle of the day. The deer were rutting, so the chance of spotting a buck moving was good.

We stopped and checked in with the landowner and then headed out onto the property. The wind had picked up pretty good, so we adjusted our plan. My dad stayed close to the field edge on top, I dropped into the middle, and Chuck went 150 yards or so below me, with all of us heading into the wind.

I was walking through some small jack pines with a nice grass floor and got onto a game trail. With the breeze, I could move through the woods deadly silent. I moved extremely slow, stopping every few steps to observe, when I reached an area that had six rubs in a 20-yard radius. I thought to myself that a couple of the rubs had to have been made by a really large buck.

Suddenly, I caught movement out of the corner of my eye. When I turned, I knew instantly that it was a big buck. He was on full sneak, coming through the brush and jack pines at 60 yards and closing. At 30 yards, he ducked under a pine tree and came up with grass in his antlers. I shouldered my Featherweight .300 WSM and the buck froze, with his head up and quartering toward me.

Through my scope, I noticed that his long fourth and fifth points made a big fork. With a handful of mule deer in the area and me having a whitetail-only tag, I lowered my .300 WSM for a split-second to confirm he was in fact a whitetail. He was, and I shot quickly. He dropped like a rock.

As I was trying to calm down and take in what had just happened, I walked another 75 yards to an opening where I thought I would be able to see Chuck or my dad. Then I just sat down, somewhat overwhelmed.

After all was said and done, it was obvious the smart old buck stayed in cover until my dad had passed him, and then got up to sneak farther down into the draw for more cover. I was just lucky enough to be in the right place at the right time.

**Michael Albright's big-framed buck was one of the biggest bucks taken in Idaho in 2009.**

# Fred H. Muhs
### 190-1/8 B&C Non-Typical
### Kootenai County, 1956

LARS EIDNES

**Idaho Non-typical Rank: 66***  **Abnormal Points: 35-4/8**  **Points (R,L): 9,8**
**Inside Spread: 26-5/8**  **Widest Spread: 28-6/8**
**Main Beams (R,L): 22-7/8, 22-6/8**  **Bases (R, L): 5-1/8, 5-1/8**

I had seen this buck a couple of times early in the fall of 1956 and decided to try and nail him. I was 16, and when I'd arrive home from school, I'd change clothes, grab my peep-sighted 8mm and cautiously move through a 40-acre patch of timber that bordered some alfalfa hay ground. Twice I spotted him on the far edge of the field, but without a scope, I chose not to shoot.

A few days before Thanksgiving, I crept up to the edge of the field. I saw him 75 yards away with a couple of does and a forked horn. Two times I shot and dropped him, and each time he'd get up and shake his head (I was trying for a head shot, as meat in our family was not to be wasted). On my third try, I aimed for his chest and took out his heart. I had grazed him two times at the base of his antlers.

FRED MUHS

**Taken over 50 years ago, Fred Muhs' trophy buck is one of the widest in Idaho.**

# Miranda Ross
## 189-5/8 B&C Non-Typical
### Benewah County, 1990

| | | |
|---|---|---|
| **Idaho Non-typical Rank: 67*** | **Abnormal Points:15-0/8** | **Points (R,L): 8x7** |
| **Inside Spread: 19-1/8** | | **Widest Spread: 21-6/8** |
| **Main Beams (R,L): 26-4/8, 27-5/8** | | **Bases (R, L): 4-7/8, 5-2/8** |

**M**iranda Ross was just an early teen when she shot one of the most massive white-tail bucks in the state of Idaho. What's even more amazing is that she was hunting alone when she did it.

According to her dad, Bill, she grabbed a .35 Whelen and hiked from her front doorstep into the timber near their home. Once there, she sat quiet and waited, hoping to shoot her first-ever deer.

It was November, and the deer were moving. Pretty soon this giant trophy came within range and she knocked it down. She didn't really know what she had, and with limited experience, she came back down to the house, where her brother helped her get it taken care of and out of the woods.

While she didn't have a true grasp for what she had done, her dad and other hunters who saw it sure did. The buck was a monster, with super mass, long-reaching beams that curled around beautifully, and outrageous eyeguards.

133

# David W. Carver
## 188-6/8 B&C Non-Typical
## Clearwater County, 1978

**Idaho Non-typical Rank: 68**          **Abnormal Points:15-4/8**          **Points (R,L): 7,7**
**Inside Spread: 22-2/8**                                                     **Widest Spread: 28-1/8**
**Main Beams (R,L): 24-0/8, 25-3/8**                                          **Bases (R, L): 4-4/8, 4-4/8**

Twenty-five-year-old David Carver was on a late season hunt close to home when he crossed paths with this giant buck. A storm had just passed through, and David headed out alone into the wet and the mud, hoping to catch a buck moving.

The area had plenty of timber and brush, but was only average thick. In fact, the ridge he was hunting was fairly open but very steep.

He had seen a bunch of deer – probably pushing 50 – including some smaller bucks that were sparring, but nothing that interested him greatly. Finally he saw two bucks about 500 yards away. They were both huge, and were gradually feeding away from a meadow into a smaller finger ridge. David followed, and quickly jumped a couple more nice bucks. Any other day, he might have been tempted to shoot, but with what he had just seen, it was an easy decision to let them walk.

He was stepping over a log when he nearly stepped on a doe at the same time. She jumped and spooked one of the big bucks David was after. Without much time to think, he shouldered his .270 and fired at 60 yards not all that far above the doe's back that had started this whole melee. The shot hit him in the shoulder and he ran out of sight.

David started tracking, but there were so many deer in the area that it quickly became futile. In addition, he couldn't find blood. This sent him into a panic. He could see that huge buck in his mind, and began to get sick to his stomach at the thought that he might have missed him. He'd never in his life seen a buck that big.

He kept looking and finally found blood. He continued in that direction and found him piled up 40 yards ahead. David had an overwhelming feeling of both relief and excitement. The buck was everything he thought it was and more. Big tall tines, extra points – this buck had it all.

Even though he was alone, he was able to drag it whole-bodied back to his vehicle. Maybe all the adrenaline helped.

David's huge buck, from way back in 1978, has a tremendous frame. The G-2s, measuring 14-2/8 and 15-2/8 inches, are among the longest in Idaho.

# Jason E. Gomes
## 188-4/8 B&C Non-Typical
### Nez Perce County, 2002

**Idaho Non-typical Rank: 69***  **Abnormal Points:11-7/8**  **Points (R,L): 6,7**
**Inside Spread: 21-5/8**  **Widest Spread: 24-1/8**
**Main Beams (R,L): 25-3/8, 27-0/8**  **Bases (R, L): 5-0/8, 5-4/8**

t was a promising October afternoon - a day for a good hunt with good friends. Kyle Andrews, Thomas James, and I climbed into my pickup and headed for a canyon where I occasionally see a few head of elk.

The country I prefer to hunt, though surrounded by wheat fields, can be fairly rugged terrain, mostly consisting of steep canyons, heavy brush, scattered timber, and a lack of roads. This makes it unappealing for some hunters, as it is a difficult hunt, and packing game out requires a pack board and is seldom easy.

Worn out from our earlier hunting efforts, Thomas decided to sit this hunt out and grab some sleep in the pickup – a decision he was to later regret! Kyle and I headed down the ridge to get a good view of the opposite hillsides and glass until dark.

The canyon on the left was steep and brushy, with the occasional fir tree on our side, and open with star thistle and rocky outcroppings on the other. The far side of the canyon to our right was open on our side and scattered with brush and timber on the other. To the left, 30 yards from the crest of the ridge, there was a 20-foot bluff that ran for a couple hundred yards. The only brush between us and the bluff was a scattering of waist-high red bushes that we passed twenty feet above.

We had just passed the little brush patch when we spotted several cow elk and a pretty good six-point bull feeding along the creek in a nice little flat. I laid my BAR .300 Win.-mag. down across a big rock, as did Kyle with his Ruger .30-06.

I placed the point of the duplex crosshairs high on the shoulder and squeezed off a shot. The rifle jumped in my hands, and the bullet went right over the bull's back, kicking up dust in the creek bottom.

The elk spooked and ran to the base of the hill on our side. I went back the way we came to try to get a better line of vision along the bottom of the canyon. I was now about ten yards from the little brush patch that we had passed earlier, and heading back toward it.

As I got nearer, the biggest whitetail buck I had ever seen stood up broadside right in the middle of the brush patch! I wasn't prepared for such a close encounter, but eventually fired. He took a couple of quick steps and I fired again. He then ran up and to my left, heading over the ridge! I thought I had somehow missed the first two shots, so I aimed just behind his shoulder from 50 yards away and shot again! He looked hit as he dropped out of sight at the top of the ridge!

I finally got to the top of the ridge, where I'd last seen him, and began to look for blood. My heart sank when I didn't see any, but I did see a fresh set of running tracks. I followed them up the hill for 45 yards and there he was.

I couldn't believe how big he was! I called out to Kyle and he came up. He was confused about what was going on, since he had never even seen the buck. He had been looking down the hill the whole time, still trying to spot elk!

The two of us just stared in silence for a few moments, in awe. Once the initial shock wore off, we began the excited handshakes and slaps on the back. It was a great day.

# Mike Rudeen
### 187-5/8 B&C Non-Typical
### Latah County, 1952

COURTESY OF BOONE AND CROCKETT CLUB

| | | |
|---|---|---|
| **Idaho Non-typical Rank: 71*** | **Abnormal Points: 13-4/8** | **Points (R,L): 7,6** |
| **Inside Spread: 23-3/8** | | **Widest Spread: 25-4/8** |
| **Main Beams (R,L): 22-3/8, 25-3/8** | | **Bases (R, L): 5-3/8, 5-3/8** |

many years have passed since Mike Rudeen killed his big buck in Latah County. As such, information was hard to come by. Darrell Tonn, who has two whitetails in this book, happened to bring up Mike's name and I keyed in on it instantly. Darrell owned Husky Sport Shop in Moscow, which was a big sporting goods store for many years in the heart of whitetail country. As such, Darrell was pretty well acquainted with most people in the area and knew Mike. He said that Mike was a logger, and that Mike killed this buck on Burnt Ridge in a canyon behind his house. Darrell knew this because he hunted the same area and sometimes visited with Mike when he was out there.

I also lucked out a little bit in finding some more information about this buck. Back in 2005, I was working for Boone and Crockett Club as Assistant Director of Big Game Records. I often found myself digging through old archives, and had an idea for a book. Based on getting glimpses into private B&C files and seeing some great vintage hunting history and photos, *A Whitetail Retrospective* was born.

I spent weeks digging and selecting photos, interesting letters, and other unique memorabilia, and writing many of the captions and the preface to the book. One item of great interest to me was Mike Rudeen's file. It had been one of those that had dropped out of the records book when the minimums had been raised, but had not been reinstated when the lower Awards period minimum was instituted.

Inside was a great vintage photo of the deer on an antiquated but interesting mount, along with a letter to B&C from legendary outdoor writer Jack O'Connor. Jack was a measurer for B&C, and had measured Mike's trophy. Following is a letter Jack wrote to the Club, along with a response from Grancel Fitz, who headed up the Records Program at that time. It adds some interesting history to the trophy, and I figured that since Jack lived in Lewiston and has a big fan base in Idaho, our readers might enjoy it as well.

Special thanks to B&C Club for sharing this private look into the file for this book. If you are interested in seeing more of this type of history and would like to order *A Whitetail Retrospective*, go to www.booneandcrockettclub.com or call 406-542-1888.

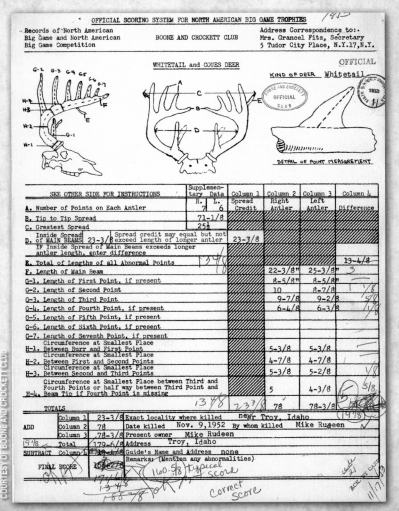

# Outdoor Life

*First Choice of Discriminating Sportsmen*

353 FOURTH AVENUE · NEW YORK 10, N.Y.

April 20, 1 9 5 4

SHOOTING DEPARTMENT
JACK O'CONNOR, EDITOR

Dear Grancel:

My pal Mike Rudeen of Troy, Idaho, who had a hell of a big whitetail in the contest that I measured is all of a dither because his head did not wind a prize. He had card from Betty saying his head scored 188 2/8 and was non-typical. No photo was sent with the measurements I sent in, but Mike now has had a photo taken and I am enclosing it. Mike thinks his head should be classed as typical, <u>not</u> non-typical. I tell Mike I don't even work there, that it is up to the committee.

I have also suggested that Mike take his head up to Don Hopkins and have Don look at it.

Please thank Betty for sending me the list for the last competition. Brother, you really got some trophies this last time! Herb Klein got a nice Stone this last fall, quite long but slender. He just got back from a trip to India and Iran.

My best,

Jack

Box 382
Lewiston
Idaho

*I got a fine kudu and one hell of a sable when I was in Africa*

**Jack O'Connor's letter to B&C regarding Mike Rudeen's trophy, along with Grancel Fitz' response.**

Dear Jack:

In re your note on the Rudeen whitetail, let's first have a look at how the Scoring System works. The question of whether a head is typical or non-typical is solved quite automatically, without the need of any personal judgment. The scores for questionable specimens are easily computed for both classes, and the head is then ranked in the class in which it rates the higher place.

The Rudeen trophy shows a non-typical score of 174 6/8:13 4/8= 188 2/8, and this, of course, is good but by no means startling. On the other hand, if it were scored as a typical head, the 13 4/8 which is the total of the abnormal point lengths would be deducted from the 174 6/8, leaving a net score of 161 2/8. There were 22 typical heads with higher scores entered in the Competition, which was won by a new world record scoring 183 7/8, although several heads we asked for were not sent in to the show. In the non-typical class, the lowest score of the five exhibited was 15 points ahead of the Rudeen trophy.

While the Rudeen buck is unquestionably large for an Idaho specimen, it hardly stacks up with the really big ones. For instance, it has beam lengths of 22 3/8 and 25 3/8. Compare this with the 29 5/8 and 31 1/8 beams of the Pennsylvania buck which won only 4th prize in the non-typical class. Actually, these two trophies are alike in that they are too freakish to get far in the typical class -- which emphasizes normal conformation -- and they are not nearly freakish enough to stack up with the real non-typicals such as this year's winner, which shows 28 antler points and a score of 178 2/8: 59 1/8 = 237 3/8. I hope that this will clarify the picture for your friend.

All best wishes, and congratulations on your fine African trophies.

Yours sincerely,

Grancel Fitz

GF:H

# Brad Corkill
## 187-1/8 B&C Non-Typical
### Kootenai County, 1990

**Idaho Non-typical Rank: 73**   **Abnormal Points: 38-4/8**   **Points (R,L): 9,10**
**Inside Spread: 20-5/8**   **Widest Spread: 30-0/8**
**Main Beams (R,L): 24-1/8, 24-5/8**   **Bases (R, L): 4-7/8, 5-0/8**

T hanksgiving weekend, 1990, was our first fall in our new home, and also one of my son Nathan's first times accompanying me on a deer hunt. He was eleven years old, still too young to carry a rifle. My father was also hunting with us. The weather was cold and wet; no snow, just rain and low clouds.

We are fortunate to live where we do. The land behind our house is split between public land, timber company land, and friendly neighbors. As such, we had plenty of area to hunt and explore.

Nathan and I climbed high up the mountain behind our house and my father stayed low. We hunted for a long time that morning, moving quietly through the wet brush and timber, eventually becoming soaked and cold. For several hours we saw nothing, and all we heard - besides the sound of the rain - were the flocks of geese heading south. Regardless, I have always felt that the rain gives me a bit of an edge when hunting deer.

I have always had trouble sitting still when I hunt deer and elk. I much prefer moving slowly, watching and listening. This technique is perhaps not the most productive, but I like it. Even though the weather was miserable, it was a great day for hunting and we thoroughly enjoyed ourselves.

I was carrying a .250/3000 Savage that was owned by my grandfather. It was the same rifle I had used to take my first deer in 1963. It had a 2-1/2-power scope that would eventually fog up in the rain. I still use that rifle today; some things just cannot be improved on. However, I have changed scopes.

At 10 a.m., Nathan and I were heading back home, contouring the mountain and moving through patches of pine and serviceberry. Even though we were heading home, we were still hunting.

I saw the buck before he saw me, which even at that moment I thought was unusual. He was facing away from us, not even 20 yards away, and the only shot I had was at his neck. He began to turn his head, sensing that something was up. I fired immediately and he disappeared into the brush. We waited for just a moment and then headed downhill in the direction he went. He didn't go 50 yards.

We found him in the open, and it was then I realized that this buck was special. It was also then when I began to realize why I had seen him first. His front teeth were worn to the gum line and his hide was almost totally gray. He was very old and had probably lost some of his senses. He had no doubt been dodging hunters for years, and on that day his luck just ran out. He was the patriarch of that area and his bloodline is still there.

We field dressed him and then dragged him to the house. It began to sink in more and more that his antlers were spectacular. I doubt I will ever harvest a big game animal that will match this buck. Since that day, Nathan and I have taken several bucks in the same area, but not one of them comes close to this one.

*Note: Brad Corkill's awe-inspiring trophy buck, with a 30-inch spread, is the second-widest whitetail in Idaho, behind only the state record non-typical.*

**Brad Corkill (right) and his son, Nathan, hold up Brad's incredible whitetail buck, taken southeast of Coeur d' Alene on a rainy day on Thanksgiving weekend.**

# Tami M. Van Ness
### 186-7/8 B&C Non-Typical
### Latah County, 1990

**Idaho Non-typical Rank: 74**     **Abnormal Points:20-6/8**     **Points (R,L): 8,6**
**Inside Spread: 17-5/8**     **Widest Spread: 21-0/8**
**Main Beams (R,L): 24-0/8, 24-3/8**     **Bases (R, L): 4-2/8, 4-1/8**

 was just 16 years old when I shot this deer on November 13, 1990. I remember that hunting was something my father and I did together from the time I was an early teen until I had children of my own.

     That particular morning I remember my dad taking me out behind our house (20 minutes past Viola) before I got ready for school that day. It was overcast and cool, and he felt the deer might be rutting. I also remember thinking there wouldn't be enough time to hunt! We had been standing outside on my parents' property for 20-30 minutes when I decided I needed to go and get in the shower to get ready for school.

     I turned around at 7 a.m. and headed back to the house, and my father stayed out to watch for deer. I got about 50 feet down the hill when I heard my dad calling me back.

I turned and saw him motioning that there was a deer coming. I ran back up the hill, and when I reached my father, I saw the buck. I remember thinking how big it was, and I was amazed that this buck had come out right in front of us!

He was about 30 yards away and coming toward us. When he turned broadside, I shot him in the right shoulder with a Marlin .44-Magnum lever-action rifle. He fell not far from where he'd been shot. I remember my dad telling me to shoot again to finish him, so I hit the buck again and put him down for good.

When we walked up to him, Dad and I were both pretty surprised. His two droptines on his right side are pretty amazing.

**A young Tami Van Ness poses with her gorgeous whitetail buck, taken on a very brief hunt before school only a rifle shot from their home.**

# Earl Nelson
## 186-1/8 B&C Non-Typical
### Kootenai County, 2005

EARL NELSON

| | | |
|---|---|---|
| **Idaho Non-typical Rank: 79*** | **Abnormal Points:30-6/8** | **Points (R,L): 8,9** |
| **Inside Spread: 19-3/8** | | **Widest Spread: 24-3/8** |
| **Main Beams (R,L): 25-3/8, 25-2/8** | | **Bases (R, L): 4-6/8, 4-5/8** |

**E**arl Nelson was 56 years old when he moved to northern Idaho, and was a bona fide neophyte to whitetail hunting. He accepted the challenge, learned quickly, and took his hunting very seriously.

In fall of 2005, Earl was focused on a big buck. He had seen it twice right at dark, but the big, wide buck had thus far outfoxed him.

That morning, he left from his house and drove to a friend's property, where he would be hunting a mix of public and private land. It was foggy, and Earl wasn't sure how the hunt might go.

He got into position, and when the fog lifted, a big buck appeared 150 yards away. Unaware of Earl's presence, the buck bounced out into a clearing and was starting to alternately feed and look around for danger. Earl didn't hesitate; he fired his .257 Roberts and brought down his best trophy buck ever. It was a tremendous non-typical buck, and it had a 13-inch-long extra point coming out of the base of the left antler.

Ironically, the buck he shot that day wasn't the same buck that he had seen on the previous occasions - the buck he wanted so badly. Judging by the size of the one he settled for, it's probably safe to assume he's okay with it.

# Adrian Lane
### 185-6/8 B&C Non-Typical
### Bonner County, 1961

ADRIAN LANE

**Idaho Non-typical Rank: 81\***      **Abnormal Points:33-2/8**      **Points (R,L): 10,7**
**Inside Spread: 21-2/8**      **Widest Spread: 25-2/8**
**Main Beams (R,L): 21-6/8, 25-1/8**      **Bases (R, L): 5-0/8, 4-6/8**

The day after Thanksgiving 1961, thirteen year-old Adrian Lane was hunting with his father, Roy Lane, and his older brother, Jerry. They had driven up the Talache Road south of Sandpoint, parked their pickup, and hiked up the mountain. They hunted most of the day, but didn't see anything.

They were headed back down to the pickup when Jerry said he wanted to make one more pass. Adrian and his dad returned to the truck and were waiting for Jerry when they heard several rifle shots. Roy told Adrian to run up the old logging road where they had parked and maybe his brother would chase something down to him. He ran 200 yards up the road when a big buck jumped out, stopped and took one last look Adrian's way. One shot to the neck put him down. Adrian was using a Model 141 Remington .35 pump rifle his father had given him the previous year.

The Lanes were hunting for meat, so Adrian didn't appreciate the size of his deer until years later. It wasn't until 1976, when co-worker Clarence Davis showed off a large buck he had taken, that Adrian thought of the rack still in his mom's garage. Adrian made the comment that he had one bigger, but Clarence didn't believe him, so he urged Adrian to get it scored, and that's when he found out that he had a record-class whitetail.

*Note: While officially scoring 185-6/8, this buck actually grosses 200-7/8.*

# Nik Galloway
### 185-4/8 B&C Non-Typical
### Clearwater County, 1992

**Idaho Non-typical Rank: 82***     **Abnormal Points:15-7/8**     **Points (R,L): 9,9**

**Inside Spread: 17-7/8**                                          **Widest Spread: 20-5/8**

**Main Beams (R,L): 24-7/8, 24-2/8**                           **Bases (R, L): 4-7/8, 5-0/8**

I t was breaking daylight in the foothills of northern Idaho on November 26, 1992. I decided to go watch over an area where I had seen a nice heavy buck enter a small brush patch the previous day.

As I worked my way slowly to the crest of the hill, I stopped one last time to check the wind, and that's when it all happened. I glanced over to my right and instantly my heart dropped. Bedded 50 yards away and looking right at me was the biggest whitetail I had ever seen.

I knew I was busted and had little time to react, so I took aim quickly with my scoped .243. I settled my crosshairs on the base of his neck and pulled the trigger. The rest is history.

I was just 13 years old when I killed this buck. To this day I can't believe my good fortune, and I thank God for the incredible experience.

*Author's note: The first time I met Nik Galloway (and his friend Nate Manfull) was on top of a mountain the day before elk season in 2006. I was packing in on horses with my dad, and let's just say that the day hadn't exactly gone as planned. Near dusk, I ran into them feeling a little disheveled and hurried. The first thing they did was invite us to share their camp, and the second thing they did was dig us out a tent spot while I was back getting my dad. It's one of the nicest and best encounters I've ever had in the mountains, with two of the best people. It's only fitting that things come full circle, and I'm very happy to be able to include a much older and wiser Nik Galloway in this book. See the field photo section for some of his other big whitetails. He's one of the best hunters around.*

**Thirteen-year-old Nik Galloway had seen this big buck in a brush patch the day before. He came back the next day and saw the buck bedded 50 yards away.**

# Darrell Tonn
### 185-1/8 B&C Non-Typical
### Benewah County, 1975

**Idaho Non-typical Rank: 83***    **Abnormal Points:14-7/8**    **Points (R,L): 8,9**

**Inside Spread: 17-0/8**    **Widest Spread: 19-1/8**

**Main Beams (R,L): 24-4/8, 26-4/8**    **Bases (R, L): 4-7/8, 4-6/8**

D arrell Tonn, who owned Husky Sport Shop in Moscow for many years, was an experienced hunter who was always on the lookout for a chance at a good buck. Being keen, he had taken many good trophies over the years.

He was driving down the highway one day near Plummer when he saw some bucks. It was a long shot, but he decided to talk to the landowner.

He had a conversation with an older gentleman who owned the farm, and after sharing a cup of coffee and getting the okay, he went out. It was a pretty simple hunt, and as Darrell says, "This big buck just sort of showed up." Sometimes, that's all there is to it.

# Nick Roberson
### 185-1/8 B&C Non-Typical
### Nez Perce County, 1977

**Idaho Non-typical Rank: 83**  **Abnormal Points:15-2/8**  **Points (R,L): 8,8**
**Inside Spread: 21-1/8**  **Widest Spread: 24-1/8**
**Main Beams (R,L): 24-1/8, 24-0/8**  **Bases (R, L): 5-2/8, 5-4/8**

W hen the blood trail and sign – both plainly visible in the knee-deep snow – just up and vanished into thin air, Nick Roberson had to have wondered, short of being abducted by aliens, just what the heck was going on and what happened to his buck.

He had started out that morning hoping to kill a doe. After driving a short distance to a starting point, he had pushed through an early season snow two miles to a likely spot. It was mostly comprised of steep, brushy draws breaking off from wheat fields.

After a couple of hours, Nick heard something crashing through the brush, busting limbs as it went. Then he saw it; a big buck was streaking across the canyon 400 yards away.

It turns out that a man who had been hunting that particular buck for a number of years had bumped it right to him. Nick took the shot with his .30-06 Remington 760 pump rifle and hit the buck right in the left eye.

Nick navigated down the canyon through the snow and climbed up the other side. He found blood and followed the mottled sign until, magically, it disappeared. He looked in every direction but could find no further evidence of any disturbance in the snow.

He had looked for about an hour, and coincidentally looked up. There, hanging by his antlers as if someone had strung him up for skinning, was his buck. After the shot, the buck had evidently tumbled down the hillside, gaining momentum with the snow. After hitting a small lip in the terrain, the buck had been launched right into the side of a big Douglas-fir, about twelve feet up from the base.

Nick surveyed the scene for a while, but as much as he'd have liked to see that buck come down on its own, it wasn't going to happen. Nick had to climb the tree and break branches until the buck finally came freefalling out. When the buck hit the ground, just to add insult to injury, the buck slid another 150 yards right down into the bottom of the creek.

The look on Nick's face must have been priceless as he wondered if anything about this buck was going to be easy. It wouldn't be the pack out; Nick and his brother-in-law, Gordon Halsey, had to come back in and quarter the buck. Once the job was finished, they got the honor of packing it out on their backs in that deep snow.

# Steve D. Spletstoser

### 185 B&C Non-Typical
### Bonner County, 2004

STEVE SPLETSTOSER

**Idaho Non-typical Rank: 85**  **Abnormal Points:33-5/8**  **Points (R,L): 11,7**
**Inside Spread: 23-5/8**  **Widest Spread: 25-6/8**
**Main Beams (R,L): 23-0/8, 25-0/8**  **Bases (R, L): 5-3/8, 5-1/8**

I have lived in Idaho my entire life, and spent my school years in Priest River. My hometown of 30 years, LaClede, is a small town between Sandpoint and Priest River, along the Pend Oreille River.

Mid November is usually the peak of the whitetail rut here, and also usually when the northern waterfowl migrate through. As the weekend of November 14, 2004 approached, Christy and Casey, my wife and daughter, headed to Boise to check out college opportunities. The weather had been cool and wet, with temperatures just above freezing. The river was full of ducks and geese and I told Christy that my plan for the weekend was to head up and shoot the first four-point I could find; then get after the ducks with my Labrador retrievers.

I went to an area my family and I have been hunting since the mid '70s. The land has changed hands between several lumber companies and borders Forest Service. It is prime whitetail country, with heavy cover. This area is only five miles from my home and real handy for morning and evening hunts.

Riley Creek Lumber Company (now Idaho Forest Group) owns the land bordering the Forest Service ground. I have worked for the company for many years and often quiz the foresters about harvest plans and deer sightings. In 2002, one of the foresters had mentioned that a logging crew had seen a big non-typical in the area, but we never heard of him being harvested.

The morning of November 14 was cool and wet. It had rained the night before, but I was glad it had stopped. The spot I wanted to hunt required about a four-mile ATV ride - just long enough to get soaked.

After parking the ATV, I hiked about half a mile around a ridge and broke over toward the creek as first light broke. There are several crossing points where the deer drop from the ridge to the creek or flank the ridge, so it's a good area to sit on stand or move slowly through.

I was disappointed because the wind, which was a very light breeze, was quartering down the ridge toward the creek. This would not allow me to drop down very far without being winded by flanking deer.

Tactics changed to finding the best viewpoint from above and listening. Usually in this spot, you will hear them coming long before you see them - especially after a good frost.

After sitting for 20 minutes, I thought I heard a limb snap down below. Shortly after, I heard the unmistakable grunt of a buck in the bottom. There is usually a line of scrapes there and it appeared he was following the creek bed. I knew the only chance I had was to let him get ahead of me a little and then flank the ridge. If he crossed the creek and came up my side of the ridge, I might get a look.

This buck was really rutting, grunting often. The ridge I was on had been thinned a few years earlier and there was a skid trail angling toward the creek. I broke around a finger ridge where I could see to the end of the skid trail, but the buck had stopped grunting. Did he see or wind me? The only thing I could do was wait.

A few minutes later I caught movement in the creek bed. It was him, and he was going to cross at the far end of the trail! He stopped just below the trail, presenting a broadside view. Through the scope I could see he was a good buck.

The shot was 100 yards and there was no time for a rest. I tripped the safety on my Ruger No. 1 and squeezed. The 7x57 went off and the buck did the classic rodeo kick, spun to his left, and started running right at me!

During the shot, the view through my 2-7x Leupold gave me no clue to his size, but as he ran toward me, I remember thinking, "Wow, that buck is wide!"

I was so startled that I didn't even think about reloading for a second shot until he turned and ran below me. He crashed into a pile of brush 30 yards from where I shot. After I got a good, up-close look at him, there was a quick cell phone call to my wife to let her know we were having a whitetail mount done (our first).

This was a big-bodied deer. After field-dressing and dragging him to a point where I could get the ATV, it took me over an hour to get him loaded. I had to pull him up a bank and lay some stout poles from the bank to the rear rack to load him.

Several guys at work took one look at the pictures and asked if I was able to eat him. Actually, he made great steaks! Cravens Taxidermy in Sagle did the head mount. They estimated the buck's age at 8-1/2 years.

# Frank Hester

### 183-2/8 B&C Non-Typical
### Latah County, 2005

 **F**rank Hester killed this awesome whitetail in Latah County in 2005. He was hiking along with his nephew, Andrew Michaels, who was tagging along but still too young to hunt.

They were hunting some rocky and brushy CRP ground where a family member had seen a big buck the day before. The day was beautiful, and in four hours of hunting, they had seen a few mediocre bucks.

As they sat and glassed, Frank spied this giant lying in the tall grass by a creek bottom. The minute they made eye contact, the buck stood up. Frank promptly put him back down with his .270.

His trophy scores 183-2/8 B&C net non-typical as a 7x8. The outstanding taxidermy was done by Nick Clark in Lewiston.

# Paul Snider
## 182-4/8 B&C Non-Typical
### Nez Perce County, 2000

B oyd Gruell and I had just dropped off my brother, Jack, half an hour before daylight to trudge across a muddy field. We were hoping the rain would stop before we got across the canyon and had to get out ourselves.

The three of us had made this same hunt many times. Jack would hunt over the top as Boyd and I crossed the canyon to position ourselves underneath him, and then we would sidehill over to the open star thistle hillside where an old salt box sat next to a big Ponderosa pine.

We were hunting steep terrain that day. The canyon mostly consisted of brushy draws and star thistle on one side, and timber and brush on the other. Thorn brush and wild rose brush covered both sides.

It was one of those wet days where your pants weigh about 30 lbs. and your suspenders dig troughs into your shoulder blades. It was also so slick that it was difficult to keep our feet under us. My scope was constantly getting smeared and visibility was terrible due to the fog. Other than that it was a great day.

I was the first one to make it to our rendezvous point. By the time Jack and Boyd made it, I had a big fire going. There was plenty of talk of going home, but the fire warmed up our bones. Also, we had been kicking up plenty of deer, but most of them were holding tight unless you got right on top of them. The truck was clear across the canyon, so we didn't really have that much choice anyway.

We split up and started out on our routes again. I made it across the creek and up the steep hillside and was thinking of that warm pickup when I spotted some does. Up until right then, I had seen about 20 deer that day, but not one decent buck. I was glassing the timber behind the does and finally spotted what looked like a nice five-point with good mass. All I could see was the rack and his neck. Now, the three of us were all trophy hunters, and I really wasn't sure I wanted this buck. I've walked up to big bucks before and had major ground shrinkage. However, I hadn't taken an elk that year, and thoughts of an empty freezer filled my head.

Before I had fully made up my mind, the does decided they'd had enough and ran off. Panicked, I ran over to the draw and to my surprise, the buck and does were still at the head of the draw. The buck was about 175 yards above me in a little opening, and I could tell he was ready to bolt. I got down on a knee, aimed quickly, and fired my .270. The buck rolled straight down the hill and kept coming until he came to a rest only 20 yards from me! It was only then that I really had any idea what I had just done. There would be no ground shrinkage that day. He had actually grown – from a five-point into this great non-typical.

**Paul Snider, Jr. (right) and Lee Gruell pose with Paul's tremendous non-typical.**

# Ed Hartbarger
## 182-3/8 B&C Non-Typical
### Kootenai County, 2000

**P**art of hunting whitetails in northern Idaho is dealing with misery. The hunt is late, in cold weather, and in thick vegetation. A hunter either has to get used to it or pick up a different hobby.

Ed Hartbarger shot this big Kootenai County non-typical in November 2000 in just such a way. It was late afternoon, and the weather was changing to a miserable freezing rain and snow.

With not much time left, he got aggressive with rattling and calling. Out of nowhere, this giant buck appeared with his head down, running right at him, apparently ready to show him who was boss.

Ed reached for his rifle, but the buck saw him and turned to run. He fired quickly and luck was on his side.

# Lance Uppendahl
## 180-7/8 B&C Non-Typical
## Nez Perce County, 1997

On the day after Thanksgiving, 1997, my brother-in-law, Mike Brocke, our friend, Ron Damarell, and I set out for another day of hunting. We had already been out for eight days, and the largest buck that we passed up was a solid 160, which of course, was saw on our very first day!

On this particular day, we were going to a new location. It was on a place that Ron was given permission to hunt, so it was new territory.

Everything happened quickly. We parked and proceeded down a narrow road. Not even 200 yards from the truck, Mike spotted a buck running below us. I just happened to be in front of them, so I readied my rifle. I got a good look at him through a small opening in the timber and knew he was a gagger. I found an opening ahead of him, and as he ran through it, I swung through and shot, but missed.

Mike and Ron never really saw him, and they kept asking me about his size. I was going crazy and yelled, "He's not a Randy Clemenhagen buck, but he's close!"

We continued on down the ridge to see if we might get lucky enough to spot him again. We finally hit an open area where we could look down into the drainage and over to the next ridge. Five minutes passed, but it felt like a lifetime. Ron then said, "There's a deer right there in the wide open star thistle!"

It was him! Mike shot and missed and the race was on; we traded shots. Our trophy buck ran straight up the opposite side on the open ridge. With time running out, I fired and dropped him. He's everything a hunter dreams about and more.

# Idaho's Greatest Typical Whitetails

# Idaho's Greatest All-Time
## Typical Whitetails
## (Boone and Crockett Scoring System)
*Indicates that it has been officially scored but not submitted to B&C

| Rank | Score | Hunter | Location | Year | Main Beams R | Main Beams L | Inside Spread | Widest Spread | Bases R | Bases L | Points R | Points L | Abnormal Points |
|------|-------|--------|----------|------|------|------|------|------|------|------|------|------|------|
| 1 | 186-7/8 | Ronald M. McLamb | Bonner County | 2001 | 27-5/8 | 26-7/8 | 19-2/8 | 21-3/8 | 4-5/8 | 4-7/8 | 7 | 6 | 1-5/8 |
| 2 | 186-4/8 | Mark A. Schilling | Shoshone County | 2005 | 26-1/8 | 25-3/8 | 20-6/8 | 23-1/8 | 5-3/8 | 5-1/8 | 6 | 6 | 0 |
| 3 | 182-5/8 | Aaron M. McNall | Boundary County | 1993 | 24-0/8 | 23-7/8 | 20-1/8 | 24-0/8 | 5-4/8 | 5-3/8 | 5 | 5 | 0 |
| 4 | 181-7/8 | Richard E. Carver | Clearwater County | 1985 | 26-5/8 | 27-3/8 | 21-5/8 | 22-6/8 | 4-4/8 | 4-4/8 | 5 | 5 | 0 |
| 5* | 181-4/8 | Picked Up by Steve Kluver | Bonner County | 1988 | 24-2/8 | 24-3/8 | 21-0/8 | 24-7/8 | 4-6/8 | 4-5/8 | 5 | 6 | 7-6/8 |
| 6* | 181-0/8 | Richard Hart, Sr. | Nez Perce County | 1967 | - | - | - | - | - | - | - | - | - |
| 7 | 178-7/8 | Tony L. Siron | Kootenai County | 1998 | 24-6/8 | 26-0/8 | 18-7/8 | 21-2/8 | 5-2/8 | 5-1/8 | 5 | 5 | 0 |
| 8 | 177-5/8 | Donna M. Knight | Idaho County | 1986 | 26-0/8 | 25-6/8 | 21-3/8 | 24-2/8 | 4-5/8 | 4-5/8 | 5 | 5 | 0 |
| 9* | 177-1/8 | Andy Short | Benewah County | 2003 | 26-2/8 | 25-7/8 | 19-1/8 | 23-0/8 | 4-5/8 | 4-6/8 | 6 | 6 | 7-2/8 |
| 10 | 176-6/8 | Edward D. Moore | Idaho County | 1986 | 22-3/8 | 23-6/8 | 16-2/8 | 18-2/8 | 4-1/8 | 4-1/8 | 7 | 7 | 3-2/8 |
| 10 | 176-6/8 | Frank J. Loughran | Idaho County | 1987 | 26-5/8 | 25-6/8 | 17-0/8 | 20-1/8 | 5-2/8 | 5-1/8 | 7 | 7 | 3-0/8 |
| 12* | 176-0/8 | Thomas Lougee | Nez Perce County | 1987 | 29-0/8 | 28-4/8 | 23-2/8 | 26-0/8 | 4-5/8 | 4-6/8 | 5 | 5 | 0 |
| 13 | 175-7/8 | Joe Sparks | Nez Perce County | 1987 | 27-2/8 | 26-0/8 | 18-0/8 | 22-3/8 | 4-6/8 | 4-6/8 | 5 | 7 | 3-1/8 |
| 13 | 175-7/8 | Rusty P. Kirtley | Nez Perce County | 2000 | 24-5/8 | 23-1/8 | 18-7/8 | 20-6/8 | 5-1/8 | 5-0/8 | 6 | 6 | 0 |
| 15 | 175-5/8 | Carl Groth | Benewah County | 1982 | 25-5/8 | 25-0/8 | 17-7/8 | 23-3/8 | 4-5/8 | 4-5/8 | 6 | 7 | 0 |
| 16 | 175-3/8 | Daniel R. Merrill | Jefferson County | 2001 | 26-4/8 | 26-6/8 | 22-1/8 | 24-0/8 | 5-2/8 | 5-1/8 | 5 | 5 | 2-4/8 |
| 17* | 174-4/8 | Jason W. Woods | Lewis County | 1987 | 25-2/8 | 27-4/8 | 20-6/8 | 22-6/8 | 5-1/8 | 5-0/8 | 5 | 5 | 0 |
| 18* | 174-3/8 | Terry W. Jerome | Kootenai County | 1986 | 23-1/8 | 23-1/8 | 17-0/8 | 21-1/8 | 4-6/8 | 5-0/8 | 8 | 8 | 4-3/8 |
| 19 | 174-2/8 | Douglas B. Crockett | Clearwater County | 1983 | 26-1/8 | 26-5/8 | 22-6/8 | 25-2/8 | 5-0/8 | 4-7/8 | 7 | 6 | 2-2/8 |
| 20 | 174-0/8 | Don Southern | Nez Perce County | 1986 | 23-4/8 | 23-4/8 | 18-2/8 | 21-1/8 | 5-1/8 | 5-1/8 | 5 | 5 | 0 |
| 21 | 173-6/8 | Unknown | Bonner County | 1967 | 26-6/8 | 27-6/8 | 20-3/8 | 22-7/8 | 5-7/8 | 5-4/8 | 9 | 6 | 8-1/8 |
| 22* | 173-4/8 | Thomas D. Wakefield | Kootenai County | 1988 | 25-5/8 | 26-3/8 | 20-4/8 | 23-3/8 | 4-7/8 | 4-7/8 | 5 | 5 | 0 |
| 23 | 173-1/8 | John D. Kauffman | Latah County | 1991 | 25-1/8 | 26-0/8 | 18-1/8 | 20-3/8 | 4-6/8 | 4-5/8 | 5 | 8 | 3-4/8 |
| 24 | 172-7/8 | Kevin L. Lundblad | Kootenai County | 1992 | 25-2/8 | 24-3/8 | 18-0/8 | 20-7/8 | 4-2/8 | 4-1/8 | 7 | 7 | 3-5/8 |
| 25 | 172-5/8 | Shane Moyer | Kootenai County | 1996 | 26-1/8 | 26-0/8 | 20-7/8 | 25-5/8 | 4-6/8 | 4-5/8 | 5 | 5 | 0 |
| 25* | 172-5/8 | Ty Bell | Boundary County | 2006 | 23-7/8 | 24-3/8 | 21-1/8 | 23-0/8 | 5-0/8 | 5-1/8 | 7 | 7 | 6-2/8 |
| 27 | 172-0/8 | Jim Felton | Idaho County | 1965 | 24-6/8 | 24-6/8 | 17-2/8 | 21-5/8 | 4-3/8 | 4-4/8 | 6 | 5 | 0 |
| 28 | 171-5/8 | Glen D. Barnett | Latah County | 2000 | 26-0/8 | 26-7/8 | 18-7/8 | 21-3/8 | 4-2/8 | 4-2/8 | 6 | 5 | 1-4/8 |
| 29 | 171-4/8 | Picked Up by Darwin L. Baker | Latah County | 1986 | 24-7/8 | 25-2/8 | 19-4/8 | 21-5/8 | 4-7/8 | 5-2/8 | 6 | 6 | 1-6/8 |

| Rank | Score | Hunter | Location | Year | Main Beams | | Inside Spread | Widest Spread | Bases | | Points | | Abnormal Points |
|------|-------|--------|----------|------|------|------|------|------|------|------|------|------|------|
| | | | | | R | L | | | R | L | R | L | |
| 30* | 171-3/8 | Richard L. Henderson | Idaho County | 1963 | 27-1/8 | 26-6/8 | 19-5/8 | 21-4/8 | 4-6/8 | 4-7/8 | 5 | 5 | 0 |
| 30* | 171-3/8 | Norm Mathewson | Bonner County | 1984 | 26-0/8 | 27-1/8 | 19-3/8 | 21-5/8 | 4-2/8 | 4-1/8 | 8 | 8 | 9-6/8 |
| 30 | 171-3/8 | Donald B. Vickaryous | Boundary County | 1995 | 24-3/8 | 24-2/8 | 17-5/8 | 20-0/8 | 5-1/8 | 5-1/8 | 6 | 7 | 4-6/8 |
| 33* | 171-0/8 | William Bennett, Jr. | Clearwater County | 1986 | 26-6/8 | 27-3/8 | 21-1/8 | 24-4/8 | 4-2/8 | 4-4/8 | 5 | 8 | 4-5/8 |
| 33 | 171-0/8 | Paul A. Eke | Nez Perce County | 1993 | 27-5/8 | 27-0/8 | 19-2/8 | 21-2/8 | 4-6/8 | 4-6/8 | 7 | 7 | 3-2/8 |
| 35 | 170-6/8 | Clarence Hagerman | Shoshone County | 1947 | 28-6/8 | 28-4/8 | 27-1/8 | 29-1/8 | 5-2/8 | 4-7/8 | 6 | 6 | 3-7/8 |
| 36 | 170-4/8 | George F. Bourgeois III | Shoshone County | 2007 | 25-5/8 | 25-4/8 | 24-2/8 | 26-2/8 | 4-6/8 | 4-6/8 | 6 | 5 | 0 |
| 37 | 170-3/8 | Unknown | Idaho | 2002 | 26-2/8 | 25-3/8 | 17-7/8 | 20-1/8 | 5-0/8 | 5-1/8 | 5 | 6 | 0 |
| 38 | 170-1/8 | Theodore Millick, Jr. | Latah County | 1969 | 25-4/8 | 25-2/8 | 16-2/8 | 19-1/8 | 4-4/8 | 4-5/8 | 6 | 5 | 1-5/8 |
| 38* | 170-1/8 | Ed Bradbury | Benewah County | 1988 | 25-5/8 | 26-4/8 | 19-3/8 | 23-2/8 | 5-0/8 | 5-0/8 | 5 | 5 | 0 |
| 40 | 170-0/8 | Lewis L. Turcott | Latah County | 1974 | 28-4/8 | 27-3/8 | 21-4/8 | 24-1/8 | 4-7/8 | 5-0/8 | 8 | 7 | 10-4/8 |
| 40* | 170-0/8 | Picked Up by William Leach | Boundary County | 1978 | 24-1/8 | 24-4/8 | 17-4/8 | 20-0/8 | 4-5/8 | 4-4/8 | 5 | 5 | 0 |
| 42* | 169-4/8 | Ed Kuchynka | Clearwater County | 1982 | 25-4/8 | 25-5/8 | 22-0/8 | 23-4/8 | 4-2/8 | 4-2/8 | 6 | 5 | 0 |
| 42* | 169-4/8 | Richard McLeod | Kootenai County | 1987 | 24-3/8 | 23-5/8 | 20-4/8 | 22-4/8 | 5-1/8 | 5-1/8 | 5 | 5 | 0 |
| 42 | 169-4/8 | Frederick R. Staab | Clearwater County | 1990 | 26-4/8 | 26-0/8 | 19-0/8 | 22-3/8 | 4-4/8 | 4-4/8 | 7 | 8 | 5-4/8 |
| 45* | 169-2/8 | William Wilson | Kootenai County | 1986 | 25-4/8 | 25-2/8 | 20-3/8 | 24-6/8 | 5-2/8 | 5-1/8 | 6 | 5 | 2-1/8 |
| 45 | 169-2/8 | Jeremy L. Badertscher | Idaho County | 1992 | 26-7/8 | 25-6/8 | 20-6/8 | 23-0/8 | 4-5/8 | 4-4/8 | 5 | 7 | 2-4/8 |
| 47* | 169-1/8 | Mitchell Vogl | Boundary County | 1984 | 23-6/8 | 23-7/8 | 16-2/8 | 19-0/8 | 5-1/8 | 4-7/8 | 7 | 6 | 4-2/8 |
| 47* | 169-1/8 | Terry Copper | Kootenai County | 1986 | 25-4/8 | 25-6/8 | 20-2/8 | 24-6/8 | 5-2/8 | 5-1/8 | 6 | 5 | 2-1/8 |
| 49* | 168-7/8 | Barry McMinn | Nez Perce County | 1981 | 24-4/8 | 23-0/8 | 18-3/8 | 22-1/8 | 4-7/8 | 5-1/8 | 5 | 5 | 0 |
| 49 | 168-7/8 | Arthur H. Baker | Clearwater County | 1997 | 26-0/8 | 26-3/8 | 19-6/8 | 21-7/8 | 4-7/8 | 5-0/8 | 6 | 6 | 1-3/8 |
| 51* | 168-4/8 | Denise Lyman | Kootenai County | 1979 | 25-4/8 | 24-0/8 | 16-4/8 | 19-6/8 | 4-5/8 | 4-6/8 | 5 | 5 | 0 |
| 51* | 168-4/8 | Carey Campos | Idaho County | 1982 | 23-6/8 | 24-4/8 | 19-2/8 | 21-6/8 | 4-2/8 | 4-3/8 | 5 | 5 | 0 |
| 51* | 168-4/8 | Clint G. Bush | Kootenai County | 1984 | 22-3/8 | 24-4/8 | 17-6/8 | 23-0/8 | 4-4/8 | 4-3/8 | 6 | 7 | 5-2/8 |
| 54* | 168-3/8 | Nick Butler | Latah County | 1998 | 23-7/8 | 24-3/8 | 18-3/8 | 19-1/8 | 4-1/8 | 4-2/8 | 5 | 6 | 0 |
| 55 | 168-1/8 | Emerald J. Hutchins | Clearwater County | 1994 | 26-6/8 | 26-0/8 | 18-0/8 | 21-0/8 | 4-7/8 | 5-0/8 | 6 | 6 | 2-1/8 |
| 55* | 168-1/8 | John Meschko | Unknown | n/a | 23-6/8 | 23-4/8 | 19-7/8 | 22-6/8 | 4-7/8 | 4-6/8 | 6 | 6 | 8-4/8 |
| 57* | 168-0/8 | Lonna Ruark | Clearwater County | 1977 | 25-3/8 | 24-7/8 | 19-4/8 | 21-5/8 | 4-3/8 | 4-3/8 | 6 | 7 | 1-6/8 |
| 58* | 167-4/8 | Scott Goodson | Kootenai County | 2005 | - | - | - | - | - | - | - | - | - |
| 59* | 167-1/8 | Mike Poe | Boise County | 1978 | 24-4/8 | 23-6/8 | 19-5/8 | 22-3/8 | 5-1/8 | 5-1/8 | 7 | 7 | 11-0/8 |
| 59* | 167-1/8 | Del Drapeau | Boundary County | 1988 | 25-7/8 | 26-2/8 | 18-5/8 | 21-5/8 | 5-0/8 | 5-1/8 | 6 | 5 | 0 |
| 61* | 167-0/8 | Unknown | Kootenai County | 1974 | 23-1/8 | 21-5/8 | 20-4/8 | 22-5/8 | 4-6/8 | 4-5/8 | 5 | 5 | 0 |
| 61* | 167-0/8 | Casey Valliere | Bonner County | 2006 | - | - | - | - | - | - | - | - | - |

| Rank | Score | Hunter | Location | Year | Main Beams | | Inside Spread | Widest Spread | Bases | | Points | | Abnormal Points |
|---|---|---|---|---|---|---|---|---|---|---|---|---|---|
| | | | | | R | L | | | R | L | R | L | |
| 63* | 166-7/8 | Denny Cooper | Boundary County | 1987 | 24-1/8 | 24-6/8 | 18-2/8 | 21-0/8 | 4-2/8 | 4-2/8 | 6 | 5 | 3-7/8 |
| 63* | 166-7/8 | Danny Griffin | Latah County | 1991 | 24-4/8 | 25-0/8 | 21-7/8 | 24-5/8 | 4-5/8 | 4-6/8 | 5 | 7 | 5-0/8 |
| 65* | 166-6/8 | A.B. Cocklin | Bonner County | 1980 | 23-7/8 | 24-2/8 | 17-2/8 | 19-5/8 | 4-6/8 | 4-5/8 | 6 | 6 | 2-6/8 |
| 65* | 166-6/8 | Walter Asbe | Idaho County | 1990 | 22-6/8 | 22-4/8 | 18-2/8 | 21-2/8 | 4-4/8 | 4-4/8 | 5 | 5 | 0 |
| 67* | 166-5/8 | Mike W. Riley | Bonner County | 1988 | 24-1/8 | 22-3/8 | 21-1/8 | 24-0/8 | 5-0/8 | 5-2/8 | 7 | 6 | 9-4/8 |
| 68* | 166-4/8 | Don Gollen | Bonner County | 1966 | 23-5/8 | 23-7/8 | 19-3/8 | 21-4/8 | 4-7/8 | 5-1/8 | 6 | 7 | 1-1/8 |
| 68* | 166-4/8 | Glenn Hollett | Bonner County | 1979 | 26-1/8 | 25-1/8 | 20-3/8 | 22-7/8 | 4-5/8 | 4-4/8 | 5 | 6 | 1-3/8 |
| 68* | 166-4/8 | Nick Randall | Lewis County | 2004 | 23-7/8 | 24-0/8 | 17-7/8 | 21-0/8 | 4-2/8 | 4-2/8 | 5 | 8 | 3-7/8 |
| 71* | 166-2/8 | Kenneth Hawly | Gifford | 1967 | 23-1/8 | 22-6/8 | 18-6/8 | 22-4/8 | 5-1/8 | 5-1/8 | 5 | 5 | 0 |
| 71* | 166-2/8 | Mark Carter | Kootenai County | 1987 | 26-4/8 | 25-6/8 | 18-7/8 | 21-2/8 | 4-2/8 | 4-0/8 | 5 | 5 | 1-1/8 |
| 73* | 166-1/8 | Denny Hall | Bonner County | 1980 | 24-2/8 | 24-3/8 | 19-4/8 | 22-6/8 | 5-0/8 | 4-7/8 | 8 | 7 | 9-5/8 |
| 73* | 166-1/8 | Roger R. Davis | Shoshone County | 1986 | 24-1/8 | 25-1/8 | 19-5/8 | 21-6/8 | 4-5/8 | 4-5/8 | 5 | 5 | 0 |
| 75* | 166-0/8 | Paul Finney | Kootenai County | 1970 | 23-0/8 | 23-0/8 | 19-2/8 | 21-2/8 | 4-1/8 | 4-0/8 | 6 | 6 | 0 |
| 75* | 166-0/8 | Everett Hagen | Latah County | 1973 | - | - | - | - | - | - | - | - | - |
| 75* | 166-0/8 | Ernest E. Clanton | Bonner County | 1987 | 24-1/8 | 23-6/8 | 18-2/8 | 22-0/8 | 4-4/8 | 4-7/8 | 5 | 5 | 0 |
| 75* | 166-0/8 | Todd Felton | Nez Perce County | 2003 | 22-7/8 | 22-6/8 | 18-6/8 | 20-4/8 | 4-5/8 | 4-4/8 | 7 | 5 | 2-6/8 |
| 75* | 166-0/8 | Karl Neumann | Bonner County | 2007 | - | - | - | - | - | - | - | - | - |
| 80* | 165-7/8 | Betty Arnett | Latah County | 1965 | 26-0/8 | 25-1/8 | 18-5/8 | 20-5/8 | 5-1/8 | 5-1/8 | 6 | 5 | 4-0/8 |
| 80* | 165-7/8 | Vern Breazeal | Nez Perce County | 1984 | 24-7/8 | 23-5/8 | 18-7/8 | 21-5/8 | 5-2/8 | 4-7/8 | 6 | 6 | 0 |
| 80* | 165-7/8 | Richard Wolff | Clearwater County | 1994 | 27-2/8 | 26-3/8 | 16-0/8 | 18-3/8 | 4-2/8 | 4-3/8 | 6 | 5 | 1-2/8 |
| 83* | 165-6/8 | Darrell D. Tumelson | Clearwater River | 1972 | 27-1/8 | 27-1/8 | 20-4/8 | 22-4/8 | 4-7/8 | 4-7/8 | 4 | 4 | 0 |
| 84* | 165-5/8 | Les Schilling | Clearwater County | 1986 | 24-7/8 | 24-4/8 | 19-1/8 | 21-0/8 | 4-2/8 | 4-2/8 | 5 | 5 | 0 |
| 84* | 165-5/8 | Doug Farrell | Benewah County | 2007 | 25-0/8 | 25-6/8 | 21-3/8 | 23-4/8 | 4-5/8 | 4-7/8 | 7 | 7 | 10-4/8 |
| 86* | 165-1/8 | Richard D. McCoy | Shoshone County | 1973 | 24-2/8 | 24-2/8 | 20-5/8 | 22-7/8 | 5-1/8 | 4-2/8 | 5 | 7 | 5-0/8 |
| 86* | 165-1/8 | Richard A. Blagden | Kootenai County | 1982 | 25-2/8 | 25-0/8 | 17-5/8 | 23-0/8 | 4-1/8 | 4-2/8 | 7 | 6 | 1-4/8 |
| 88 | 165-0/8 | Gregory R. Pimentel | Teton County | 2007 | 23-2/8 | 22-6/8 | 17-2/8 | 19-2/8 | 4-2/8 | 4-2/8 | 6 | 6 | 0 |
| 89* | 164-7/8 | Don E. Fiedler | Bonner County | 1962 | 23-7/8 | 24-3/8 | 22-5/8 | 25-1/8 | 5-2/8 | 5-2/8 | 8 | 8 | 7-6/8 |
| 90* | 164-6/8 | Steve Aller | Bonner County | 1992 | 26-2/8 | 27-2/8 | 20-0/8 | 24-0/8 | 4-4/8 | 4-5/8 | 6 | 7 | 8-2/8 |
| 91* | 164-5/8 | Mack Newbanks | Boundary County | 1981 | 23-2/8 | 23-6/8 | 20-6/8 | 22-0/8 | 5-1/8 | 5-2/8 | 6 | 7 | 1-3/8 |
| 92* | 164-3/8 | Mike Fitzgerald | Unit 11A | 1986 | 26-2/8 | 26-0/8 | 21-0/8 | 27-6/8 | 5-2/8 | 5-1/8 | 8 | 7 | 7-3/8 |
| 92* | 164-3/8 | Jim McManus | Clearwater County | 1986 | 25-3/8 | 24-6/8 | 16-6/8 | 19-0/8 | 3-7/8 | 4-0/8 | 7 | 8 | 4-1/8 |
| 94* | 164-2/8 | Jim Jensen | Clearwater County | 1988 | 28-0/8 | 28-2/8 | 18-4/8 | 20-6/8 | 4-3/8 | 4-5/8 | 4 | 5 | 0 |
| 95* | 164-1/8 | Joseph H. Hester | Bonner County | 1981 | 24-7/8 | 24-4/8 | 19-4/8 | 22-3/8 | 4-6/8 | 4-7/8 | 6 | 7 | 1-7/8 |

| Rank | Score | Hunter | Location | Year | Main Beams | | Inside Spread | Widest Spread | Bases | | Points | | Abnormal Points |
|---|---|---|---|---|---|---|---|---|---|---|---|---|---|
| | | | | | R | L | | | R | L | R | L | |
| 96 | 164-0/8 | Gary Esser | Latah County | 1979 | 23-6/8 | 23-0/8 | 18-4/8 | 20-2/8 | 4-4/8 | 4-4/8 | 6 | 6 | 1-2/8 |
| 96* | 164-0/8 | Brion Poston | Boundary County | 1979 | 24-5/8 | 23-5/8 | 17-6/8 | 20-0/8 | 4-3/8 | 4-4/8 | 5 | 5 | 0 |
| 96* | 164-0/8 | Sonny Hairston | Unit 8 | 1983 | 24-4/8 | 26-1/8 | 19-4/8 | 22-4/8 | 5-3/8 | 5-3/8 | 6 | 5 | 1-6/8 |
| 99* | 163-7/8 | Picked Up by Clarence Cook | Nez Perce County | 1973 | 24-4/8 | 24-1/8 | 21-0/8 | 23-1/8 | 5-0/8 | 5-1/8 | 5 | 6 | 3-1/8 |
| 100* | 163-6/8 | Bruce Dawson | Bonner County | 1977 | 24-6/8 | 24-6/8 | 19-5/8 | 21-5/8 | 5-0/8 | 5-0/8 | 6 | 6 | 4-3/8 |
| 101* | 163-5/8 | August Barfuss | Bonner County | 1966 | 25-5/8 | 23-6/8 | 17-7/8 | 20-1/8 | 4-2/8 | 4-2/8 | 7 | 5 | 2-6/8 |
| 102* | 163-4/8 | Bill White | Clearwater County | 1973 | 25-0/8 | 25-0/8 | 20-0/8 | 22-0/8 | 5-5/8 | 5-4/8 | 5 | 5 | 0 |
| 103 | 163-3/8 | Steven J. Funke | Latah County | 1997 | 25-0/8 | 26-0/8 | 18-3/8 | 20-2/8 | 4-5/8 | 4-5/8 | 4 | 4 | 0 |
| 104* | 163-1/8 | Lorene Anderson | Clearwater County | 1988 | 25-3/8 | 25-0/8 | 17-3/8 | 19-3/8 | 4-2/8 | 4-3/8 | 5 | 6 | 2-0/8 |
| 105* | 163-0/8 | Lee Mullins & Paul Ison | Unit 8A | 1983 | 25-3/8 | 25-5/8 | 21-3/8 | 28-2/8 | 5-0/8 | 4-6/8 | 6 | 8 | 6-7/8 |
| 105 | 163-0/8 | David A. Neighbor | Kootenai County | 1994 | 26-2/8 | 26-3/8 | 19-6/8 | 22-0/8 | 4-2/8 | 4-3/8 | 6 | 5 | 1-2/8 |
| 107* | 162-6/8 | Earnest Allgood | Kamiah | 1960 | 25-0/8 | 25-0/8 | 22-6/8 | 26-1/8 | 5-0/8 | 5-1/8 | 6 | 6 | 0 |
| 107* | 162-6/8 | Warren Misner | Kamiah | 1981 | 25-0/8 | 25-4/8 | 21-4/8 | 26-0/8 | 4-7/8 | 5-3/8 | 7 | 6 | 8-6/8 |
| 107 | 162-6/8 | Larry Stohs | Latah County | 1986 | 24-4/8 | 24-3/8 | 22-4/8 | 24-0/8 | 4-5/8 | 4-6/8 | 6 | 6 | 2-6/8 |
| 110* | 162-5/8 | Woody Myers | Bonner County | 1974 | 23-7/8 | 23-7/8 | 18-1/8 | 20-0/8 | 5-4/8 | 5-6/8 | 6 | 6 | 6-6/8 |
| 111* | 162-4/8 | Lane Barney | Nez Perce County | 1972 | 24-4/8 | 25-4/8 | 23-4/8 | 25-3/8 | 4-6/8 | 4-7/8 | 5 | 5 | 1-6/8 |
| 111* | 162-4/8 | Dan Flerchinger | Unit 11 | 1985 | 24-1/8 | 24-2/8 | 18-3/8 | 21-3/8 | 4-7/8 | 4-6/8 | 7 | 6 | 3-4/8 |
| 111* | 162-4/8 | Mike Dahl | Clearwater County | 2000 | 23-1/8 | 23-1/8 | 16-6/8 | 18-6/8 | 4-2/8 | 4-2/8 | 6 | 6 | 0 |
| 114* | 162-3/8 | Tim O'Connell | Benewah County | 1970 | 23-3/8 | 24-4/8 | 23-6/8 | 26-3/8 | 4-7/8 | 4-6/8 | 6 | 8 | 7-5/8 |
| 115* | 162-1/8 | Greg Wilhelm | Nez Perce County | 1990 | 23-2/8 | 24-5/8 | 18-5/8 | 20-1/8 | 4-3/8 | 4-3/8 | 8 | 8 | 8-0/8 |
| 116* | 161-6/8 | Mike Stephens | Boundary County | 1983 | 25-1/8 | 24-5/8 | 17-5/8 | - | 4-4/8 | 4-5/8 | 5 | 6 | 1-7/8 |
| 116 | 161-6/8 | Jared Johnson | Bonneville County | 2007 | 24-1/8 | 24-1/8 | 20-0/8 | 21-6/8 | 4-1/8 | 4-4/8 | 5 | 5 | 0 |
| 118* | 161-4/8 | Aaron Smith | Nez Perce County | n/a | 24-1/8 | 24-4/8 | 16-0/8 | 20-0/8 | 4-7/8 | 4-7/8 | 5 | 5 | 0 |
| 119* | 161-3/8 | Richard Holmberg | Snake River | 1952 | 25-1/8 | 25-0/8 | 19-7/8 | 21-5/8 | 4-4/8 | 4-4/8 | 10 | 7 | 6-6/8 |
| 119 | 161-3/8 | Douglas Lamm | Idaho County | 1978 | 24-4/8 | 23-4/8 | 20-7/8 | 23-0/8 | 4-5/8 | 4-3/8 | 5 | 5 | 0 |
| 119 | 161-3/8 | Jack S. Snider | Nez Perce County | 2000 | 22-5/8 | 22-6/8 | 16-6/8 | 19-1/8 | 4-1/8 | 4-3/8 | 7 | 7 | 4-3/8 |
| 122* | 161-2/8 | Nick Larrison | Latah County | 2005 | 25-4/8 | 25-4/8 | 18-3/8 | 20-7/8 | 4-5/8 | 4-4/8 | 8 | 8 | 8-7/8 |
| 123* | 161-1/8 | Jerry Moore | Clearwater County | 1986 | 24-6/8 | 25-3/8 | 19-1/8 | 20-7/8 | 4-2/8 | 4-2/8 | 5 | 5 | 0 |
| 123* | 161-1/8 | Andrew Schumaker | Clearwater County | 2007 | 26-3/8 | 26-7/8 | 17-6/8 | 23-6/8 | 4-5/8 | 4-5/8 | 4 | 6 | 4-3/8 |
| 125* | 161-0/8 | Kelly Vandevender | Latah County | 1998 | 26-2/8 | 24-3/8 | 18-4/8 | 21-0/8 | 4-3/8 | 4-2/8 | 5 | 6 | 1-6/8 |
| 125 | 161-0/8 | Richard C. Speaks | Bonner County | 2002 | 24-7/8 | 24-5/8 | 15-6/8 | 17-7/8 | 4-7/8 | 5-0/8 | 5 | 5 | 0 |
| 127* | 160-7/8 | Brad Ailor | Lewis County | 2004 | 22-2/8 | 20-7/8 | 18-1/8 | 23-4/8 | 4-3/8 | 4-2/8 | 6 | 6 | 0 |
| 128 | 160-6/8 | Mike Madden | Lewis County | 1992 | 26-0/8 | 26-4/8 | 21-0/8 | 23-1/8 | 4-3/8 | 4-3/8 | 6 | 5 | 4-0/8 |

| Rank | Score | Hunter | Location | Year | Main Beams R | Main Beams L | Inside Spread | Widest Spread | Bases R | Bases L | Points R | Points L | Abnormal Points |
|---|---|---|---|---|---|---|---|---|---|---|---|---|---|
| 128* | 160-6/8 | Jason E. Gomes | Nez Perce County | 2001 | 24-7/8 | 23-0/8 | 19-1/8 | 22-0/8 | 4-3/8 | 4-4/8 | 6 | 6 | 1-1/8 |
| 128 | 160-6/8 | Brian Stanley | Shoshone County | 2003 | 24-1/8 | 25-2/8 | 15-4/8 | 18-0/8 | 4-3/8 | 4-3/8 | 5 | 5 | 0 |
| 131* | 160-5/8 | Kurtis J. Hull | Bonner County | 1985 | 21-4/8 | 21-1/8 | 19-7/8 | 21-7/8 | 4-5/8 | 4-6/8 | 6 | 6 | 1-2/8 |
| 132* | 160-4/8 | Mark Mayer | Lewis County | 1972 | 23-3/8 | 23-1/8 | 22-2/8 | 25-4/8 | 4-6/8 | 4-7/8 | 7 | 6 | 5-7/8 |
| 132* | 160-4/8 | Jamie & Irene Lehman | Kootenai County | 1980 | 23-7/8 | 23-1/8 | 22-2/8 | 24-6/8 | 4-0/8 | 4-1/8 | 6 | 6 | 4-0/8 |
| 132 | 160-4/8 | Christopher Collecchi III | Boundary County | 1992 | 25-0/8 | 25-6/8 | 18-4/8 | 22-2/8 | 4-2/8 | 4-0/8 | 7 | 6 | 3-2/8 |
| 135* | 160-1/8 | George Berg | Nez Perce County | 1963 | 24-3/8 | 22-0/8 | 20-5/8 | 22-6/8 | 4-5/8 | 4-6/8 | 5 | 5 | 0 |
| 135* | 160-1/8 | Mike Dahl | Unit 10 | 1984 | 23-5/8 | 23-5/8 | 17-7/8 | 20-1/8 | 4-2/8 | 4-1/8 | 6 | 5 | 1-2/8 |
| 137* | 160-0/8 | Tracy Robinson | Kootenai County | 1986 | 24-0/8 | 23-6/8 | 19-0/8 | 21-7/8 | 4-2/8 | 4-2/8 | 5 | 5 | 0 |

| Widest Spread Typical Whitetail | | | |
|---|---|---|---|
| Rank | Hunter | Widest Spread | County |
| 1 | Clarence Hagerman | 29-1/8 | Shoshone |
| 2 | Lee Mullins & Paul Ison | 28-2/8 | Unit 8A |
| 3 | Mike Fitzgerald | 27-6/8 | Unit 11A |
| 4 | Tim O'Connell | 26-3/8 | Benewah |
| 5 | George F. Bourgeois III | 26-2/8 | Shoshone |
| 6 | Earnest Allgood | 26-1/8 | Kamiah Area |
| 7 | Thomas Lougee | 26-0/8 | Nez Perce |
| 7 | Warren Misner | 26-0/8 | Kamiah Area |
| 9 | Shane Moyer | 25-5/8 | Kootenai |
| 10 | Mark Mayer | 25-4/8 | Lewis |

| Longest Main Beam Typical Whitetail | | | | |
|---|---|---|---|---|
| Rank | Hunter | Longest Beam | Other Beam | County |
| 1 | Thomas Lougee | 29-0/8 | 28-4/8 | Nez Perce |
| 2 | Clarence Hagerman | 28-6/8 | 28-4/8 | Shoshone |
| 3 | Lewis Turcott | 28-4/8 | 27-3/8 | Latah |
| 4 | Jim Jensen | 28-2/8 | 28-0/8 | Clearwater |
| 5 | Unknown | 27-6/8 | 26-6/8 | Bonner |
| 6 | Paul Eke | 27-5/8 | 27-0/8 | Nez Perce |
| 6 | Ronald L. McLamb | 27-5/8 | 26-7/8 | Bonner |
| 8 | Jason W. Woods | 27-4/8 | 25-2/8 | Lewis |
| 9 | William Bennett, Jr. | 27-3/8 | 26-6/8 | Clearwater |
| 9 | Richard E. Carver | 27-3/8 | 26-5/8 | Clearwater |

| Largest Base Circumference Typical Whitetail | | | |
|---|---|---|---|
| Rank | Hunter | Largest Base Circumference | Other Base Circumference | County |
| 1 | Unknown | 5-7/8 | 5-4/8 | Bonner |
| 2 | Woody Myers | 5-6/8 | 5-4/8 | Bonner |
| 3 | Bill White | 5-5/8 | 5-4/8 | Clearwater |
| 4 | Aaron M. McNall | 5-4/8 | 5-3/8 | Boundary |
| 5 | Sonny Hairston | 5-3/8 | 5-3/8 | Unit 8 |
| 5 | Mark A. Schilling | 5-3/8 | 5-1/8 | Shoshone |
| 5 | Warren Misner | 5-3/8 | 4-7/8 | Kamiah Area |

# Boone and Crockett Club
## Typical Whitetail Score Chart

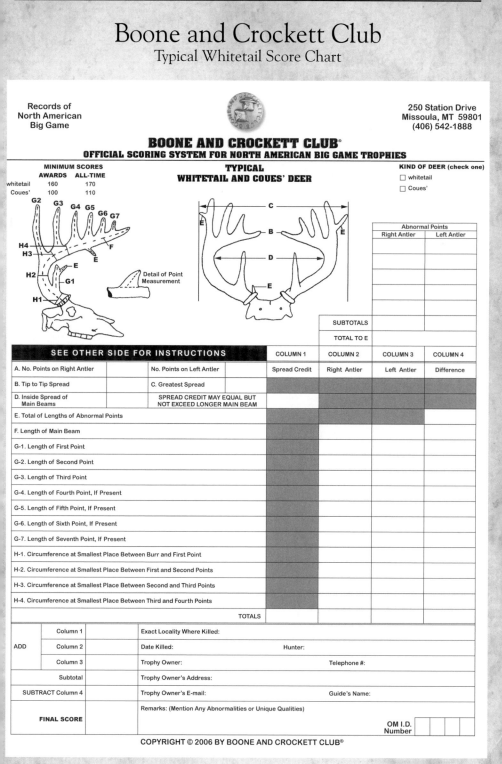

Records of
North American
Big Game

250 Station Drive
Missoula, MT 59801
(406) 542-1888

### BOONE AND CROCKETT CLUB®
### OFFICIAL SCORING SYSTEM FOR NORTH AMERICAN BIG GAME TROPHIES

**MINIMUM SCORES**

| | AWARDS | ALL-TIME |
|---|---|---|
| whitetail | 160 | 170 |
| Coues' | 100 | 110 |

### TYPICAL
### WHITETAIL AND COUES' DEER

**KIND OF DEER (check one)**

☐ whitetail
☐ Coues'

Detail of Point Measurement

| Abnormal Points | |
|---|---|
| Right Antler | Left Antler |
| | |
| | |
| | |
| | |
| | |
| | |

| | | |
|---|---|---|
| SUBTOTALS | | |
| TOTAL TO E | | |

| SEE OTHER SIDE FOR INSTRUCTIONS | | COLUMN 1 | COLUMN 2 | COLUMN 3 | COLUMN 4 |
|---|---|---|---|---|---|
| A. No. Points on Right Antler | No. Points on Left Antler | Spread Credit | Right Antler | Left Antler | Difference |
| B. Tip to Tip Spread | C. Greatest Spread | | | | |
| D. Inside Spread of Main Beams | SPREAD CREDIT MAY EQUAL BUT NOT EXCEED LONGER MAIN BEAM | | | | |
| E. Total of Lengths of Abnormal Points | | | | | |
| F. Length of Main Beam | | | | | |
| G-1. Length of First Point | | | | | |
| G-2. Length of Second Point | | | | | |
| G-3. Length of Third Point | | | | | |
| G-4. Length of Fourth Point, If Present | | | | | |
| G-5. Length of Fifth Point, If Present | | | | | |
| G-6. Length of Sixth Point, If Present | | | | | |
| G-7. Length of Seventh Point, If Present | | | | | |
| H-1. Circumference at Smallest Place Between Burr and First Point | | | | | |
| H-2. Circumference at Smallest Place Between First and Second Points | | | | | |
| H-3. Circumference at Smallest Place Between Second and Third Points | | | | | |
| H-4. Circumference at Smallest Place Between Third and Fourth Points | | | | | |
| | TOTALS | | | | |

| | | | |
|---|---|---|---|
| ADD | Column 1 | | Exact Locality Where Killed: |
| | Column 2 | | Date Killed: Hunter: |
| | Column 3 | | Trophy Owner: Telephone #: |
| | Subtotal | | Trophy Owner's Address: |
| SUBTRACT Column 4 | | | Trophy Owner's E-mail: Guide's Name: |
| FINAL SCORE | | | Remarks: (Mention Any Abnormalities or Unique Qualities) |

OM I.D. Number

# Ronald M. McLamb

186-7/8 B&C Typical
Bonner County, 2001
*Idaho State Record Typical Whitetail*

**Idaho Typical Rank: 1**
**Inside Spread: 19-2/8**
**Main Beams (R,L): 27-5/8, 26-7/8**

**Points (R,L): 7,6**
**Widest Spread: 21-3/8**
**Bases (R, L): 4-5/8, 4-7/8**

For tens of decades, and through millions of hunters and tens of millions of hunts, Idaho whitetail hunters have pursued their quarry in a variety of conditions and with a multitude of methods. They've weathered deep snows, heavy rains, and high winds; they've still-hunted, spotted and stalked, sat patiently in tree stands, and conducted drives; they've hunted in deep canyon country, heavy dog hair conifer thickets, and pushed through star thistle, blackberry, and rose brush; and they've schemed ways to get access to private ground, studied maps, and sacrificed jobs and relationships just to be out in the hills. Yet no matter how successful they've been, few have ever had the feeling of one who has been bestowed the honor of having taken the state record.

Ron McLamb was hardly of the mindset to break any records. Quite to the contrary, he and his friend Marshall Herrin left early one afternoon for a very casual whitetail hunt near the Idaho/Washington border without much intention of "hitting it hard." And maybe the irony of the whole thing is not only the best part, but it's often what sets Idaho apart. It's that notion that hunting in a state with as much opportunity and room to roam as Idaho has means that "it" could happen to any hunter at any time.

It was around 4 p.m. when Ron was driving down an old skid road and saw something move in an opening. He stopped to look and watched as a big buck lifted his head. Ron wasted no time in getting out and taking a few steps forward.

As much as he wanted to see more, all he could make out was the buck's head. He wasn't about to wait and watch the situation deteriorate, so he aimed at what was offered. It was only about 70 yards, and Ron touched the trigger on his Ruger M77 .30-06. The bullet nailed the buck right between the eyes, literally.

Ron had no idea when he walked up to his prize that it was so big. In fact, he didn't even bother to have it measured for several years.

Then, in spring of 2008, while I just happened to be doing a book signing at the Bonner County Gun and Horn Show in Sandpoint, Ron moseyed in carrying a rack that his friend kept bugging him to get measured. Needless to say, more than a few jaws dropped. When the numbers were tallied, Ron's buck was the new state record typical whitetail.

**Ron McLamb's huge typical seems to be all antlers, with a relatively small body.**

# Mark A. Schilling
## 186-4/8 B&C Typical
### Shoshone County, 2005

**Idaho Typical Rank: 2**
**Inside Spread: 20-6/8**
**Main Beams (R,L): 26-1/8, 25-3/8**

**Points (R,L): 6,6**
**Widest Spread: 23-1/8**
**Bases (R, L): 5-3/8, 5-1/8**

My 2005 elk season started like most others except for two things – the Fish and Game opened an antlered deer season with the start of elk season, and at 50 years old, I was only a few months removed from a total knee replacement. Both of these events would play a big part in my hunting that year.

My father, who was in his late 70s, had been on an old logging road and came back to camp saying he had just seen the biggest whitetail buck of his life. I didn't give it much thought since I never thought I'd see him again anyway.

Elk season started October 10, and with only weekends to hunt, I really wanted to make the most of it. On October 15, they gave us four days of either-sex elk hunting and then it was back to antlered only. On October 16, I found two cows and thought I had one but the wind switched; game over. My good friend, Don Wheatly, kept on with the chase but I backed down and decided to look elsewhere.

I headed back to the four wheeler, which was a good hour's walk. Once there, I rode back down to a lower logging road, shut the engine off and thought about what to do with the rest of the day. My mind kept nagging me to go cross-country and come out down below; it was noon and I could expect to be in camp at 5 p.m. The problem was whether or not I wanted to leave my four wheeler on the mountain overnight and make someone ride double the next morning to get it.

At this point, a third party in our camp, Bobby Kramer, showed up after an eight-mile walk up the ridge trail. By the look on his face, he was glad to see me. After all, he really didn't want to walk eight miles back to camp. The decision was made; Bobby went with the four wheeler and I went cross-country.

I made good time going downhill, but found no elk sign. A mile into my walk, I looked up and saw a big whitetail buck. Since our main focus was elk, my first thought was that my partners would not be happy if they had to stop their elk hunt to pack out deer.

While I could see him clearly, I couldn't judge his size. All I could tell was that he had a good, mature configuration. I shouldered my rifle and looked at him, instantly realizing I had a BIG buck only 100 yards downhill from me. I still didn't want to take my friends from their elk hunt, so I decided to go for a neck shot, thinking "If I hit him, we pack him out; if not, no harm done except to my pride."

The buck was head on, which was not much of a target for my 3x Weaver scope mounted on my .45/70, with a 405-grain slug. As luck would have it, down he went; the shot was dead center! Now the work began as I realized that we had meat to pack and I had to tell everybody that we had deer to pack out during elk season.

I walked over to take a look and about fell over, remembering what my father had said about the deer he saw. I knew right away I had something special.

It took me two hours to get out of there, and I ended up meeting Bobby on the trail. One look at my hands and he knew we had work to do.

Back at camp, I waited for my dad and Donny to come in. My dad was first, and as I told him the story, he asked me if I thought it was the same deer he had seen. I told him I didn't think two deer of that size could be in the same drainage.

When Donny came in, I was ready to have some fun. I told him I had shot a 6x6 but didn't mention it was a whitetail. After awhile, I told Donny it was a whitetail, only to have him look at me and mutter something about "what did I think I was doing and it was not even deer season." Donny didn't know the regulations had changed, and the look on his face was priceless.

The next day we made our way back to the deer and the boys finally understood why I shot him. Over five hours later, we were in camp. Sixty days later, I found out I had taken the new Idaho state record.*

*Mark Schilling's buck was the state record from fall of 2005 until summer of 2008, when Ronald McLamb's new state record was entered.

# Aaron M. McNall
## 182-5/8 B&C Typical
### Boundary County, 1993

**Idaho Typical Rank: 3**
**Inside Spread: 20-1/8**
**Main Beams (R,L): 24-0/8,23-7/8**

**Points (R,L): 5,5**
**Widest Spread: 24-0/8**
**Bases (R, L): 5-4/8,5-3/8**

ome of the country in the far north portion of the Panhandle can be some of the tallest and most extreme in the state. Valley floors give way to jutting high country, all of which is subject to thick vegetation and extreme weather. It was this type of country that appealed to 22-year-old Aaron McNall, and his intent was to go out and find a massive and mature mule deer buck. Northern Idaho has plenty of them, but they can be difficult to root out of that dense cover.

There were a couple of inches of snow on the ground lower down, and about six inches up top on that November day. Todd Russell was with Aaron that day, and they got up plenty early since it was a long drive into the backcountry.

They drove up the partially overgrown road as far as it would let them and then hiked farther up to a viewpoint. They watched some moose for awhile, but saw no deer, and hadn't seen much for sign.

They decided to head for the top, and a fog rolled in on them while they continued to hike. They reached the top around 11 a.m., and built a fire to warm up and have lunch.

After their brief reprieve, they broke over the other side to get out of the wind and started glassing a basin. They saw a couple of small bucks, which they quickly dismissed, and then split up to hunt their way back down. Aaron took a similar route as they had taken while climbing, while Todd was one ridge south in a brushy area.

Aaron stopped at the same point where they had been watching the moose earlier. By 2:30, he was watching the moose again. He was sitting quietly when he heard something that sounded like a buck grunt on the ridge that Todd should have been on. He walked over to look and saw a doe come through an opening. One by one in single file, four more does followed. All the while, a buck kept on grunting.

Suddenly, a big-bodied and big-antlered buck streaked through the opening and was gone. Aaron instantly knew it was a big buck. It was a long shot, and he had no rest where he was at.

Aaron's luck was exceptional that day when the buck came back up a ridge and offered him a shot. He dropped to one knee, aimed just below the top of the buck's back with his .270, and fired. The buck bowed his back and jumped forward. He shot again, spinning the buck. His antlers hung up in the alders, and Aaron was able to put a finishing shot into his giant trophy buck.

While the distance to the buck was manageable, the terrain was extreme. Aaron had to mark a spot by a subalpine fir so he could find the buck once he reached the other side of the drainage. When he got there, even though he had taken time to avoid the problem of finding the buck, there were about a dozen trees that all looked the same. He was eventually forced to hike his way all the way back to where he had taken the shot and mentally flag a few more features, including a snag.

He finally located his buck, and while he wanted to take time to appreciate a special moment, he was more worried about the impending darkness. After all, they were still back in remote country late in the year with snow on the ground. He quickly dressed out his prize and then dragged it to the bottom of the drainage. He then tried to sidehill the buck to a trail but soon found it impossible. He had no choice but to leave the buck and hike back to the truck.

When he arrived back at the vehicle, He found Todd there waiting. He had never even heard the shot, which must have been muffled by the snow and timber. Aaron asked him, "Well, how ambitious are you?"

Todd said he was game, so the two weary hunters went back up with flashlights and found the buck in the dark. They elected to take him down the creek bottom, and had to fight thick alders the entire way. They made it back to the pickup at 8:30 and were back to town at 11 p.m.

*Note: Aaron's buck was the Idaho state record typical for quite a few years. Of his 1993 buck, Aaron says, "I still think about him all the time."*

# Richard E. Carver
## 181-7/8 B&C Typical
### Clearwater County, 1985

**Idaho Typical Rank: 4**

**Inside Spread: 21-5/8**

**Main Beams (R,L): 26-5/8,27-3/8**

**Points (R,L): 5,5**

**Widest Spread: 22-6/8**

**Bases (R, L): 4-4/8,4-4/8**

ach day on the way home from school, the kids on the bus kept a lookout for old Amos Mose and his gang. No, it wasn't a pack of criminals, but a bachelor herd of whitetail bucks. Ol' Amos was the biggest of the bunch, and all of the school boys would have given just about anything to hang their tag on that deer.

Richard Carver and his boys, Charles and Rick, had been watching the group near some pea fields for about three years now, and the boys had been hunting them hard. It started with seven bucks altogether, but with each passing season, one or two would be taken and the herd would shrink.

On that fateful morning in fall of 1985, a thin blanket of snow covered the ground and weather was perfect for hunting. Richard, Charles, Rick, a friend, Guy Nielsen, and a few others hunted together as a group. Nothing happened during the morning hunt, so

Richard headed back to town to have some breakfast.

On the way back, he was almost home when a doe crossed right in front of him. Richard about had a heart attack when he saw Ol' Amos Mose hot on her heels. He went and got his rifle and quickly made a plan. He figured they were heading to feed near an apple orchard in a natural grass meadow, so he headed up that direction, stalking along the edge of the timber.

He was closing in when he saw a doe, which was locked in on him. She bolted with white flag raised. It was then that Richard saw Amos 200 yards out and quartering away. He dropped to a knee and fired a round from his 7mm-mag. as the buck was running. The shot connected solidly behind the shoulder, and the buck traveled only 30 yards before expiring.

Suddenly all was quiet. The only sound in the stillness was the sound of Richard walking slowly while he made his way to a trophy buck that had eluded hunters in the area for many years. Richard held the rack and savored the chance to finally see this legend up close for the first time.

It was the end of a legendary buck's reign. It was likely coming to an end soon anyway. At least he'd be appreciated this way.

# Picked Up by Steve Kluver
## 181-4/8 B&C Typical
## Bonner County, 1988

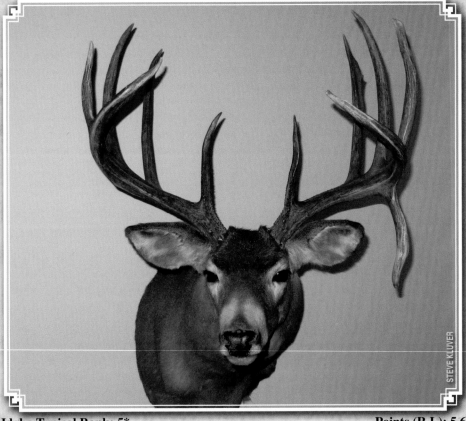

STEVE KLUVER

**Idaho Typical Rank: 5***

**Inside Spread: 21-0/8**

**Main Beams (R,L): 24-2/8,24-3/8**

**Points (R,L): 5,6**

**Widest Spread: 24-7/8**

**Bases (R, L): 4-6/8,4-5/8**

**W**hen Steve Kluver and his hunting partners, Jay and Jana Cates, left for a hunting spot near Clark Fork, whitetails were the furthest things from their minds. They were hunting elk in some higher country, and even if they did see a deer, they figured it would more than likely be a mulie.

Steve separated from the other two, with plans to meet back up a few hours down the line. He was down in a creek bottom quite a ways from the nearest road and was just getting ready to head up the other side when he looked over and saw something under a brush patch. It looked like a dead buck. With the elevation and terrain they were in, he automatically figured it was a decent mule deer buck.

His first instinct was to just leave it since the elk hunt had just started. He would have to pack it a long way, and it had been dead just long enough that it wasn't in good shape. His curiosity got the best of him, though, and he decided at the very least that he should go take a peek at it.

He hiked over to the carcass, grabbed hold of an antler, and pulled it out of the brush. That's when he about had a heart attack. It was the biggest whitetail he'd ever seen

– a giant of a buck, with long, long tines and a big droptine.

From what he could tell through his eyes and nose, it looked like the buck had been dead a week, and had a smell that was nearly unbearable. He decided to leave it for the time being, mull it over whether he wanted to deal with it, and continue on with his elk hunt. Leaving the carcass behind, he continued on his way.

Meeting up with Jay and Jana a while later, he told them about his find. He and Jay decided to grab a saw and head on back to retrieve the head.

Both men did their best to cope with the rancid and powerful smell while wrestling the carcass and sawing off the antlers. They also tried to determine how the great buck had met his demise. Steve could see the buck had a slice on his shoulder, which looked like it might have been inflicted by a cougar. The carcass had also been dragged into the brush, also indicating a big cat. The only thing that didn't fit with a cougar was that the carcass hadn't been covered, but perhaps with it being semi-hidden in the brush, the cat figured it didn't have to. There was also fine blood splatter on the antlers, as if a main artery had been severed.

Steve's great "picked up" trophy, with a 195 gross typical frame, has one of the biggest typical frames in Idaho history. If he hadn't grown the droptine, he would have scored 189-2/8 and been the Idaho state record typical.

STEVE KLUVER

# Richard Hart, Sr.
## 181 B&C Typical
## Nez Perce County, 1967

**Idaho Typical Rank: 6\***

T here's a lot to be thankful for on Thanksgiving. Beyond all the normal things – health, family, etc. – there are the important things, like a day off from work and a free extra day of hunting. Richard was working in the veneer plant at Potlatch, so a day of chasing whitetails was a welcome relief from the daily grind.

Richard, along with his brother, Bob, and dad, Clair, were hunting an area near Culdesac where they had taken many bucks over the years. Typical for November in that area, it was cool but there was no snow on the ground.

They had planned on making a drive and pushing some bucks to each other, but they had gotten no more than about 100 yards from the truck when Bob spooked up a huge buck! Richard took quick action and hit the buck high in the shoulder with his .264 Win.-Mag. The buck had been at a full run 75 yards away, making it quite a good fast-reaction shot. Richard used the old "buck for a backpack" trick and packed out the buck on his back whole-bodied.

The men had received strict orders that they were not to be late getting home for Thanksgiving dinner, and they weren't the type to disobey. Getting the buck so early in the hunt allowed them to be back in plenty of time.

# Tony L. Siron
## 178-7/8 B&C Typical
### Kootenai County, 1998

**Idaho Typical Rank:** 7
**Inside Spread:** 18-7/8
**Main Beams (R,L):** 24-6/8,26-0/8

**Points (R,L):** 5,5
**Widest Spread:** 21-2/8
**Bases (R, L):** 5-2/8,5-1/8

 wo years prior to killing this deer, I encountered him on the last day of the season. I had jumped him and followed his tracks in fresh snow. He led me through a creek bed in thick timber, and I could hear him every now and then. I eventually got on an old road and just walked slowly, hoping to see him.

Looking up a steep hill, I finally saw him standing broadside with a doe and looking down at me 60 yards away. I was amazed at the length of his tines. I took quick aim at his heart and shot. He instantly bolted over a ridge, and I ran up the hill as fast as I could, thinking I had hit him.

I got up there and all I found was a drop or two of blood and a bit of white hair; I had just grazed his chest. Upset and still breathing hard, I calmed myself down and slowly started tracking him. Now he was going down the ridge toward where I had jumped him the first time. He eventually went onto private property and I gave up, thinking my chance was gone.

I continued down the ridge and sat on a white fir that had fallen over, thinking about what to do. Soon after, I heard a snap. I looked up the hill where I just come from and saw a doe with that buck on her tail! I was amazed to be getting a second chance. The doe crossed the creek and I had my rifle up and waiting for the buck to pass through the same spot. When he did, I shot at 40 yards and missed again! What a way to end my season. I later checked and learned that my rifle was off.

The next season, I took my friend Jim there. We split up and Jim jumped the buck and shot but missed. The buck ran by me but was in the brush in low light and I couldn't get a shot. Jim dogged me for not being where he wanted me to be, even though it was my hunting spot. I dogged him back for missing in the first place; it didn't end our friendship, though.

The next year, I had been taking my son hunting with me most of the time, grooming him to be my hunting partner. He was just five, but we were having fun.

**Tony Siron's son is barely bigger than the antlers of his massive whitetail.**

We were out on Veterans Day with no real thought of actually getting a deer; it was more about being out hunting with him and trying to teach him. Nonetheless, we were hunting the same area.

Stopping, listening, and going slow, we began hearing something to our left. I told him to be quiet, and just then we saw him through the brush. He was acting like he was following us, likely due to me rattling as I was walking.

I brought my .300 Win.-mag. up quickly and shot the buck in the neck at only 50 yards. He flipped over backwards and my son said, "Hey, Pa, he did a flip like a Power Ranger." He was into the Power Rangers at that time.

I can only assume this was the same deer I had seen the previous two years. The best part of the whole thing was my son's comment; he had no idea the magnitude of what had just happened. Now, at 16, he is still my best hunting partner.

# Donna M. Knight
### 177-5/8 B&C Typical
### Idaho County, 1986

**Idaho Typical Rank: 8**

**Inside Spread: 21-3/8**

**Main Beams (R,L): 26-0/8,25-6/8**

**Points (R,L): 5,5**

**Widest Spread: 24-2/8**

**Bases (R, L): 4-5/8,4-5/8**

D onna Knight has hunted since she was just 13 years old, strictly for meat back then, and has kept with it her entire lifetime. She also really enjoys hunting alone.

However, for about eight years leading up to the 1986 season, she had been very ill. She had a muscle disease that left her weak and tired, and by the time she was properly diagnosed, she couldn't even walk. At that point, the doctors told her that she had only a 45 percent chance of even surviving.

It took surgery and a long time, but she was recovering. With only one day left in the deer season, Donna was set on getting out and trying to get her whitetail. Her family was adamantly opposed to her going, but she insisted, and promised that she "wouldn't do anything stupid."

She was walking down an old trail below a field when she looked up toward the skyline and saw a huge rutting buck keeping company with a doe. As quickly as she could, she set up on a stump for a rest and fired her .30-30 Marlin with open sights. Four shots later, she was shaky and still hadn't hit the buck. Praying for divine intervention she said, "Okay, Lord; it's up to you. If I'm gonna get a deer, I need your help."

Donna pulled up freehand and shot one final time. The deer quickly disappeared, leaving little evidence as to how successful the shot might have been.

She climbed up the steep slope, which took awhile due to a bit of slick snow and her weak condition. Once she got there, she couldn't find any sign. Out of ammo, and feeling a bit weak and a whole lot disheartened, she still looked for 30 minutes before giving up.

As she started back to go get help, she had just stepped over a rock when she looked down and saw the dead buck practically at her feet. Donna gave out a loud and excited yell – she knew instantly that her buck was a trophy of huge proportions. Her last shot had clipped the tip of the heart and the buck had died nearly instantly.

She went back to get some muscle to get her buck off the hill. Her husband, Larry, and her son, Marvin Mendenhall, figured at best that she was exaggerating from being overexcited. One quick look at the antlers proved them wrong, though. Donna had done the unthinkable. She had overcome her illness enough to go out solo and come back with one of the biggest bucks in the history of the state of Idaho.

**Donna overcame health problems and big odds in taking one of Idaho's largest typical whitetails. She was hunting alone when she encountered her buck in 1986.**

# Andy Short
## 177-1/8 B&C Typical
### Benewah County, 2003

**Idaho Typical Rank: 9***          **Points (R,L): 6,6**
**Inside Spread: 19-1/8**          **Widest Spread: 23-0/8**
**Main Beams (R,L): 26-2/8,25-7/8**          **Bases (R, L): 4-5/8,4-6/8**

I f there is one thing that sets Idaho apart from many states, it's the fact that most all of the trophies here were taken by "Average Joe" hunters. Most are general season, after work or school, "I think I might go out hunting today" stories. They are typically fairly unassuming and somewhat innocent stories about hunters with no special privileges who just went out and shot the big one – and that's how it should be.

Andy Short could be the poster child for why it's important to keep hunting an "equal opportunity" endeavor. Just 15 years old and still without a first buck, Andy was chomping at the bit. He was on a break from school for Thanksgiving and had just finished his driver's education. What's a kid do to celebrate in Idaho? Go hunting.

He walked out the door of his house, hunting alone, with plans to do a quick evening hunt. With it being so close to home, there wasn't much to worry about for safety.

Four inches of snow carpeted the ground as he slowly hiked up the hill through the timber and into an area of logging roads and old skid trails. Being careful to watch for deer movement, he got to a likely spot only about 300 yards from the house and then stopped. He broke out a deer call "can"and gave it a couple of twists, listening to the slow, drawn out bleat.

He was surprised to get an instant response; a doe came in to investigate. Right behind her, a buck followed closely. With Andy's youth and inexperience at judging whitetails, he had no idea the magnitude of what was about to happen. He just thought it looked like a "nice" buck.

He aimed behind the shoulder with his .300 RUM from 80 yards away and promptly hit the buck in the neck, killing it instantly. As Andy walked up, he got a better look at the antlers and knew he'd taken a good one, but only much later would he learn exactly what he'd done that day.

Andy's big buck, while on display at the Big Horn Show in Spokane.

He raced down the hill and got his dad, who helped him get the buck taken care of and back to the house. Several months later, at the legendary Big Horn Show in Spokane, Andy had his buck measured at 177-1/8, making it one of the ten biggest typical in Idaho history. He also won the coveted buckle awarded to the top trophy. Not bad for a kid hunting alone behind the house and taking his first buck.

*Note: Andy's buck has a huge typical frame (190-7/8 gross) but loses 13-6/8 inches to deductions (7-2/8 of which are two abnormal points).*

# Edward D. Moore
## 176-6/8 B&C Typical
### Idaho County, 1986

**Idaho Typical Rank: 10**                                             **Points (R,L): 7,7**
**Inside Spread: 16-2/8**                                         **Widest Spread: 18-2/8**
**Main Beams (R,L): 22-3/8,23-6/8**                     **Bases (R, L): 4-1/8,4-1/8**

 d Moore was 28 years old and living in Lewiston in 1986. His grandma was living in Clearwater, a very small community up the South Fork of the Clearwater, right in the heart of good whitetail hunting. While seeing your grandma should be reason enough to make a trip, a mid November whitetail hunt doesn't hurt, either. November 16, 1986 found Ed in just such a situation, thinking more about where he might find a good whitetail buck during the rut.

He had passed the middle part of the day by taking his mom for an easy countryside drive. As evening approached, he dropped his mom off at his grandma's and headed out for a quick evening hunt.

Ed had been seeing a lot of deer in an open and mixed brush area near an old apple orchard, so he headed that way. As he drove his little Toyota pickup to the area where he wanted to stop, he saw a huge buck in a field from his pickup. It took off, and Ed almost instantly dismissed the buck, figuring the chances of seeing it again were nil.

He went ahead and parked, took his time getting his gear ready, and then set out. He had scarcely covered 50 yards when the buck came right back over the hill toward him – "a gift", as Ed describes it.

At about 200 yards, Ed fired his 7mm-mag. and hit the buck right in the neck. The buck rolled downhill, but got up, so Ed fired and hit him once more before he lost sight of him. He had six inches of snow to help in tracking, but as last light faded, he still hadn't caught up to it. He had no choice but to back out and come back in the morning.

That night was a restless one for Ed. Visions of big antlers, as well thoughts about the uncertainty of the buck's condition, filled his mind.

The next morning he came right back to where he had left off, and found his buck lying there in the snow within minutes of starting his search. It was a feeling of both relief and excitement.

While he knew it was a nice buck, Ed admits that he really had no idea how significant a trophy he had taken. Even after having it measured and seeing where it sits from a historical perspective, he's pretty modest about it.

**"A gift" is how Ed describes the big deer he took in 1986. He had just parked and started walking when this buck came running over the hill right at him.**

# Frank J. Loughran
## 176-6/8 B&C Typical
### Idaho County, 1987

**Idaho Typical Rank: 10**  
**Inside Spread: 17-0/8**  
**Main Beams (R,L): 26-5/8,25-6/8**

**Points (R,L): 6,7**  
**Widest Spread: 20-1/8**  
**Bases (R, L): 5-2/8,5-1/8**

L iving in the middle of whitetail country, Frank Loughran has the luxury of keeping his eyes peeled for big bucks. During the mid '80s, he had his eye on a couple. He had given it everything he had trying to outwit them, but had thus far come up short.

He was hunting with his son Jason one day in early November, and most of the way through the hunt, Jason left to go get the pickup and meet Frank. As he crossed an open field, he jumped a big-bodied buck out of a pile of rocks and brush in the middle of the open. It was dark before they could do anything, so they dismissed it from their minds.

The next day they hunted a different area in the morning. About noon, Frank and Jason were in town and ran into Eddie Sears. The three of them decided to go to that spot where Jason had jumped the big buck the day before.

They drove up that way and asked the rancher for permission to hunt. He granted it, and mentioned that he'd seen some big bucks on the place.

185

Jason and Eddie took one side of the draw; Frank took the other. He waited until they reached the other side so they could start working the draw. Once they were across, Jason started throwing some rocks into the draw in hopes of kicking something up. On his fourth throw, a buck – a HUGE buck – jumped up. Jason yelled, "Big!"

In an attempt to escape, the buck ran with his head down straight for Frank. It It was an unbelievably close encounter that resulted in Frank snap-shooting the buck with his 7mm-mag. at a matter of only a few yards.

The buck veered to the left and made it about 100 yards into some thick brush before collapsing. Jason and Eddie got to the buck before Frank, and started whooping it up. In a matter of minutes, Frank was doing the same thing.

Taken near the top of the draw, it was an easy drag back to the rig. The buck's body was also fairly small – only 174 lbs. field dressed – apparently putting most of its growing efforts directly into its enormous and handsome headgear.

**Frank Loughran holds the results of his 1986 hunt near Kooskia. He shot the buck at extremely close range as the buck nearly ran him over.**

# Thomas Lougee
## 176 B&C Typical
### Nez Perce County, 1987

BUD LOUGEE

**Idaho Typical Rank: 12***

**Inside Spread: 23-2/8**

**Main Beams (R,L): 29-0/8,28-4/8**

**Points (R,L): 5,5**

**Widest Spread: 26-0/8**

**Bases (R, L): 4-5/8,4-6/8**

It was the last week of hunting season in 1987. Two of my uncles, two of my good friends, my dad, and I met early in the morning to go on a big hunt that they had been planning.

I was told that I was going to have to hike up the hill, and I remember being mad, because I didn't like hiking up hills. Then I found out it was just going to be me and I started to get excited. They dropped me off, and then everyone else took the drive up the hill. The plan was to try to drive some deer down to me.

When I arrived at my location, it was just starting to get light, and I had a special feeling that something good was going to happen. I started sneaking up an old logging road and wasn't even halfway up the hill when I saw a deer walk behind a bush. It was 100 yards away and I had seen a quick glimpse of antler.

I slowly sat down and rested my rifle on my knee, and the deer walked out into the open. I once again got a quick glimpse of antler, and quickly aimed and pulled the trigger. The deer fell immediately, and as it did, I got a real good look at the antlers. I began to get very excited.

I sat there for several minutes with my crosshairs on him, but he never moved, so finally I hiked up to him. I couldn't believe how large he was.

I was pretty excited, so I fired off two shots to try and signal my hunting party. I waited awhile and then started hiking up the hill. Thirty minutes later, I found my friend Coby. He and I would always bet five dollars on who would get the biggest buck, and I told him I got a nice five-point. When we got to it, he hit me. "It's huge!" he said.

Uncle Ben came down the hill and was equally impressed. He said, "Yep, he's the one that's been making the tracks I've been seeing around here."

I bailed down the hill and met my dad, Uncle Ned, and my friend, Billy. I told them I got a nice five-point.

A young Bud Lougee, with his amazing trophy buck, in 1987.

We got permission to drive the pickup up to my deer. Billy and I were in the back, and I told him it was bigger than all the bucks in my parents' house, and I must say, there were some nice ones. He said there was no way, and I said, "Bet me."

We arrived at my buck, and my dad got out of the truck and walked over to him. He tipped up the rack and said, "I might as well burn all my horns, because I have never gotten anything this big."

We took the buck to the taxidermist, where we entered the big buck contest and had it caped out. The buck won the contest and the prize was a free mount.

To this day, I've never seen another whitetail that was even close to this one. I am lucky and proud to say that the largest buck I ever saw was the one I killed.

*Note: Thomas Lougee's jaw-dropping buck has a very interesting build. Not one single point is ten inches, but it has some of the longest main beams in Idaho. When coupled with a wide inside spread, these two traits more than make up for it.*

# Joe Sparks
## 175-7/8 B&C Typical
### Nez Perce County, 1987

**Idaho Typical Rank: 13**
**Inside Spread: 18-0/8**
**Main Beams (R,L): 27-2/8,26-0/8**

**Points (R,L): 5,7**
**Widest Spread: 22-3/8**
**Bases (R, L): 4-6/8,4-6/8**

eaving Lewiston early that morning and winding their way up the mountain in an old '73 Ford pickup, 26-year-old Joe Sparks and Jack McLaughlin were planning on hunting some steep country near the confluence of the Salmon and Snake Rivers. It was true "breaks country", with steep, grassy slopes, punishing elevations drops, and isolated Douglas-fir and pine stands.

They had been still-hunting along through a small, thick bedding area and had also been rattling from time to time when they saw a 4x4 whitetail. Joe was getting ready to shoot it, but Jack talked him out of it. It was still early in the hunt.

As they moved on, a deer jumped up; it had been bedded there 20 yards away the entire time. It went over the hill and Jack went over to head it off, but it never came out. Then it started sneaking back down, and when Joe threw a rock, it came out and ran into an opening at only 50 yards.

It all happened so quickly that Joe had no chance for a shot. He couldn't really even tell how big the buck was, other than it was "nice." With only one more opening available, Joe zeroed in on that spot, praying the buck would waltz on through it. A few seconds later it did, and when it filled his scope, he let loose with his .300 Win.-mag.

It was as lucky a shot as a hunter could ever ask for, since the buck was flying at full speed through the opening, but that doesn't matter to Joe. It connected right behind the shoulder and the buck dropped within 75 yards.

Joe is a dedicated hunter with plenty of experience, but he was speechless when he saw what he had just taken. The massive frame was more than he'd ever seen, and maybe more than he'd ever even hoped for. The beams were so long and curled in so well that they nearly touched. It was an amazing day, made even better by a more amazing trophy.

The two hunters lugged Joe's trophy buck a quarter-mile to the truck and then, since there was plenty of daylight left, Joe gave Jack a while to hunt. Jack used it to the fullest, taking a nice 4x4 mulie. That must have been one nice-looking load in the back of that old Ford pickup.

*Note: IDFG did a tooth sample on this buck and determined he was 9-1/2 years old.*

# Rusty P. Kirtley
## 175-7/8 B&C Typical
### Nez Perce County, 2000

RUSTY KIRTLEY

**Idaho Typical Rank: 13**
**Inside Spread: 18-7/8**
**Main Beams (R,L): 24-5/8,23-1/8**

**Points (R,L): 6,6**
**Widest Spread: 20-6/8**
**Bases (R, L): 5-1/8,5-0/8**

I f all you heard was that Rusty Kirtley drove all the way up from Fruitland and killed a big whitetail, your first instinct might be to just dismiss it as luck. However, the truth is that even though he was living in southern Idaho, Rusty went to school in Lapwai and knew all the surrounding whitetail country extremely well. Beyond that, Rusty had invested time in several scouting trips, which led to him spotting a huge typical buck on two separate occasions.

Rusty and his friend, Ron Thompson, headed up to Rusty's old stomping grounds, basing their "camp" out of the Super 8 in Lewiston. There was enough good hunting close by that they could reach decent hunting spots within an hour's drive each morning.

On the second day of their hunt, November 16, both hunters hopped into the Toyota pickup dressed and ready to go. It had snowed a few inches overnight and the fresh snow was now coupled with crisp weather and blue skies.

They arrived at their chosen location - the edge of a stubble field framed by a timbered draw and some CRP ground - just as light was breaking. When Rusty opened the door, he had left the key in the ignition, and it started "dinging". He knew that was bad news and instantly looked around to see if any deer were within earshot. He instantly spotted two does, which were now staring at him. At the same time, Rusty noticed antler tips coming over the horizon. Before he could see what it was, the does blew out of there, taking the buck with them.

Luckily, Rusty was pretty much ready to go, so he grabbed his rifle and was gone in a flash. Ron took off as well, but in a slightly different direction. Rusty followed

the deer over the rise and down through some cattails near an old homestead. He saw the deer, and at that moment he heard Ron shoot in a different location at a different deer. It normally would have been inconsequential, but it just happened to stop the lead doe. When she stopped, so did the second doe, and the buck plowed right into the back of the second doe. The chaos stopped all three deer just long enough for Rusty to touch off a shot from

**This photo is one of the best field photos ever taken of a giant whitetail in Idaho. What a big, beautiful buck.**

**Rusty Kirtley's buck, taken in Palouse country farm ground in 2000, has one of the most massive, mature, and developed typical frames in the state.**

his Ruger M77 7mm-mag. It was a 225-yard shot that hit home, causing the buck to kick and then sail out of sight.

He ran up to the spot and found where the buck had hit the snow-clad slope and slid to a stop. At the end of the slide lay his trophy, a big, beautiful, long-tined monarch that would later prove to be one of the best the state had ever produced.

Ron, fresh off the sting of missing his buck, came over to see how Rusty did. Both hunters stared in awe at the giant buck, and then began the process of getting it out of there. Rusty says being weighed down on a pack out never felt quite so good.

**There's no better feeling as a hunter than to have the weight of a trophy buck on your back.**

193

# Carl Groth
## 175-5/8 B&C Typical
### Benewah County, 1982

AMY DEGON

**Idaho Typical Rank: 15**
**Inside Spread: 17-7/8**
**Main Beams (R,L): 25-5/8,25-0/8**

**Points (R,L): 6,7**
**Widest Spread: 23-3/8**
**Bases (R, L): 4-5/8,4-5/8**

 arl Groth was a farmer and machinery dealer, and was 58 years old when he took his historic whitetail buck. Sadly, he died in 2004, but his son-in-law, Bergen Bothman, was with him on the hunt and helped with the story of a very special day of hunting.

That late November morning before dawn, they jumped in a Chevy pickup and headed toward Plummer Mountain. The area was not particularly high in elevation, and was fairly brushy, with plenty of CRP ground. It was perfect whitetail habitat.

When they got there, they started walking up into a draw. They were scarcely ten minutes into the hunt when a great big buck and seven does ran across a CRP field blanketed with a few inches of snow. Carl raised his Remington .25-06 and took a shot at the running buck, making a solid hit on it at 300 yards.

Carl saw that the buck had been hit and proceeded to track him for 2-1/2 hours. During that time, the buck did some serious traveling. Up and over the hill he went, back down, and up again. They jumped the buck four times during that span. Snow on the ground helped, but it was melting, and the longer the tracking went on, the less their chances were of recovering the buck.

Finally, they came to a clearing. "There's that buck!" Bergen shouted.

Carl shouldered the rifle again and made a solid hit. His mind could now relax; the buck was his.

Being experienced whitetail hunters, they knew it was a good buck, but it seemed that the more people they showed the buck to, the more everyone kept getting all excited over it.

The next spring, they took the buck up to the Big Horn Show in Spokane and got it scored. It did pretty well, winning the coveted buckle for the top trophy.

**This photo really symbolizes a lot of what northern Idaho is all about. Pickups, big tractors, rolling hills, and big whitetails. Whether by coincidence or design, this is a great photo.**

195

# Daniel R. Merrill
## 175-3/8 B&C Typical
### Jefferson County, 2001

DANIEL MERRILL

**Idaho Typical Rank: 16**                    **Points (R,L): 5,6**
**Inside Spread: 22-1/8**                     **Widest Spread: 24-0/8**
**Main Beams (R,L): 26-4/8,26-6/8**           **Bases (R, L): 5-2/8,5-1/8**

 t was the last weekend of the shotgun deer season, and my family and I decided to give it one last push. My wife, my in-laws, and my brother all went to the river bottoms near our home. My brother and I were the only ones with tags left for the season; everyone else was just along for the walk and to make some extra noise.

I gave my brother the choice of two different locations to sit and watch for deer. He took the draw, so I sat at the point near the river. At 2 p.m., after waiting for 30 minutes, I heard a ruckus across the main channel of the Snake River. I began looking to see what it was when I noticed a float boat about 600 yards up the river.

Suddenly, I heard a splash. I looked up and saw the biggest whitetail buck I had ever seen running right at me. I remember thinking that if he continued on his path, he'd be within ten yards of me when he popped up on the bank.

He was halfway across the river when he noticed the boat coming at him. He suddenly stopped, turned around, and began running away from me. I started thinking, "I can't believe that just happened!"

Then the buck stopped broadside 100 yards away and looked at the boat. I raised my 20-gauge shotgun, preparing myself for the shot. I knew the boat was getting closer and that my window of opportunity was slipping away.

Boom! I knew it was a good shot, hitting the buck behind the shoulder. He hunched up and ran over to the edge of the trees and was struggling. The boat stopped near where I was standing and the men in the boat said, "You hit him good!"

With my adrenaline rushing, I asked the men in the boat to give me a ride across the river, so I wouldn't get wet. I wasn't even thinking about waiting for my family. They took me across, wished me good luck and continued down the river.

I went into the trees and found the blood trail. By then, my family had heard the shot and made it to where I was when I shot. They wanted to help me, but they needed a boat to cross. While I waited for them to go get a boat, I began following the blood trail. He had lain down in the grass and I must have spooked him. I backed off to give him more time.

Once they returned, we started on the blood trail again. This led us to the edge of a hay field. The field was thick and it was hard to see blood, but there was a thicket of willows on the other side of the field and I wondered if he might be hiding in there. My wife and I started in that direction.

We were approaching the willows and I could see the tines of his antlers sticking out. I pointed him out to my wife and she asked, "That's him? That big?"

By this time, he had spotted us. He began trotting, headed right back toward the river. We caught up to the others, and found out they had watched him cross a slough and jump a fence. We all started that way and hadn't been walking long when I glanced ahead and saw his antlers alongside of a log. He was finally done.

Once we returned to the truck and were loading the buck, other hunters gathered around. Some were excited by the size of the buck, while others boasted tales of bigger whitetail bucks they had supposedly seen that day.

The shotgun I used to shoot the buck was borrowed from my father. He later gave it to me as a birthday present.

*Note: While Dan Merrill's whitetail is significant in regard to Idaho's records, it's even more significant to eastern Idaho. His buck is the only whitetail to ever make the all-time record book from that half of the state, and is larger than any other whitetail known to have come from that region.*

# Douglas B. Crockett
## 174-2/8 B&C Typical
### Clearwater County, 1983

**Idaho Typical Rank: 19**
**Inside Spread: 22-6/8**
**Main Beams (R,L): 26-1/8,26-5/8**

**Points (R,L): 7,6**
**Widest Spread: 25-2/8**
**Bases (R, L): 5-0/8,4-7/8**

D oug Crockett took this exceptional trophy in Clearwater County late in the 1983 season. This is one of those bucks that photos don't do justice to. The buck is very massive throughout the entire rack, and is a very impressive trophy when viewed in person.

Many of Idaho's best whitetails were taken in the two-decade span from 1986 through 2005. This buck, taken a few years earlier, was one of the top whitetails in the state at the time.

# Don Southern
### 174 B&C Typical
### Nez Perce County, 1986

**Idaho Typical Rank: 20**
**Inside Spread: 18-2/8**
**Main Beams (R,L): 23-4/8,23-4/8**

**Points (R,L): 5,5**
**Widest Spread: 21-1/8**
**Bases (R, L): 5-1/8,5-1/8**

W hile you might think that living close to deer would mean you get to hunt more, the truth is that when it's that close to you, sometimes it turns into one of those things that you try to fit in when you have time.

Don Southern had been working all day for the road department that November day in 1986. After he got off work, he decided on a whim to try and take advantage of the last half-hour of daylight.

A storm had come through and blanketed the ground with a full 18 inches of snow, and Don figured that maybe it might have the deer moving. He jumped in his '84 Chevy without too much of a plan. He jetted down the highway and saw a small draw he'd hunted before and decided to give it a shot. After all, light was fading fast and he was mostly looking for meat anyway.

He parked the truck and started up a fairly open, grassy swale centered between two fields. A light snow was still falling, limiting visibility to a slight degree.

He had walked all of about 100 yards when he rounded a bend and had the shock of his life. A mammoth buck was in the bottom of the small drainage with a doe. They locked eyes on Don about the same time and took off. Don focused on the buck through his Weaver scope, fired his Winchester .30-06 at 100 yards and promptly missed. His second shot followed at 150 yards and had the same horrifying result. With his window of time shutting at an alarming rate, he touched off one more desperation shot at 200 yards and hit the buck, steamrolling it.

Don made good time to his trophy buck, which was now nearly buried in 18 inches of snow. He had no idea what to expect when he lifted the head, and the antlers were so big that his first instinct was that he'd made a huge mistake and shot a mule deer. A quick check reassured him it was a whitetail and then he about went crazy. He probably would have been heard clear in Lewiston if he'd have had anyone to share the moment with.

He dragged the buck back, but it was so big and heavy he couldn't get it loaded by himself. He raced back down the road and grabbed his pregnant wife to help him. It's probably a pretty safe bet that he was much more excited by that than she was.

**Don Southern was on a last-minute evening hunt close to home in deep snow, and encountered this buck right off a highway.**

# Unknown
## 173-6/8 B&C Typical
## Bonner County, 1967

**Idaho Typical Rank: 21**
**Inside Spread: 20-3/8**
**Main Beams (R,L): 26-6/8,27-6/8**

**Points (R,L): 9,6**
**Widest Spread: 22-7/8**
**Bases (R, L): 5-7/8,5-4/8**

his outstanding typical was one of the top-ranked whitetails in Idaho for many years. Even now, well over 40 years later, it still occupies a prominent place in the Idaho listings.

This buck was killed near Garfield Bay by an unknown hunter. It has been incorrectly listed for all these years as having been taken by Robert L. Campbell. However, Robert informed me that he did not actually kill the buck. He had just taken it in to get scored, and that it was a simple error on the score chart.

The score on this massive buck is deceiving. It has an outstanding 190-6/8 gross typical frame.

# John D. Kauffman
### 173-1/8 B&C Typical
### Latah County, 1991

**Idaho Typical Rank: 23**  
**Inside Spread: 18-1/8**  
**Main Beams (R,L): 25-1/8,26-0/8**

**Points (R,L): 5,8**  
**Widest Spread: 20-3/8**  
**Bases (R, L): 4-6/8,4-5/8**

 trychnine Ridge, several miles east of Harvard, Idaho, had become one of my favorite whitetail hunting areas in the mid 1980s. The area had a nice mix of thick timber, brush patches, and fairly open slopes, and well-used game trails that contoured around finger ridges for several miles along the main ridge. In addition to the game trails, several old, partly overgrown skid roads made it a great place to quietly sneak along. I shot several nice bucks in the area, but none that were record size.

On November 24, 1991, I headed out that way for a hunt. It was moderately cold with a few inches of snow on the ground, but not too crunchy underfoot. I walked up the ridge a mile or so from the Forest Service road, stopping at some favorite spots along the way for half an hour or more at a time, then moving on to others.

About noon, I picked a spot under some big ponderosa pines near the top of the ridge where I could see quite a ways ahead. There were scattered large trees and grassy areas on top, with thicker timber and brushy draws on either side of the ridge.

After an hour, my feet were starting to get cold and I had about decided to move on. Suddenly, I noticed movement behind me and off to my right about 30 yards away. A nice buck was sneaking along the main ridge trail and looking in my direction, but apparently didn't see or smell me.

When he moved slightly ahead of me, I slowly raised my Sako .270, put the crosshairs just behind the shoulder and fired. He quickly jumped off the trail and disappeared into the brush. I was dumbfounded. I couldn't possibly have missed, could I?

I walked over and found him dead in the brush not far from where he had disappeared. It turned out to be a heart shot.

Now came the "fun" of dragging him the mile back down the ridge to the pickup. By myself, that ordeal took several hours, even with the snow that made dragging easier. I alternated carrying my rifle and pack ahead 50 yards, then went back and dragged the deer a ways, leap-frogging loads all the way out, around deadfall and brush patches.

At the time, I thought it was a pretty nice buck, but didn't think much more about it. Several years later, I started noticing mounts in sporting goods stores that looked smaller than this deer, so I finally had it measured late in 1994. I found out it scored well enough to make the all-time record book.

# Kevin L. Lundblad
## 172-7/8 B&C Typical
### Kootenai County, 1992

KEVIN LUNDBLAD

**Idaho Typical Rank: 24**

**Inside Spread: 18-0/8**

**Main Beams (R,L): 25-2/8,24-3/8**

**Points (R,L): 7,7**

**Widest Spread: 20-7/8**

**Bases (R, L): 4-2/8,4-1/8**

It was a cold, wet November day in 1992 when 31-year-old Kevin Lundblad and his dad, Gary, took off for a local hunting trip in Kootenai County. Eight inches of snow blanketed the ground in the relatively open country where they chose to hunt that day.

They had hiked in about two miles and were scanning the mostly white terrain when Kevin saw a big buck chasing a doe 300 yards out. With timing about as bad as it could get, a bank of fog rolled in before Kevin could even decide what to do. He had no choice but to sit and wait it out.

An hour passed as father and son tried to stay warm and keep their nerves in check. The fog finally lifted, and miraculously, the buck was still there! As much as that was exactly what they had hoped for, neither of them could believe it.

Kevin and Gary both shot a number of times as the buck made a run for the timber. On Kevin's last possible shot from the old aught-six, he broke the buck's back just before it hit the trees.

Kevin ran the entire 300 yards to the deer, which was mostly finished. However, Kevin was out of ammo, so he had to finish the job with a hunting knife.

The long drag through the creek bottom and back to their rig wasn't easy, but the fact that Kevin was with his dad made the job much easier - that, and they had just managed to take one of Idaho's biggest whitetails.

Note: Kevin isn't the first member of his family to get a record book whitetail in Idaho. His great-grandfather, Alfred Hegge, took a 203-4/8 non-typical in Kootenai County in 1929.

# Shane Moyer
172-5/8 B&C Typical
Kootenai County, 1996

**Idaho Typical Rank: 25**
**Inside Spread: 20-7/8**
**Main Beams (R,L): 26-1/8,26-0/8**

**Points (R,L): 5,5**
**Widest Spread: 25-5/8**
**Bases (R, L): 4-6/8,4-5/8**

T he plan was that Shane Moyer would soon be joining his father-in-law for a four-day hunt up in the Bonners Ferry area. So much for plans. The minute Shane saw this giant buck, his plans changed entirely.

Not thinking that much would probably come of it, Shane decided to venture out for a quick hunt on November 20 with his friend, Jamie Jenicek. Jamie had seen some mulies up high and really wanted to go after them. Shane quickly obliged.

They drove in Jamie's pickup and plowed snow with the front bumper until they got the pickup stuck. From there, they hiked in to the hunt area and trudged around in deep snow for about six hours, with noth-

**This photo defines the word "perspective."**

ing to show for it.

They spent a little while getting the truck out, and started back down the road. They had only gone about a mile when they started talking about the fact that there was still a bit of light left and that maybe they should stop the rig and at least hunt until dark. They pulled over and decided to give it a try.

They had barely started walking when a small buck stepped out and Jamie shot it. They quickly took care of it, loaded it in the truck, and drove on down into some lower, more open ground.

Finding another likely spot, they again pulled over. Miraculously, it was almost a repeat performance. Shane instantly saw a

doe, and while he was looking at her, he nearly had a heart attack when this breathtaking buck stepped out.

As Shane started to kick his mind into overdrive, the buck disappeared back to where he had just come from. It hadn't seen them; the buck was just rutting and moving. Within seconds, the buck came back out to check the exposed doe, and Shane cranked off a round from his .30-06 at 75 yards. The wounded buck took off across the hillside, and Shane fired off two more rounds in vain. It didn't matter; the buck piled up within a matter of seconds.

Of his most successful hunt, Shane says, "It's almost embarrassing. I've had hunts that I lie in bed at night and think about – hunts that really tested me - but this just wasn't one of them. Sometimes it just happens. Getting a buck like this spoils you. You can't help but expect that you can do it again, but it's not possible. Now I just get out and enjoy it."

**As with most big whitetails taken in Idaho, an intense rutting instinct was this buck's downfall.**

# Ty Bell
## 172-5/8 B&C Typical
### Boundary County, 2006

**Idaho Typical Rank: 25***       **Points (R,L): 7,7**
**Inside Spread: 21-1/8**       **Widest Spread: 23-0/8**
**Main Beams (R,L): 23-7/8, 24-3/8**       **Bases (R, L): 5-0/8,5-1/8**

 t was the morning of November 10, 2006. I had spent the night at my grandparents' house so that I could go hunting with my grandpa, Stan Sweet, who is a well-respected figure and hunter in the Bonners Ferry area.

We had made a game plan to hit the Queen Mountain Loop because I wanted to shoot a nice mule deer buck. In order to do that, we had to get up high, where there was a lot of snow.

After a few hours of trudging through over two feet of snow, I decided to give up for the time being and head back to the pickup. My toes and fingers were frozen and my clothes soaked; the heater in the Ford pickup and the Butterfinger candy bar were amazing! We decided to finish the loop and head back to the house for lunch and figure out what to do for the afternoon.

While sitting at the house, wet, heavy snowflakes began to fall. Grandpa said it was perfect whitetail buck weather and that he had a hunch on where we should go. We headed for an area that had been logged over and might be a good spot to rattle in a buck.

When we got to a fork in the road, and went to the right, but someone was already parked there and hunting. We backtracked and went down the left fork, and half a mile up the skid trail stood a big bodied whitetail doe. We stopped and looked to see if there was a buck tagging along, but nothing showed, so we moved on. Between there and the end of the road, we didn't see another deer or any fresh sign.

When we got to the end of the skid trail, we ran into another pickup! Frustrated, we backed up and decided to just start hunting. We headed down the trail toward where we had just seen that doe, and right before we got there, my grandpa said, "I'll bet there was a…Holy…there he is, Ty! He looks like a good one!"

Not ten yards from where we had seen the doe, there was a huge buck standing in the snow. It looked like a picture you would see in a hunting magazine. I grabbed my Ruger M77 chambered in .300 Winchester magnum and put a round in the chamber.

I had to move back up the trail, because he had stepped behind a tree, and all I had was a neck shot. Every time I looked at him, he looked like a massive 4x4, so I decided to take him. I settled the crosshairs under the white patch on his neck and squeezed.

**Ty Bell and his grandpa, Stan Sweet, pose for a photo at the Sandpoint Gun & Horn Show in 2008. Ty and Stan were hunting together that fateful and very special day.**

As the recoil rocked me back, I quickly chambered another shell, but the buck had disappeared. I thought I had missed him, so I sprinted up there and found the biggest buck I had ever seen lying right where he once stood!

I yelled down to grandpa that it was a huge buck, and when he got up there, he gave me the biggest bear hug you could ever imagine. I was the happiest boy in the world, and it was the most memorable moment of my life.

My buck won a lot of awards, including at Bonners Ferry, Sandpoint, and Spokane. While those are nice, none of it compares to the moments that my grandpa and I spent out there together. Those moments will always be cherished by both of us. Thank you, grandpa. Maybe next time we can put a mulie in the books!

**Ty Bell's grandpa, Stan Sweet, holds a nice 7x7 whitetail he took in Boundary County in 1955. Notice how much Stan and Ty look alike? Stan probably wishes their bucks looked more alike, too. Stan's dad, Red Sweet, also took a record book animal – a 191-7/8 typical mule deer taken in 1939 – that will be in the 2nd Edition of *Idaho's Greatest Mule Deer*, along with a classic old-time field photo.**

# Jim Felton
## 172 B&C Typical
### Idaho County, 1965

**Idaho Typical Rank: 27**
**Inside Spread: 17-2/8**
**Main Beams (R,L): 24-6/8,24-6/8**

**Points (R,L): 6,5**
**Widest Spread: 21-5/8**
**Bases (R, L): 4-3/8,4-4/8**

A s I left Lewiston on the morning of October 12, 1965, there was a light rain falling. Knowing it would be turning to snow, I headed south toward Joseph Plains. This was a two deer area at the time, with an abundance of both whitetail and mule deer.

As my ol' faithful '61 Scout and I climbed farther up the grade from the Salmon River, it was starting to snow harder by the mile. I was looking forward to a good day of hunting.

Arriving on top, there were four inches of new snow, and it was still snowing hard with a brisk wind. I passed a pickup parked alongside the road with its engine running and the windows all fogged up. It was still 45 minutes away from shooting light and I knew how they intended to hunt that patch of timber.

It was about half a mile through the patch, with an abandoned homestead, some outbuildings, and hay fields on the other side. Knowing I still had some darkness left and knowing how to get into the homestead, I was there before they ever left their truck.

I was able to get Ol' Red inside the barn through the large doors. As I climbed into the loft area, I thought about how great this was going to be, protected from the falling snow and brisk wind. The doors where the rail came through for bringing in the hay were open, allowing a full view of the open hayfield and surrounding timber.

As daylight broke, there were several deer in the field, with a few more just passing through. The stage was set and now it was just a waiting game.

Suddenly, with his nose to the ground and walking close to the timber, a beautiful buck came by at 150 yards. Leaning against the open doorway, I shot. The deer jumped straight up, ran 50 yards, and fell near the timber's edge.

After field-dressing and starting the skinning process, two hunters came out of the timber and said they had been following the buck since daylight. They proceeded to help me finish skinning the trophy and we loaded it up in my Scout. Afterward, I offered them a ride back to their truck.

After being in my home and office for several years, I was talked into selling it to an antler buyer in Orofino, who then sold it to a buyer near Missoula. If you recognize this set of antlers, please contact the author of this book, as we would like to get them back in our family.

# Picked Up by Darwin L. Baker
## 171-4/8 B&C Typical
## Latah County, 1986

DARWIN BAKER

**Idaho Typical Rank: 29**
**Inside Spread: 19-4/8**
**Main Beams (R,L): 24-7/8,25-2/8**

**Points (R,L): 6,6**
**Widest Spread: 21-5/8**
**Bases (R, L): 4-7/8,5-2/8**

D arwin Baker was going to college at the University of Idaho in Moscow and was actively involved in the Forestry program. As such, he spent quite a bit of time on the university's experimental forest.

It was late December and they had been doing some logging. Mike Reggear and Darwin were driving down the road when Darwin looked over and yelled, "Stop!"

He had seen what looked like a big buck sleeping near the road. When it didn't move, they realized it was dead. The buck was fairly emaciated, weighing only about 90 lbs. when it died, by Darwin's estimation. Whether it was by injury or disease isn't known.

Darwin, being a young and starving undergrad, sold the rack for $500 so he could by a new Weatherby 7mm-mag. Looking back, he wishes he'd held on to it instead.

# Richard L. Henderson
## 171-3/8 B&C Typical
### Idaho County, 1963

RICHARD HENDERSON

**Idaho Typical Rank: 30***

**Inside Spread: 19-5/8**

**Main Beams (R,L): 27-1/8,26-6/8**

**Points (R,L): 5,5**

**Widest Spread: 21-4/8**

**Bases (R, L): 4-6/8,4-7/8**

 was just 20 years old when I killed this whitetail buck in October of 1963. Del Phillips and I had been hunting elk up high in the snow above Slate Creek all day, and were on our way home.

I was packing a pre-'64 .264 Winchester Model 70 with me that day. I had purchased it just two years prior from Fred Warren down at Warren's Sport Shop in Lewiston in 1961.

We were pretty well resigned to having had an unsuccessful day, but knew that there was still a bit of a last chance, as there always seemed to be deer down toward the bottom of the grade. As we came around a bend in the road down in the lower but still steep grassy hills, a buck was on the point of a ridge above the road across a small draw from us.

He had been crossing from the south side of the creek, but as we came up to a gate and cattle guard on the road, he started running up a narrow ridge.

He had a head start, so he was probably two or three hundred yards up the ridge and doing his best to make it even farther. I jumped out of the vehicle and scrambled up the cut bank of the road, so that I would have an unobstructed view.

It was right at dusk, and the sun had already set. Light was not great, but it was still plenty. I picked him up in my scope, put the crosshairs between his antlers as he ran straight away from me, and pulled the trigger. I was lucky enough to hit him and bring him down with that one shot.

I knew it was a pretty good buck, but was even more thrilled when I got up to where he lay. He was a beautiful and perfect 5x5, and the biggest I had ever taken.

**Richard Henderson and his big record book trophy whitetail, taken near Whitebird in 1963.**

# Donald B. Vickaryous

## 171-3/8 B&C Typical
### Boundary County, 1995

DONALD VICKARYOUS

**Idaho Typical Rank: 30**
**Inside Spread: 17-5/8**
**Main Beams (R,L): 24-3/8,24-2/8**

**Points (R,L): 6,7**
**Widest Spread: 20-0/8**
**Bases (R, L): 5-1/8,5-1/8**

I t was getting close to the end of the whitetail season in November of 1995, and I still had my tag burning a hole in my pocket. My son, Barry, and son-in-law, Dan, were home for the holiday, and we had made plans to hunt together during Thanksgiving week.

The weather was almost too nice – very clear and mild – and we were bemoaning the lack of any snow. However, the rut was still in full swing, we were seeing plenty of deer every day, and were having a great time.

This particular day we decided to each still-hunt a different area of the same broad ridge that overlooked the beautiful Kootenai Valley. Late in the afternoon, around 3 p.m., I stood on a stump in head-high regrowth of an old clearcut to gain some height and view.

I locked right in on a huge set of antlers bouncing along in my direction. The brush was just high enough that the animal's body was kept concealed and I could only occasionally get a glimpse of his rack as he trotted along toward me.

I had the wind in my favor and my luck held as the buck finally moved across an opening where I could get a clear shot at him. He dropped out of sight after taking a bullet to the lungs from my Husqvarna .30-06.

Not until I got to where he was lying could I really appreciate what an exceptional whitetail I had just taken. He was very heavy, with well developed points all the way around.

To my surprise, when the boys and I thoroughly examined the big buck later, we found him to be younger than we expected. He still had good teeth and plenty of body fat.

**Don Vickaryous was hunting an old, grown-over clearcut when this buck came bouncing along through the brush. The antlers are very dark, typical to mountain deer in the area.**

# William Bennett, Jr.
## 171 B&C Typical
### Clearwater County, 1986

DONALD VICKARYOUS

**Idaho Typical Rank: 33\***
**Inside Spread: 21-1/8**
**Main Beams (R,L): 26-6/8, 27-3/8**

**Points (R,L): 5,8**
**Widest Spread: 24-4/8**
**Bases (R, L): 4-2/8,4-4/8**

Willliam Bennett was a logger, and as such, spent most of his time in the woods. Even so, any chance to get back out and do some deer and elk hunting is hard to pass up.

He and Al Lockman left Deary very early that morning, headed toward Elk River. It was an elk hunting trip, but deer was still a secondary option and they both had tags.

He had been hiking quite a bit, but was actually reasonably close to a road when this tremendous buck jumped up in front of him in an area of small openings among some smaller trees. He fired his 7mm-mag. in quick fashion as the buck ran straight away, and a well-placed and lucky shot hit the buck in the back of the neck, dropping it instantly.

# Paul A. Eke
## 171 B&C Typical
### Nez Perce County, 1993

**Idaho Typical Rank: 33**
**Inside Spread: 19-2/8**
**Main Beams (R,L): 27-5/8,27-0/8**

**Points (R,L): 7,7**
**Widest Spread: 21-2/8**
**Bases (R, L): 4-6/8,4-6/8**

I t was opening day of both deer and elk season, and some friends and neighbors were hunting on Paul's property. Everyone wanted an elk, so no one was focusing in on whitetails. This left Paul all alone in hoping for a big buck.

Other than the rut, there are few times to catch a mature buck unaware, but opening day might be that one exception. Paul was hoping for exactly that. He had been cowboying on his property and had seen three big bucks, and had found a big shed antler, too. He had that in the back of his mind as he set out that morning.

He parked his truck and had walked half a mile through lower, steep canyon country below a field. It was mostly open country, with plenty of yellow star thistle.

That's when he looked out and saw this buck still out feeding. A 100-yard shot with his .300 Weatherby did the trick. The buck ran a few hundred yards before collapsing, but Paul had no problem tracking down his trophy.

# Clarence Hagerman
## 170-6/8 B&C Typical
### Shoshone County, 1947

BONNIE MYERS

**Idaho Typical Rank: 35**
**Inside Spread: 27-1/8**
**Main Beams (R,L): 28-6/8,28-4/8**

**Points (R,L): 6,6**
**Widest Spread: 29-1/8**
**Bases (R, L): 5-2/8,4-7/8**

larence Hagerman was born in 1916. He married his wife, Rose, during the Great Depression, and migrated from South Dakota to Washington, where they picked fruit. When their daughter Bonnie was born, they felt the need for more permanence. Clarence took a job at the Bunker Hill smelter in Kellogg around 1940, and worked there for 44 years.

Clarence took full advantage of all the great hunting that could be found in the area. He was primarily a bear hunter, but also took many deer and elk. He was a true, ethical sportsman who believed in full use of the animals he killed.

One fall day in 1947, he took off for a quick hunt before his swing shift was to start. He had four kids to feed, and was determined to fill the freezer. He headed for an area near Pritchard, left his car, and headed into snowy, foggy conditions.

He ended up taking this buck, and because of its size, decided to keep it – a rare occurrence for someone who had little interest in antlers.

BONNIE MYERS

# George F. Bourgeois III
### 170-4/8 B&C Typical
### Shoshone County, 2007

SKIP BOURGEOIS

**Idaho Typical Rank: 36**
**Inside Spread: 24-2/8**
**Main Beams (R,L): 25-5/8,25-4/8**

**Points (R,L): 6,5**
**Widest Spread: 26-2/8**
**Bases (R, L): 4-6/8,4-6/8**

After a day of muzzleloader hunting for whitetails in the Panhandle, I was on my way back to meet Uncle Ned at our rendezvous point several miles up a logging road. This was my second year of hunting, but I had yet to fill a tag.

I decided to pause and survey a large clearing. After a few uneventful moments, I turned and started back toward Uncle Ned and the car, taking only a few steps before realizing that a doe was walking toward me. I froze, as she appeared to be staring directly at me the entire time she was walking.

With my concentration on her, I nearly missed the huge buck that suddenly came strutting out of the woods behind her. He walked with a swagger that could only be likened to royalty. He was the king of the woods and he knew it.

His steady strut carried him across the old road in seconds, but those seconds seemed like hours. My stomach knotted up as he turned to look at the doe. His rack was massive, and though I couldn't count the points that quickly, I knew he had a bunch. His body was just as impressive, yet he moved with great stealth.

If I had made a move to shoot, I would have spooked the doe, which would have spooked him. Finally, he disappeared into the woods, followed by the doe. Darkness closed in, and certain that they had been oblivious to my presence, I slipped back to the car hoping to remain undetected.

Uncle Ned was calmly excited as I relayed the encounter. He was energized with the idea of such a large buck and was optimistic we would get him. On the drive back to the motel, we formulated a strategy for the next day.

The following day was Thanksgiving, and after several unsuccessful hours, I retreated back up the road to a tree stand Uncle Ned had prepared that morning. Perched 25 feet up a lodgepole pine, I listened and waited as the gentle breeze rocked the tree. On the left was the old road, which I could see for 100 yards until it turned behind a cluster of pines. On my right was a clearing surrounded by pine and aspen trees.

Suddenly, I heard the crack of a breaking branch. The noise came from several hundred feet behind me, but it wasn't immediately apparent if it was from the wind or an animal. My senses kicked into high gear.

A minute later, I was once again graced by the presence of royalty. Goose-

**George "Skip" Bourgeois saw this buck the day before, but couldn't get a shot off. He had some amazing luck in getting a second chance at one very impressive whitetail.**

bumps ran up my spine as he walked underneath me, approaching from behind and walking out in front of my stand. Looking down on the buck, my stomach dropped just like it had the first time I saw him. The buck's one mistake had been breaking the branch. If he hadn't committed that one foul, it's likely he would have walked underneath me and into the woods before I could have readied a shot.

The buck walked into a clearing, at which time I hurriedly attempted to line up a shot. At 40 yards, the buck slowed, preparing to jump over a log. At that instant, the crosshairs fell into position and I squeezed the trigger.

In a flash, the recoil of the .50-caliber Thompson Center Encore slammed the scope against my eye. The sting from the scope was instantly forgotten. To my delight, I heard the deer drop only seconds later. Though certain the deer had gone down, I couldn't see him. I decided to wait half an hour before following. After the longest 30 minutes of my life, I went over and found him right where I'd expected.

The animal's body mass was the first thing that struck me. He seemed like an elk. The buck's 5x6 rack was polished from wear and spanned wider than my shoulders. This deer, my first, will not soon be forgotten, and I'll likely have to spend many years in the mountains to have a chance at another one like him.

222

# Theodore Millick, Jr.
## 170-1/8 B&C Typical
## Latah County, 1969

| | |
|---|---|
| **Idaho Typical Rank: 38** | **Points (R,L): 6,5** |
| **Inside Spread: 16-2/8** | **Widest Spread: 19-1/8** |
| **Main Beams (R,L): 25-4/8,25-2/8** | **Bases (R, L): 4-4/8,4-5/8** |

I n 1969, Ted Millick, then about 22 years old, was working as a ranch hand for Dale Gottschalk near Potlatch. Ranching can be a tough business; just ask Ted's younger brother Drake, who was busy trying to recover from busting up his leg when he slipped off of a combine ladder that summer.

On November 17, all three men anxiously climbed into Drake's new 1968 red Chevy pickup and headed south from Potlatch, driving down a graveled country road through some farm and pasture ground around 10 a.m. It was a cold, frosty morning and the rut was on.

A big buck and a doe jumped across the road in front of them, and all three men piled out of the vehicle. The followed a very short distance, and then all three men shot at the buck almost simultaneously - Ted with is .270, Drake with his .30-06, and Dale with a

.30-30. The buck dropped, and unsure of who shot it, Drake tagged the buck.

For a long time after that, no one thought much more about it. Drake had taken it to a sports show or two and won a few trophies with it, but that was about the extent of it.

Then one day a long time later, their mom, Betty, approached Drake and handed him something. It was a spent .270 bullet. She said, "Do whatever you think is right." It's not known how she knew whose bullet it was.

A few years later, after Betty had passed away, Drake had his chance. They had started an annual ritual of having a potluck in February, where they would award a traveling trophy to whoever had taken the biggest buck the previous fall. Drake took the opportunity to announce that Ted was actually the one who had hit the big buck.

Ted was obviously very surprised, and didn't really know what to say. It had been a long time, and he suddenly had to readjust his mind about how to think of it and how to "re-remember" what happened on that day.

Regardless of who hit it, they were all there and all a part of it; it could have been any one of them. In that respect, they all had a hand in making it happen, and for sure, they will all always be closely connected to the buck and by what happened on that one-of-a-kind day when they got that big trophy whitetail.

# Lewis L. Turcott
## 170 B&C Typical
### Latah County, 1974

**Idaho Typical Rank: 40**

**Inside Spread: 21-4/8**

**Main Beams (R,L): 28-4/8,27-3/8**

**Points (R,L): 8,7**

**Widest Spread: 24-1/8**

**Bases (R, L): 4-7/8,5-0/8**

nder normal circumstances, one might think that a buck of this caliber would have to be exceptionally reclusive in order to reach such stature. Such was not the case with this great buck. A number of people had seen him, and many were after him.

Lewis Turcott had been working in the area, falling timber for a logging outfit. Over the course of the summer, most of the guys on the crew had seen the buck, and a couple of them had even shot at him but missed. It seemed as though the buck's days were numbered unless he moved on. Lewis had even seen him drink from a stock pond on more than one occasion.

Lewis put in a full day of falling trees and decided to see if he could find that buck that evening. He had a general idea of where the buck was, and had been trying to figure out his patterns and where his escape routes might be.

It was raining, but Lewis worked in the woods every day, so it made little difference to him. He figured that it was a good thing, as it would silence his footfalls and knock down scent.

He made his way in there, and sure enough, he managed to jump the buck at 50 yards in a brushy area where the buck had a major advantage. However, instead of pursuing, Lewis sprinted toward a spot where he thought the buck might run to. It was a big gamble, but luck was on his side. It worked to perfection, and the buck came sneaking through an opening. Had the buck kept his speed up, he'd have gotten away scot free, but his wariness ultimately failed him on this particular occasion. Lewis dropped the hammer on his .30-06 at 150 yards. The buck crumpled, and their short game of cat and mouse was over.

Lewis was able to get his Ford pickup pretty close, which was a welcome relief. The buck's carcass weighed 235 lbs., and would otherwise have been quite a chore to extract.

*Note: this buck has a monstrous 190-4/8 gross typical frame, but gets knocked clear down to 170 due to a slew of deductions.*

# Ed Kuchynka
## 169-4/8 B&C Typical
### Clearwater County, 1982

**Idaho Typical Rank: 42***
**Inside Spread: 22-0/8**
**Main Beams (R,L): 25-4/8, 25-5/8**

**Points (R,L): 6,5**
**Widest Spread: 23-4/8**
**Bases (R, L): 4-2/8,4-2/8**

**B**ack in the 1970s and early '80s, it was all about elk hunting. The question was always, "Did you get your elk yet?" Nobody intentionally hunted just for deer, at least not until you had your elk down.

Ormal Ward and I were good friends who worked together at a local plywood mill. It just so happened that we were laid off for two weeks, right in the middle of hunting season. We decided to go up near Pierce to a spot where he knew elk liked to bed in some big timber. After arriving, he told me to drive down to a saddle where I could park the Toyota and drop off into the timber. I then drove him back to the top and let him off, returned to the saddle, and dropped down 300 yards to find a good position.

227

     I found a well used game trail and sat down against a tree ten yards above the trail. The plan was that Ormal would hunt the basin above, and if he jumped the elk, they would head in my direction.

     It wasn't very long until I could hear something coming, so I raised my rifle to get ready for the elk. I could see about 100 yards up the trail, so I had plenty of time. Soon I could see him coming, sneaking down the trail with his head about two feet off the ground. The problem was that it wasn't an elk, but a big whitetail buck.

     I had a one-week vacation scheduled for a late mule deer hunt down on the Salmon River, so I didn't want to shoot this whitetail. However, the closer he came and the more I saw, I could tell that he was pretty nice! Finally, when he was about to pass by me, I pulled the trigger on my .300 Weatherby at no more than ten yards. He dropped in his tracks.

**Ed was on an elk hunt when he took this gorgeous whitetail buck as it ran by him. In the process, he sacrificed an upcoming mule deer hunt he was scheduled to go on. It was a good choice. This photo is one of Idaho's best field photos.**

Hearing the shot, Ormal hurried on down, thinking we would be packing out elk meat. In those days, you just didn't shoot at a deer when you were hunting elk. When he arrived, he couldn't believe I shot the deer, especially since he knew of my plans for the mule deer hunt.

After admiring the buck, I field dressed him and then we hiked back to the truck. Our plan was to drive to another location and continue with a short elk hunt. We hunted until about 2 p.m., and then decided to go back and drag the buck out.

It wasn't until we reached the buck again that we really realized just how big he actually was. We knew we couldn't drag him up the hill, so we returned to the truck for the pack frames. We came back and then halved him, with me packing the front half (90 lbs.) and Ormal taking the back half (80 lbs.). We had to head back down for a return trip so we could pack out the head, antlers, and cape.

After the drying period, I took the head to the Fish and Game office to have it scored. I was surprised to find out that it ranked #7 in the state at that time. This turned out to be the buck of a lifetime for me. Now, 27 years later, I'm still looking for a big buck, but none have compared to this buck that was supposed to be an elk.

**Ed Kuchynka (right) and Ormal Ward take a breather while packing out Ed's great trophy.**

# Frederick R. Staab
## 169-4/8 B&C Typical
### Clearwater County, 1990

**Idaho Typical Rank: 42**

**Inside Spread: 19-0/8**

**Main Beams (R,L): 26-4/8,26-0/8**

**Points (R,L): 7,8**

**Widest Spread: 22-3/8**

**Bases (R, L): 4-4/8,4-4/8**

uck Staab is an experienced whitetail hunter who lives in the middle of good whitetail country and has a habit of crossing paths with big bucks. He and his family have several bucks of significant size, but this buck, taken in 1990, is the cream of the crop.

Buck had a couple of friends, Darrell Lowery and Lance McCoy, coming over from Washington to join him for an early November whitetail hunt. It was a rainy weekend, which was just about on par with normal weather for that time of year.

The area they were going to hunt was only a short drive from where Buck was living at the time. It had a good combination of habitat – plenty of timber and brush for bedding, some farming activity, and a low elevation that kept the local deer population fit in the winter. There were some steep, grassy slopes that could be tricky walking when it was slick, but Buck had seen a decent buck there a few days before, and figured the spot was as good as any. There were also networks of rosebrush, blackberry, and other vegetation that made it tough to ferret a deer out if it chose to hang tight.

They stepped out of the Ford pickup after a short drive, ready to hit a drainage well known for good bucks. They were greeted by a foggy, rainy, windy day and plenty of mud.

Walking down into the bottom of the canyon and up the other side, they began to methodically push brush patches and conduct small drives. In that area, it's about as effective a hunting method as you can find.

At around 11 a.m., they were in the middle of one push through a brush patch when Buck heard a deer take off. He took off at a sprint, hoping to see what it was before it was too late. He barely saw the top of some antlers heading down a steep draw. He got to an area where he could finally see the entire deer and knew right away it was a great buck. With the steep angle, his best shot was to aim right in the upper center of the back, and his 50-yard shot with his 7mm-mag. dropped the deer like a rock.

**Buck Staab and his trophy whitetail in 1990. It was a wet, muddy, miserable day to hunt, but was plenty worth it when this buck busted out of the brush in front of him.**

# Jeremy L. Badertscher
169-2/8 B&C Typical
Idaho County, 1992

**Idaho Typical Rank: 45**

**Inside Spread: 20-6/8**

**Main Beams (R,L): 26-7/8,25-6/8**

**Points (R,L): 5,7**

**Widest Spread: 23-0/8**

**Bases (R, L): 4-5/8,4-4/8**

ne thing that makes Idaho special is the wealth of opportunity. After school hunts, over-the-counter tags, and tons of public land make it an explorer's paradise. Jeremy Badertscher's big buck, taken by walking right outside his door the day after a high school football game, is a perfect example of what hunting should be about.

Tired from the rigors of the previous day's game, Jeremy slept in late that morning. It was a Saturday, and though days off for hunting are few when dealing with fall sports, he was just dogged tired.

He woke up at 10 a.m. in a panic, knowing he'd already missed out on prime deer hunting hours. He quickly threw on a camo shirt and some blue jeans, grabbed his Ruger .243 and a backpack, and ran out to catch what was left of that day's hunting hours.

It took an hour and a half to get across the canyon they lived in. Once there, he walked along the road, stopping often to look, listen, and glass.

After awhile, he dropped off the road and propped his rifle on a fence post and glassed across the canyon. He glimpsed a set of antlers and then identified a big buck backing into its bedding area. As it was settling into its bed, Jeremy took aim and shot. The bullet clipped its upper back and the big buck dropped instantly, falling right into a big patch of thorn brush.

It was an extremely steep hill, and it took three people and a lot of effort to get him out of the brush. The thorn brush didn't make it an better.

Jeremy says his big Idaho County buck from 1992 had only three teeth left, and two of those were loose. The buck had reached the end of his reign one way or another, and Jeremy is thankful to be able to take a buck of that size and age class.

**Jeremy Badertscher took this buck after waking up late on a Saturday, still tired and sore from a high school football game the previous day.**

# Mitchell R. Vogl
## 169-1/8 B&C Typical
### Boundary County, 1984

**Idaho Typical Rank: 47***
**Inside Spread: 16-2/8**
**Main Beams (R,L): 23-6/8,23-7/8**

**Points (R,L): 7,6**
**Widest Spread: 19-0/8**
**Bases (R, L): 5-1/8,4-7/8**

itch Vogl was working at a furniture refinishing shop back in 1984. He and his boss, Rich Beck, both loved to hunt, so they went out to Rich's property in the afternoon of the deer opener.

They headed out in his boss's van, and pulled up to the property, which was fairly mild on top, but broke down into a creek bottom. It was an area with a little bit of everything – timber, openings, some brush but not thick, and plenty of whitetails.

He was walking down an old road when he saw a buck hightailing it away from him over the hill. It was a good buck, but Mitch pretty well wrote him off.

Imagine his surprise when the buck came prancing right back up the hill right at him! By the time he squeezed the trigger on his old .30-30, the buck was only ten yards away from him. It all happened unbelievably quickly, but he made his shot count. Mitch was amazed at the buck's massive rack and body size, and just as amazed at everything that had just happened.

They were able to back the van right up to the deer and load him whole. Mitch says the buck weighed 210 lbs. field-dressed when they weighed it out at Alt's Meat Processing in Bonners Ferry.

# Emerald J. Hutchins
## 168-1/8 B&C Typical
## Clearwater County, 1994
### *Idaho State Record Typical (Archery)*

| | |
|---|---|
| **Idaho Typical Rank: 55** | **Points (R,L): 6,6** |
| **Inside Spread: 18-0/8** | **Widest Spread: 21-0/8** |
| **Main Beams (R,L): 26-6/8, 26-0/8** | **Bases (R, L): 4-7/8,5-0/8** |

merald Hutchins had been watching some deer over the summer, and they were frequenting a field that his uncle owned. He asked for permission to hunt it, which he was given, and decided to try and hunt it with a bow. This way he might get the jump on those bucks before they got wise and before anyone else might get a crack at them. While he had taken elk with his bow before, hunting whitetail with one would be a whole new adventure.

There was a pond on the place where the deer had been coming in to drink, so Emerald (55 at the time) decided to set up a tree stand about 20 feet up a white fir and 45 yards from the pond. He set the stand up a week before the season opened, and didn't go back.

On opening day of the bow season, he grabbed his High Country bow, hopped on his Fat Cat, and rode to within 200 yards of his stand. He then walked to his stand in the dark so that he'd be ready for any action at first light. He was so close to town that he could actually hear random human-caused noise in the otherwise still morning air.

As dawn finally broke, he watched as some deer came in to drink. They drank and then vanished as quickly as they had appeared. Soon after, a nice buck followed suit. Emerald was thinking of taking a shot at him when the buck turned. It offered a good shot, so Emerald drew back, aimed, and fired. The shot was low! The buck bolted for a few yards, stopped, and then stomped.

Just as the buck stopped, a much bigger buck sauntered in to drink, completely unaware of what had just happened. Emerald suddenly was fighting a lot of emotions at once. He was upset about his miss, excited at the arrival of a larger buck, and adrenaline was overtaking him. Fresh off of a miss to the low side, he overcompensated and shot high over the monster typical. His arrow and broadhead stuck right into the mud. The buck ran off about 75 yards.

Emerald was now really kicking himself when the buck did the unthinkable. He strolled right back in to the pond to get his drink. Emerald was shaky by now, but he knew the distance. He took aim again and squeezed. The arrow hit the buck in the spine, dropping him like a rock. A follow-up shot secured the deal and Emerald's hunt was over in a matter of minutes on the first day of the season.

Emerald's whim of trying to take the big buck with a bow had proven to be right on the money. It was an amazing stroke of luck that not only got him a first-rate trophy, but also the distinction of taking the biggest archery typical whitetail in Idaho history.

EMERALD HUTCHINS

**Emerald Hutchins had never taken a whitetail with a bow, but decided to give it a try. He set up a tree stand over a watering area and it worked like a charm. His buck, taken in 1994, is the Idaho state record typical whitetail in the archery category.**

# Mike Poe
## 167-1/8 B&C Typical
### Boise County, 1978

MIKE POE

**Idaho Typical Rank: 59***        **Points (R,L): 7,7**
**Inside Spread: 19-5/8**        **Widest Spread: 22-3/8**
**Main Beams (R,L): 24-4/8, 23-6/8**        **Bases (R, L): 5-1/8,5-1/8**

I t all started on the morning of October 11, 1978. My dad, mom, older sister, and I got in our 1958 Jeep CJ2A (I hated riding in that thing, with the hard top and the metal fender seats in the back). I really didn't know where we were going, but I knew it was to shoot a deer. I was 15 at this time and had never taken one.

We went up toward Banks, across the river and up the hill. Before we got to the top, we pulled over and Dad said that we were walking from there.

Mom stayed in the Jeep as we headed across a draw and walked on an old logging road. My dad decided to go up a skid trail, so I followed. My sister was behind us a ways.

Suddenly, my dad said, "There's a deer!" I looked over and there was buck with his head down, sneaking away at about 100 yards. He went behind a tree, and all I could see was his body.

I shot him with my dad's police-issued .30-30. The buck ran toward us, down through a draw and 20 yards from us, toppling over a stump and dying right there.

I found out later that there had been a lot of talk locally among some of the loggers and log truck drivers who had been seeing a larger whitetail in the area. And some punk kid shot him.

*Note: Mike Poe's 1978 whitetail is one of the largest whitetails ever taken in southwestern Idaho. It is likely a descendent of a transplanted population of whitetails to the Banks area by IDF&G in the late 1940s following a major fire in the area, with the idea that the whitetails might fare better in that vicinity.*

# Casey Valliere
## 167 B&C Typical
### Bonner County, 2006

**Idaho Typical Rank: 61***

iving on the Idaho/Montana state line in the middle of great hunting country is a great thing for people like Casey Valliere. Quick whitetail hunts can be had at a moment's notice, and a person has the chance to become much more intimately familiar with the country.

Casey had been hunting in the Hope area that day, and had to hustle to get back for Thanksgiving dinner. His driveway is a couple miles up in the woods, and on his way home, he saw some does on his in-laws' property. He decided to make a last-minute check before completely giving up for the day.

He jumped this big buck at last light and took a shot with his .45-70 at 50 yards. The buck trotted off, seemingly unscathed. Not knowing if he had hit it, he ran home and changed, hoping to get one errand done while he gave the buck some time to settle down, just in case. He came back and did a sweep through there and found the buck piled up.

Casey thinks it's pretty ironic that he busted his rear end all day long for nothing, only to be coming up the driveway and see a big buck. Most people would probably agree.

# Walter Asbe
## 166-6/8 B&C Typical
## Idaho County, 1990

**Idaho Typical Rank: 65***      **Points (R,L): 5,5**
**Inside Spread: 18-2/8**      **Widest Spread: 21-2/8**
**Main Beams (R,L): 22-6/8, 22-4/8**      **Bases (R, L): 4-4/8,4-4/8**

hile Walter Asbe would love to be able to tell you a big tale of great adventure, the fact is that's just not what happened in the fall of 1990 when he killed his biggest buck. In fact, he barely left home.

It was November 24, and 55-year-old Walter opened his front door and started walking real easy down toward the creek with his Ruger M77 .30-06. He alternately sat and walked, being quiet and patient while waiting to see what might unfold.

Walter had been a bird hunter until he moved to Idaho, so his quick instincts with a gun were helpful in whitetail hunting, where quick decisions are the norm. He was prepared for just such an encounter when quite the opposite happened. He was sitting and watching when a lone buck came strolling along, headed for somewhere unknown.

Walter had taken enough deer in his life to recognize exceptional headgear, so when opportunity was presented, he wasted no time. He fired at 125 yards, and the buck, now hit in the shoulder, fell within a few feet. All this, of course, was nearly within view of his home.

# Nick Randall
## 166-4/8 B&C Typical
### Lewis County, 2004

**Idaho Typical Rank: 68***

**Inside Spread: 17-7/8**

**Main Beams (R,L): 23-7/8, 24-0/8**

**Points (R,L): 5,8**

**Widest Spread: 21-0/8**

**Bases (R, L): 4-2/8,4-2/8**

he morning started late - or the afternoon started early - however you want to look at it. My father, Blake, and I had woken up rather late on October 13, 2004 after a late night the previous night. My dad had killed a dandy 150-class buck the day before and we felt some celebrating was in order. This decision, little did we know, would play a key role in having one of the biggest whitetail buck's I've ever seen show up in my scope the next day.

It was a nice clear day and still relatively warm. Dad and I slipped into the canyon on the private ground we've been allowed to hunt for several years. The ground is full of steep, timbered, brushy draws that those big whitetails like to hide in. Oftentimes we'll spend hours glassing these steep draws, which can sometimes be a mile away. Good optics and patience are key for this type of hunting. To this day, I still haven't figured out that whole patience thing.

The day was starting to grow old, so we decided to head to a closer draw that we'd always wanted to" bird dog" in. It is a very intimidating and steep draw but can offer some good shooting if the deer cooperate. Since Dad had already killed his deer, he decided to bird dog for me. Thanks, Dad! I positioned myself in a spot I felt would give me the best chance to catch a big sneaky whitetail trying to escape my dad's push.

Not long into the hunt, I spotted a deer a couple hundred yards up the draw trying to sneak out of there. One look through my binos confirmed it was definitely a shooter, and once a shot presented itself, I took aim with my trusty .300 Win.-mag. and fired. The big deer shifted from low gear into high; I had missed. Now panic set in and I quickly settled in for my second shot. The deer was 250 yards now and the only shot I had was quartering away, so I took a deep breath and fired. I could tell I hit him good, as he immediately changed his course from going uphill and away to directly at me.

I momentarily lost sight of him in a slight depression on the hillside, and when he reappeared, he was only 75 yards away and standing still facing me. I held on the brisket and touched another one off. At the sound of the shot, he ran into a little thicket and never reappeared.

I worked my way up and found the big boy dead. I couldn't believe the size of buck lying before me. Pretty soon I could hear Dad working his way up to me. When he reached the deer, he couldn't believe his eyes either. He had jumped the deer at only a few feet and knew it was a good buck, but didn't realize it was that big.

My dad has always been there for me, and it was fitting that he was the one that ultimately put this buck in front of me. We celebrated for a bit then started the quartering for the long pack out of that nasty spot. What an experience and what a buck; I can't think of anyone I'd rather share it with than my dad.

# Denny Hall
### 166-1/8 B&C Typical
### Bonner County, 1980

DENNY HALL

**Idaho Typical Rank: 73***
**Inside Spread: 19-4/8**
**Main Beams (R,L): 24-2/8, 24-3/8**

**Points (R,L): 8,7**
**Widest Spread: 22-6/8**
**Bases (R, L): 5-0/8,4-7/8**

It was the Thursday before Thanksgiving, and the rut was finally on. So far the season had been dry and cold, and the leaves were all on the ground from the winds. I had seen quite a few deer out and about, but no shooters yet.

The weather was supposed to change, with a forecast of snow overnight. I decided to try hunting some small hayfields about a mile from my home, as I thought the small fields might have a little bit more activity since they were surrounded by thick timber. The snow would muffle my movements.

I was on the edge of the first opening at daylight. It had snowed some, but was now raining. The fog was rolling in and out, and it was very quiet.

Right off the bat, there was a small buck in the meadow. He had his nose to the ground and didn't see me. It was plain to me that he was onto a doe. I circled the edge of the meadow and soon saw a second buck. He had the same basic behavior as the first, with his mind on one thing only. Neither was what I wanted, so I watched them travel around a bend to the next field.

I followed along the edge of the timber to the same bend, and saw a doe walking toward me. She stopped right in front of me and looked back toward where she came from as the fog still rolled slowly through the field. Showing over the edge of a small ridge in the field was the figure of a deer.

The fog lifted a little and I could now see his rack. I didn't stop to count points; I knew he was "the one." I was standing at the edge of the field, so I had to shoot quickly and offhand. He was facing me, so I placed the crosshairs on the base of his neck and pulled the trigger. With the sound, he slowly turned and ran down the ridge, cleared a fence, and disappeared.

My instincts were that the shot was good, so I waited a few minutes and then followed. When I came to the fence, there he lay. The buck was big bodied, with what appeared to be only one side of a rack. I climbed through a fence and picked up his head, and as I did, I said to myself, "It would be nice if both sides were that big." They were!

He was the biggest buck I had ever taken. I took my trophy to the IDFG office in Coeur d'Alene, where Jack McNeel did the scoring. His non-typical score was 184-7/8 inches; typical was 166-1/8 inches. At the time, he informed me that the typical score placed it #13 in their listings. I was excited about that! I entered it at the local Bonner County Sportsmen's Association Horn Show, and it placed first in its class. Later, I entered it in the Big Horn Show in Spokane. The rack placed second to one taken on the Washington-Canada border. I could live with that, too.

DENNY HALL

# Roger R. Davis
## 166-1/8 B&C Typical
### Shoshone County, 1986

**Idaho Typical Rank: 73***      **Points (R,L): 5,5**

**Inside Spread: 19-5/8**      **Widest Spread: 21-6/8**

**Main Beams (R,L): 24-1/8, 25-1/8**      **Bases (R, L): 4-5/8,4-5/8**

R oger Davis is one of the best hunters you may have never known about. He's older now and doesn't get around well, but in his prime, he spent as much time studying animal behavior and learning about the animals he hunted as anyone ever has.

Proof of that is easy. He also has a 197-2/8 B&C typical mule deer and a 388-6/8 B&C non-typical elk (these stories are featured in *Idaho's Greatest Mule Deer* and *Idaho's Greatest Elk*). Amazingly, almost all of his trophies were taken in a very small area not far from his home.

Roger didn't honestly have much to say about this handsome whitetail. Of the hunt, Roger just said that he jumped a buck, it ran uphill, and then it turned around "like they never do."

It was taken with a bow, meaning if it is ever officially entered, it would be the second-largest typical ever taken in Idaho with archery equipment.

# Paul Finney
## 166 B&C Typical
### Kootenai County, 1970

**Idaho Typical Rank: 75***
**Inside Spread: 19-2/8**
**Main Beams (R,L): 23-0/8, 23-0/8**

**Points (R,L): 6,6**
**Widest Spread: 21-2/8**
**Bases (R, L): 4-1/8,4-0/8**

L ogging has always gone hand in hand with Idaho history. Many generational families in Idaho were loggers, and the Finney family was no different. In fact, it was being out in the woods every day that led William Finney to be able to point his 16-year-old son, Paul, in the direction of this beautiful buck.

When Paul woke up to the question, "Wanna go hunting today instead of school?", it was like music to his ears. His dad told him about some big buck tracks he had seen on the job, and so Paul accompanied his dad up to the job site.

William went to work sawing logs while Paul hiked up the drainage and drifted slowly away from the buzzing of the chainsaw. He had a lever-action .30-30, perfect for those quick shots in heavy cover.

He was in just such a place – a place so thick, in fact - that he was literally forced to crawl on his hands and knees for 200 yards. Finally breaking free, he looked up into an opening and saw a big buck 100 yards away. The buck was really socking it to a defenseless piece of brush, likely explaining why Paul was able to get that close completely unnoticed while fighting his own brush battle.

He pulled up and cranked off a round, and watched as the buck took off unscathed. He took another wild desperation shot and then the buck vanished in record time. As quickly as it had happened, it was over – or so Paul thought.

Almost as if it was suicidal, the buck suddenly came running right back at him! Paul figures that maybe the second shot hit a tree beyond the buck, turning him right back around.

The wide-eyed buck sprinted down the trail on a crash course for Paul when he suddenly slammed on the brakes and slid to a stop in the mud – an impromptu 60-yard staredown to see who would blink first. Paul "drew" first, and shot as the buck turned tail. Instantly exhausted from the intense encounter and the overwhelming buck fever, Paul sat down and crossed his legs, head down, completely overwhelmed.

With no indication of a hit, he thought he had really blown it and that no one would believe him. After taking a moment to collect himself, he started tracking the buck, and was stunned beyond words when he saw one side of the buck's antlers sticking up over some downed trees.

After looking over his prize, he walked down to his dad, who was bucking a log. William turned off the chainsaw and listened to Paul's wild story about "the biggest buck he'd ever seen." Father and son then walked up the hill together, at which point William said, "Son, that's the biggest deer I've ever seen, too."

They hauled the buck into Cy's Meats in Coeur d'Alene, where it weighed 204 lbs. minus the head and forelegs. The buck was aged at ten years old.

**This photo is about as vintage as it gets. Paul, just 16 years old at the time, was one lucky hunter when the buck ran toward him after a missed shot. Paul sent this slide just in time for the book, and I was very excited to be able to include it.**

# Todd Felton
166 B&C Typical
Nez Perce County, 2003

**Idaho Typical Rank: 75***

**Inside Spread: 18-6/8**

**Main Beams (R,L): 22-7/8, 22-6/8**

**Points (R,L): 7,5**

**Widest Spread: 20-4/8**

**Bases (R, L): 4-5/8,4-4/8**

I t was November 1, 2003 on an overcast day when my dad, Allan Felton, and I went deer hunting. We had been hunting the area for many years, and I had seen this buck for the last five years. He was very wily to live so long.

We talked it over and decided to split up to cover more ground. I headed into thick timber and still-hunted through some pocket openings. We hunted for three hours, but nothing seemed to be moving, so we met back up at midday and talked about what we wanted to do next. I decided to head down into a drainage and Dad would stay up on top. With any luck, maybe we would push something between us.

I got to the bottom and started to walk next to the creek. I saw a doe with a buck behind her, and they were moving through the trees 250 yards out. I hurried down the creek toward them and caught them as they were going back up the ridge.

I was now 75 yards away, but they were going back into the trees. I knew if I didn't shoot now, he was going to get away for yet another year. I took an uphill shot and hit him. He took off and sidehilled 50 yards before turning and looking at me! I put another round in my Remington .30-06 and shot him again, and down he came.

After all this time, I finally got him. To be able to walk up and see him up close was amazing. What a buck he is!

# Karl Neumann
### 166-0/8 B&C Typical
### Bonner County, 2007

**Idaho Typical Rank: 75\***

I took this buck on the morning of November 29, 2007. There was a foot of fresh snow on the ground, and I was hunting some rolling hills near the river. It was right at the base of the mountains.

I had been watching a couple of does feeding and noticed that they were acting nervous. That can be a good thing or a bad thing, depending on whether it's another hunter or maybe a buck that's been pestering or courting them. With the rut in full swing, I was hoping there might be a buck nearby occupying their thoughts.

About that time, my hopes were confirmed when I spotted a big, beautiful buck coming out from some thick cover. He was everything a hunter hopes for, and more. He headed right for the does and started chasing them around. As much as I wanted to, I just couldn't get a good shot. He then vanished into some small trees.

I thought he was gone, so in desperation, I gave a couple of doe bleats with my Primos deer call can. I really didn't think it had much of a chance of working, and boy was I surprised when he came back out!

This time I was able to get a good look, and I leveled down on him with my .22-250 at 125 yards. One good shot and he went right down.

Up until then, I didn't really know how big he was, other than he seemed plenty big enough. When I walked up to him and saw those long, symmetrical tines and overall size of his rack, I knew right away that he was a special deer.

248

# Doug Farrell
## 165-5/8 B&C Typical
### Benewah County, 2007

**Idaho Typical Rank: 84\***
**Inside Spread: 21-3/8**
**Main Beams (R,L): 25-0/8,25-6/8**

**Points (R,L): 7,7**
**Widest Spread: 23-4/8**
**Bases (R, L): 4-5/8,4-7/8**

D oug Farrell is a rancher in the St. Maries area. As with any occupation, there are obvious pluses and minuses, and ranching is no different. One of the upsides is the freedom, and if a guy wants to get out and do some hunting, he doesn't have to beg for the time off.

Doug decided to do just that – get out and do some hunting – and knew where he wanted to be. Doug is a seasoned and accomplished hunter, having taken a nice buck or two in his time. It was evening, and with it being November, the rut was on and the deer were moving.

He was walking down an old road and saw a buck standing in the brush, thinking he was hidden. He could see right away it was a big one. He took a quick shot with his .300 Win.-mag. and the rest was history.

*Note: This buck makes the B&C minimums at both 165-5/8 (typical) and 186-5/8 (non-typical). Since the typical score is higher in relation to the minimum, we listed it this way for the book. The typical frame alone nets 176-1/8.*

# Richard A. Blagden
### 165-1/8 B&C Typical
### Kootenai County, 1982

RICHARD BLAGDEN

**Idaho Typical Rank: 86\***
**Inside Spread: 17-5/8**
**Main Beams (R,L): 25-2/8,25-0/8**

**Points (R,L): 7,6**
**Widest Spread: 23-0/8**
**Bases (R, L): 4-1/8,4-2/8**

R aised in northern California, Rick Blagden was an avid deer hunter. For many northern Californians, hunting out of state is nearly a rite of passage. Rick was no different, and started hunting Idaho in the late '60s. He enjoyed it so much that he moved to Idaho in 1974.

He was originally focused on mule deer, and hunted in central Idaho quite frequently despite living in Kootenai County. However, being in the middle of the best whitetail hunting in the Northwest, he wasn't about to turn a blind eye to it.

He had seen a big whitetail buck the year before, in 1981, and was amazed at both the size and the light color of the antlers. He hunted hard for his shed antlers that spring, with no luck.

In the fall of 1982, Rick went on his annual pilgrimage to central Idaho, but came back empty-handed. That was no big deal back then, as he could still hunt whitetails late with the same tag.

Later that fall, he was on a hunt with his brother Danny in Unit 3 when he was fortunate enough to run into this giant. He shot him on the last day of the season with his Remington Model 700 .30-06.

*Note: This is one example of a big buck with a score that belies the true size. The total gross score is 191-3/8, but is riddled with deductions.*

# Jim McManus
164-3/8 Typical
Clearwater County, 1986

**Idaho Typical Rank: 92***  **Points (R,L): 7,8**
**Inside Spread: 16-6/8**  **Widest Spread: 19-0/8**
**Main Beams (R,L): 25-3/8,24-6/8**  **Bases (R, L): 3-7/8,4-0/8**

Not all hunts are death marches or take several years or even days of chasing the same buck. If you pick a good spot and do the right thing at the right time, sometimes they can practically drop right into your lap. Jim McManus is pretty modest about how it all happened, but if he hadn't been willing to be in the rain and hadn't chosen to rattle, he may never have killed this beautiful buck.

Jim and his wife drove out to his chosen area, but faced with walking out in the rain and mud, she chose to stay in the pickup. Jim headed out alone, with his rifle and rattling horns, and walked several hundred yards before setting up under a tree at first light. It was a brushy area sliced with old skid trails, perfect for whitetails.

He rattled for about 30 seconds and then stopped to listen and watch intently. Scarcely a minute or two later, a big buck walked right into the scene "like he owned the world", according to Jim. It was hard to judge him straight on because he was narrow, but when the buck turned his head to the side, there was no doubt.

He peered down the peep sights of his .308 Winchester Model 88 and let it bark. The buck crumpled, and just as fast as the hunt had started, it was now over. That didn't upset Jim any. Now he could get out of that miserable rain.

# Bill White
## 163-4/8 B&C Typical
### Clearwater County, 1973

**Idaho Typical Rank: 102***
**Inside Spread: 20-0/8**
**Main Beams (R,L): 25-0/8,25-0/8**

**Points (R,L): 5,5**
**Widest Spread: 22-0/8**
**Bases (R, L): 5-5/8,5-4/8**

ith the November rut coming on, Bill White and the sheriff, Leroy Altmiller, headed up on Orofino Creek for a whitetail hunt. It had snowed a little bit a few days before, but most of it had melted back off.

They split up and went up two separate ridges 300 yards apart, hoping to kick deer between them. The area was plenty brushy, with a canopy of large trees over them.

They weren't that far into the hunt when Bill had a big buck jump up in front of him, and he shot it with his lever-action .30-30 Winchester as it tip-toed away from him at 80 yards.

Leroy heard the shot and came over, and each man grabbed an antler. With the drag all being downhill, they had the buck back to the truck in less than half an hour.

**A happy hunter, a big buck, and a .30-30 – vintage Idaho.**

# Larry Stohs
### 162-6/8 B&C Typical
### Latah County, 1986

**Idaho Typical Rank: 107**
**Inside Spread: 22-4/8**
**Main Beams (R,L): 24-4/8, 24-3/8**

**Points (R,L): 6,6**
**Widest Spread: 24-0/8**
**Bases (R, L): 4-5/8, 4-6/8**

I t was a mid-November day back in 1986. My two buddies and I were late getting out that morning, and arrived at where we were going to hunt a couple of hours after daylight. It was an overcast day and there were a few inches of fresh snow on the ground.

Eager to get going, we hurriedly got our packs ready and rifles loaded, and headed out on an old skid road. We walked for about two miles and saw very little sign. My one buddy, Ray, decided to head into the timber and meet us up the road. My other buddy, Mike, and I continued up the skid road. We walked another half-mile up the road but saw no deer sign at all. I actually made a comment to him about it. He laughed and we continued on to meet up with Ray.

We walked around one more corner into a clearcut and that's when I saw a big buck following a doe. I raised my Ruger .270, put the crosshairs on his chest, and fired. The bullet hit the dirt right below him; I missed! He jumped straight up in the air, did a 180, and landed and stayed there. I chambered a second round, collected myself, and fired again. This time the bullet hit the mark and down he went.

I knew he was a big buck when I shot, but didn't realize how big until we walked up to where he was lying. We were awestruck.

Mike and I got him field dressed and ready to go just as Ray came to meet us. He was in awe, too. We took turns, two at a time, dragging him to my Blazer. We were all very tired when we got to the rig, but it was a happy ride home.

# Jared Johnson
### 161-6/8 B&C Typical
### Bonneville County, 2007

**Idaho Typical Rank: 116**  **Points (R,L): 5,5**
**Inside Spread: 20-0/8**  **Widest Spread: 21-6/8**
**Main Beams (R,L): 24-1/8, 24-1/8**  **Bases (R, L): 4-1/8, 4-4/8**

 had the good fortune to watch this buck grow over a three-year span. I was hoping he would survive a year or two and grow, and that I would be lucky enough to get a shot at him.

The first year I saw him, he wasn't big yet, but I could see he had great potential. I had two opportunities to shoot him, but passed. At the beginning of the second year, while doing some pre-season scouting, I found him again. He was with several deer, and I decided to pursue him after elk season. After elk hunting ended, I had one close encounter and chose to hold off. I saw him a couple more times that season and decided at that point to hope he was still around next year.

A few weeks before the next season, I spotted the same buck with four others. I was very excited to see him; he had grown into a handsome trophy buck. After days of watching these four bucks, I knew they were traveling the same trail every night. I decided he had grown enough for me and that this was the year.

Early one afternoon I decided to hunt the buck from the ground. I sat at a pinch point where they had been traveling, hoping for the best. I had been sitting there for about two hours when the deer began to work their way down the trail. The smallest buck was first, followed by the others. I waited patiently for him to approach, but he took his time.

Finally, here he came. I sat at 30 yards with my bow drawn, waiting for him. He walked slowly down the trail, and when the time was right, I grunted and stopped him. I was already at full draw, so I took my shot and hit him well. Just that fast, it was over and I had my buck. It was a great ending to a three-year hunt.

# Douglas Lamm
## 161-3/8 B&C Typical
### Idaho County, 1978

DOUG LAMM

**Idaho Typical Rank: 119**
**Inside Spread: 20-7/8**
**Main Beams (R,L): 24-4/8,23-4/8**

**Points (R,L): 5,5**
**Widest Spread: 23-0/8**
**Bases (R, L): 4-5/8,4-3/8**

I grew up in Kamiah – the heart of whitetail country. In 1970, I turned 12 and purchased my first rifle for $125. It was a Remington Model 722 in .300 Savage with a Bushnell Sportview 4x32 scope, bought with money I earned picking strawberries for my grandparents. I still use that gun to this day.

In fall of 1978, I was a junior at Northwest Nazarene College. I drove home for the weekend after the opener. I joined my dad, Phil, my younger brother, Dwight, and a family friend, Wayne Simler, to hunt elk and deer. Over the years, we had hunted together on my grandparents' farm, on Wayne's family's farm, and on neighboring farms. No matter where we hunted, we usually got game and seemed to find ourselves showing up at my grandmother's farmhouse for a late breakfast. Why would today be any different?

That particular morning we decided to hunt on some ground owned by Wayne's dad, Don. We met early and took off on our hunt. We had hunted the ground before, so we knew the lay of the ridges and draws fairly well. We split up and took different finger ridges that all led to a good crossing at the bottom.

On this morning, I had worked down the ridge and over the crossing ahead of everyone. I hunted the crossing and then headed back down the skid road toward the pickup.

After 100 yards, I remember asking myself, "Why are you heading back down the road? The crossing is behind you; whitetail double-back all the time; and the rest of the party is still working their way down. Go back and hunt the crossing until they show up."

I had barely arrived when the two biggest whitetail bucks I had ever seen busted through the crossing, coming from the direction of our party. I suspected they had seen me work my way through, and then with the pressure behind them, decided to make their escape. I would like to think that some instinct was involved in my doubling back, but dumb luck was probably more the reason.

They stopped and looked at me with what appeared to be as much surprise on their faces as I had on mine. I pulled up on them and, for what seemed like an eternity, tried to determine which was the larger of the two; they had what seemed to be identical racks. The eternity actually only lasted two or three seconds before they had enough looking at me and turned to run. The decision on which one to shoot became an instinctual shot at the one farther behind on their turn.

When I got to him, I saw what ground "growage" really is. He was monstrous and beautiful, sporting a 5x5 rack with a 23-inch spread. And guess what? We had breakfast at Grandma's farmhouse before caping him out for the taxidermist.

I was a college kid, poor and ignorant of what Boone and Crockett really meant in the hunting world. I knew it was important to some folks but I just hunted for the meat and the excitement of a good hunt with friends. The local game warden scored the buck and told me he was a 180 buck, but that meant nothing to me. I took him to a local gentleman who did taxidermy on the side and headed back to college. Later, the buck became a fixture in my apartment and became "one of the guys" until I graduated, got married, and he took up residency in our living room.

Approximately 22 years later, I took the head in to have it scored officially. After all that time, my buck still measured 161-3/8 and made the awards book. It was a nice stamp of approval on the best buck I have ever taken – so far!

**Doug Lamm and his 1978 trophy whitetail.**

# Jack S. Snider
## 161-3/8 B&C Typical
### Nez Perce County, 2000

**Idaho Typical Rank: 119**
**Inside Spread: 16-6/8**
**Main Beams (R,L): 22-5/8,22-6/8**

**Points (R,L): 7,7**
**Widest Spread: 19-1/8**
**Bases (R, L): 4-1/8,4-3/8**

I t had been a wet, cold, miserable hunt. Jack Snider and his brothers, Paul and Travis, had trudged through the snow for three hours, and all were soaked and cold. They had seen some good bucks that day, but none of the encounters were good enough to offer any shot opportunities.

Confidence and interest weren't exactly brimming as they talked about what to do next. They all would have just as soon gone home, but there was time enough for one last hunt, so they planned it out.

One person needed to be on stand to hunt it right, but no one was begging to be the one to do it, as sitting in the cold for any period of time wasn't an easy chore. It was finally decided that it would be Jack, because he knew the best place to park the truck to get to the best place to be on stand.

He drove around to the pullout, hiked around to a point, and got into position. A light snow continued to fall as he sat still with a watchful eye for an hour and a half. At about 4 p.m, he was so cold and uncomfortable that he was about ready to call it quits and head back to some warmer confines.

As he stood up, he caught a flash out of the corner of his eye. He looked down, and there in the creek bottom were three bucks running at full speed less than 100 yards away! One looked to be in the 120 class, another one was maybe even a little better, and the third – well, he was a real dandy!

He didn't have a lot of time to react or wait for a great shot, so he brought up his trusty .270 and let 'er rip. The shot hit home, and killed the buck on the spot. Jack couldn't believe it. He had never seen that buck before, and the whole scenario just seemed sort of incredible gift.

Regardless, somehow it seemed

a little warmer now than it had been just a few minutes earlier. And now, with a hunter's work yet to do, it was going to get even warmer.

**Jack Snider was about ready to call it a day when this big 7x7 buck made him forget all about how cold he was.**

# Andrew Schumaker
## 161-1/8 B&C Typical
### Clearwater County, 2007

**Idaho Typical Rank: 123***

**Inside Spread: 17-6/8**

**Main Beams (R,L): 26-3/8,26-7/8**

**Points (R,L): 4,6**

**Widest Spread: 23-6/8**

**Bases (R, L): 4-5/8,4-5/8**

s unique and special as this buck is to Andrew, it's even more special to him because of when and where it was taken. He was able to take this buck with his grandpa's .300 H&H magnum near his grandpa's cabin just a couple of years after his passing.

Andrew and Isaac Riley had been hunting out of the cabin, located about ten miles outside of Pierce, for four days on opening weekend. Saturday night they ran into a friend, Jackson Rose, and they all ended up going back to the cabin that night.

The next morning, they left the cabin after first light, with Isaac going one direction while Andrew and Jackson went another. The fog that morning was dense, and visibility was only maybe 100 feet. They stayed on a trail and decided to slowly walk up an open clearcut ridge 50 feet apart.

They got up on top where some old skid roads separated and headed into thick timber. Just then, Andrew saw an animal about 80 yards ahead. It was standing broadside, and when he raised his grandpa's rifle, he saw the rack. He shot and then heard the buck crash.

Jackson appeared and they crawled down into the brush. They could see the buck's rack, but he was still alive. The buck startled and ran, forcing a tough tracking job. They eventually caught up with the huge buck underneath a downed tree. Needless to say, all three hunters were excited and impressed at what lay before them. This great deer has one of the largest 4x4 typical frames in the state.

# Richard C. Speaks
## 161 B&C Typical
### Bonner County, 2002

**Idaho Typical Rank: 125**
**Inside Spread: 15-6/8**
**Main Beams (R,L): 24-7/8,24-5/8**

**Points (R,L): 5,5**
**Widest Spread: 17-7/8**
**Bases (R,L): 4-7/8, 5-0/8**

O n November 21, 2002, there was a light morning rain falling as I set up in a cedar thicket along a well-used game trail. I hunkered down by a big cedar stump and called with a doe bleat, hoping a rutting buck might be nearby.

About five minutes later, a doe came running by with a small four-point trailing her. I called two or three times and waited for a few minutes, hoping something better might come along.

Soon afterward, at about 8 a.m., a big mature 5x5 came walking out of the trees right at me. I shot him at 25 yards with a .30-06. Needless to say, I was very happy and excited to take such a great buck.

RICHARD SPEAKS

# Brad Ailor
## 160-7/8 B&C Typical
### Lewis County, 2004

**Idaho Typical Rank: 127\***
**Inside Spread: 18-1/8**
**Main Beams (R,L): 22-2/8, 20-7/8**

**Points (R,L): 6,6**
**Widest Spread: 23-4/8**
**Bases (R, L): 4-3/8,4-2/8**

I t was October 29, 2004, the day after my 43rd birthday. It was an overcast day and my good friend Dan Brown and I jumped into my Dodge pickup, headed out for a midday hunt.

I am blessed to live in an area where I can be hunting in a matter of minutes. Much of the country is steep rugged canyons with timbered draws and brush patches. My preferred hunting method is to glass the canyons, and an overcast day is good because we don't have to worry about the position of the sun.

We were set up at 10 a.m. and glassing one of my favorite spots. An hour later I thought I saw a shade of tan that was out of place across the canyon and in the firs. I dug out my spotting scope, set it up, and zoomed in on the spot, which through my spotting scope looked like about a 10'x12' patch.

Right away I could see it was deer fur. As I studied it, I saw part of the deer's head and rack as he groomed himself. At this point, I got Dan's attention and we continued to study him through the scope and could see that he was a good buck.

He was too far away to even think about taking a shot, but I pulled out my range-finder anyway. It would not read, so I knew it was over 800 yards.

At this point, I knew this buck was worth a closer look. We made a plan to get closer and started working our way around the hill-side and down a ridge to try and get to a spot where I could get a reasonable shot. We took our time, stopping frequently to check on the buck.

After 45 minutes, we were at 357 yards. I could see from this location that the buck was definitely a shooter. He was bedded above the base of a ten-foot snag.

At one point, as I was setting up for a shot, he stood up broadside, but the snag was directly in front of his vitals. After a couple of minutes, he bedded back down. I had a clear view of just his neck and head. Because of the confidence I have in my Remington 7mm-mag., I decided I would take careful aim and try to shoot him in the neck. I figured if I missed and he got up, I'd have an even better shot.

**Dan Brown took this 160-class buck later that same season.**

When I squeezed the trigger, I got no response. At that point, I decided to take one more shot. When I did, he immediately jumped and ran 20 yards. He then stopped facing downhill and wrapped his head around, looking back up. This put his head right at the top of his vitals. I took a deep breath and squeezed another round, and he went down instantly.

When Dan and I finally got to the buck, I realized that my second shot clipped about an inch off of the tip of his left main beam, and that piece was lying in his bed. Dan and I were both ecstatic, and after some high fives and thanking the Lord, it was time to dig out the camera. We were able to drag the deer downhill, which doesn't happen very often in this area. Looking back, Dan and I refer to that year as the year of the 160s, because the Lord blessed us both with bucks scoring 160 or better.

**Brad Ailor (right) and Dan Brown, with Brad's big typical in fall of 2004.**

# Jason E. Gomes
## 160-6/8 B&C Typical
### Nez Perce County, 2001

**Idaho Typical Rank: 128***
**Inside Spread: 19-1/8**
**Main Beams (R,L): 24-7/8,23-0/8**

**Points (R,L): 6,6**
**Widest Spread: 22-0/8**
**Bases (R, L):4-3/8,4-4/8**

I was hunting with a friend from high school, Joe Guzman. It was overcast, and we had hunted all morning with no success. After lunch we decided to go to a spot where I've seen a lot of good bucks, and had been watching a few that year.

It was a timbered flat, bordered by a wheat field. The flat sloped into a draw, eventually forming a canyon. I've jumped a lot of bucks in the flat, but hardly catch a glimpse of them before they disappear into the brushy draw.

We headed across the flat to where we could see across the head of the draw. We passed up a smaller buck and headed farther down. There were a lot of trails coming out of the draw toward the stubble field. Our chances of catching a good buck coming out of the draw to feed looked good, so we split up. Joe stayed put, and I walked along the edge and stopped to watch the draw.

Suddenly, I saw a gray face staring at me through the timber. I raised my .300 Win.-mag. and looked through the scope. My heart almost stopped!

Before I could get a rest, he took off toward the stubble field! I went across the flat, thinking I might see him going across the field. When I got to the edge, I saw him sneaking back through the timber toward the canyon. This time I got a rest and picked an opening, and sure enough, he stepped right into my crosshairs.

Joe had been on his way back when he spotted me. He spotted the buck just as I shot, and thought I missed. We headed over, just to be sure. As we got closer, I could see him lying there. At that time, he was the nicest buck I had ever killed.

# Brian Stanley
## 160-6/8 B&C Typical
### Shoshone County, 2003

**Idaho Typical Rank: 128**

**Inside Spread: 15-4/8**

**Main Beams (R,L): 24-1/8,25-2/8**

**Points (R,L): 5,5**

**Widest Spread: 18-0/8**

**Bases (R, L): 4-3/8,4-3/8**

N ovember 23, 2003 was the day I encountered my big buck. It was overcast and there was a foot of snow on the ground. I was on a trail pushing through the snow when a doe ran in front of me at full speed. I knew there was probably a buck chasing her, so I got ready. I was right, and a big buck flew across the trail in front of me so fast I couldn't get a shot.

They went down the ridge, across the creek and onto the next ridge. I was pointing my rifle to keep my aim, and they came up through the jack pines 200 yards away and still running full speed.

Luckily for me, the doe decided to cross back toward me. As soon as he came out of the timber, I grunted and he stopped on the edge of the creek. I took the 100-yard shot with my .300 Weatherby-mag. and he fell right near the creek. I went and got my friend, Davin Jennings, and he helped get the buck out. Ironically, he also shot a 7x6 the same day – almost at the same time – but almost 30 miles away.

# More Great Whitetails

DALLEN LAMBSON

# The State Record That Never Was

For a number of years, this huge whitetail was recognized as the Idaho State Record non-typical. It was shown that way in photos and in the listings in Boone and Crockett's records as well as Idaho Department of Fish and Game's records.

However, as I was writing this book and tracing down information, it became readily apparent that there was no information whatsoever indicating that this buck was ever taken in Idaho. It was listed as being from Idaho only because it was purchased from a person living in Idaho. When I contacted that person, he relayed that he had purchased the rack from a taxidermist in California, and the taxidermist had received it from someone who had found it while cleaning out an attic.

Furthermore, it has also been learned that there have been some points repaired on the rack, and that it would never have scored the 268 B&C that it had been listed as. So for now, not only is the buck not the Idaho State Record, but it also is no longer even listed in B&C.

# Found by Dr. B.H. King

### Bonner County, 1941

T he history on this buck is limited. Dr. King, a dentist from Coeur d'Alene, found the antlers on a hunting trip in 1941. It's not known for sure if it was found intact or if these are shed antlers, but it is believed to be a full set.

The huge 10x12 buck was scored at 245-6/8. B&C's modern scoring system was in its infancy, and rules regarding non-hunter-taken trophies were yet to be determined. As such, paperwork was never finished and the buck was never accepted into the records program. If it had been, it would have been the state record non-typical, and even today would rank #3.

It had a 33-2/8-inch spread (one of the widest of all time), beams of 28 and 29-2/8 inches, and a net typical frame of approximately 206.

After it was scored, he wrote the letter on the following page to Boone and Crockett Club.

**This photo was also in B.H. King's file, along with the big non-typical pictured above. There was no documentation along with it to indicate what relevance it had, but it seems logical that it would also have been an Idaho whitetail associated with Dr. King.**

**B.H. King's letter to Boone and Crockett Club, dated Nov. 17, 1948**

Nov. 17, 1948
Boone and Crockett Club
American Museum of Natural History
Central Park West at 79th St.

Catherine Sayers,
I am sending measurements and a photograph of the unusually large whitetail head that Donald Hopkins wrote you about.
This set of horns was found on a deer hunting trip Nov. 20, 1941 on a flat up in the mountains west of Cocolalla Lake, Bonner County, Idaho. They were so unusually large I kept them and had them mounted.
I hesitated about saying much about them as they were found and was not a hunting trophy.

Yours very truly,
B.H. King

*Special thanks to Boone & Crockett Club for permission to reprint this letter and photos.*

# The Dover Buck, Bonner County, 2007

N ot all of Idaho's biggest whitetail bucks are taken by hunters. A fairly high percentage of them are either too cagey, too lucky, or both. Others are taken by predators or meet other unfortunate fates.

This huge buck was hit by a car in Bonner County in late summer of 2007. It's a very unfortunate accident that not only ended the buck's life, but also any chance for a hunter to have the privilege of harvesting him.

The buck has not been scored, but looks to be in the 210-220 range, which would have placed it well up in the Idaho all-time standings. The buck now hangs at the IDF&G Regional Office in Coeur d'Alene.

# Poached, Bonner County, 2009

DAN HISLOP

**S**ound wildlife management, great habitat, ethical conduct, and sportsmanship should add up to this buck having been taken by an appreciative hunter who deserved this great trophy. Unfortunately, such is not the case with this all-time great Idaho whitetail. Instead of going to a deserving sportsman, it was poached.

A number of people in the Bonner County community had seen this titanic whitetail, and many were hoping to have the opportunity to chase him in fall of 2009. Sadly, a convicted felon, who could not legally possess a firearm, illegally shot this buck and later admitted to it, according to Idaho Department of Fish and Game. The buck was also taken without a license or tag. Perhaps the greatest part of the crime, however, is that this trophy was stolen from the citizens of Idaho, and the history and legacy of the trophy perma-

270

nently tarnished.

This case was made due to concerned and responsible sportsmen who made an effort to come forward. Tips were received through the Citizens Against Poaching (CAP) hotline at 1-800-632-5999.

True sportsmen can understand that there will never be enough conservation officers in the field. They have to step up, come forward, and help by being additional eyes and ears. Too many sportsmen seem to see conservation officers as adversaries, instead of appreciating them for what they do to protect the resource that those same sportsmen hope to benefit from.

This breathtaking 14x11 non-typical buck was green scored by an official measurer at 210-6/8 net B&C, and it may actually score higher. This would have made the buck one of the top 15 non-typical whitetails ever taken in Idaho.

Eventually, this buck will probably be entered into B&C as a "picked up" trophy, a designation aimed at still recognizing the trophy for what it was, without giving credit to those who are undeserving.

On a side note, take a look at the incredible similarities between this Bonner County non-typical and the other Bonner County non-typical on the previous page (The Dover Buck). It's amazing how similar these two bucks are. They lived in reasonable proximity, and could easily be related. Who knows, maybe they were brothers. Sadly, neither was taken by a hunter, both instead meeting unfortunate ends.

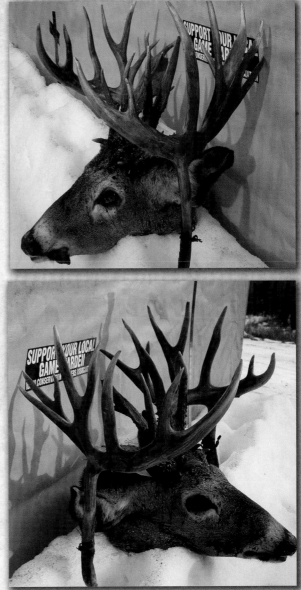

**Citizens Against Poaching**

To report wildlife violations in Idaho telephone:

**1-800-632-5999**

# Wes Stuart, 215-class
## Clearwater County, 1991

D riving down the road and looking for a big whitetail isn't normally a productive way to kill a trophy buck, but it seemed to work just fine for Wes Stuart on a November day in 1991. He just happened to look out his truck window and saw a nice buck and a doe 300 yards off. He parked the rig, leaving his rifle behind and only taking his binoculars since he was mostly just interested in watching and sizing up the deer.

There was a good-sized brush patch below them, and Wes was stunned when he watched unarmed while a giant deer came walking out of it. The other buck was obviously familiar with the new arrival because he wasted no time in retreating.

Wes was also not one to waste time, and beat feet back to his rig to grab his Ruger 7mm Mauser single shot. When he returned, the deer had disappeared.

After a short search, Wes found the buck in a clearing 100 yards away, and made a quick and easy shot to secure the tremendous 9x13 non-typical to the ground. While his buck didn't have a scratch on him other than the bullet hole, Wes noticed that he had blood on his antlers. He backtracked a ways and found an area where the buck had been in a fight just minutes earlier, obviously the victor in that battle.

*Author's Note: This great trophy was stolen from Hoot's Taxidermy shortly after Wes killed it. If you recognize this buck or have any information about what may have happened to it, please contact the author. This buck was rough scored at approximately 215, and if that score had ever been verified, it could have placed the buck in the Top 20 in the state.*

*After I had written the story above, I received this photo from Lars Eidnes, a taxidermist in St. Maries. He was a great resource for this book, and routinely sent me photos that he had collected over the years. One of them was this one, which I instantly recognized as Wes Stuart's buck. Lars couldn't remember who the person was that came in showing off the buck; he just had the photo labeled as unknown. I'd love to be able to see the face of this person, because it very well could be the person who stole the rack.*

# The Pack River Buck

R egina Hammack inherited this buck from a family friend, a man known to them as "Uncle Enoch" Garrison. According to the family, the buck was taken in 1914 in the Pack River Flats area of Bonner County.

Two men were driving along in early September killing time and hopefully a grouse. They saw a grouse alongside the road and stopped to shoot it.

When they got out, they spied this big ol' buck and decided to make better use of their bullets. They would have been using some pretty primitive rifles by today's standards, but they got the job done. It would have been quite a sight seeing this big buck in the back of some old-time car, and probably caused a good stir in town.

This great relic trophy is one of the oldest known trophies in all of Idaho. While it was taken about 35 years before the advent of a modern scoring system, I did lay a tape on it. The buck is a 13x6, has a gross score of 224 and a net of 206-6/8, with 66-4/8 inches worth of abnormal points. Not that it would have made any difference to the hunters who took the buck way back when.

# Troy Pottenger
## Benewah County, 2003 (Archery)

TROY POTTENGER

I n spring of 2003, I found a huge shed antler. From that day on, I immersed myself into scouting for this buck. I knew I was onto the buck of a lifetime. I started by breaking down the area with topo maps and gridding it on foot.

Once summer came, I had amassed a thorough knowledge of the area, so I backed out and set up two observation stands. The spying paid off in mid June when the velvet giant appeared one evening 400 yards from my observation stand. I captured him on video for nearly five minutes. I was ecstatic!

By the time the season came, I had strategically picked my spots. I hung a couple of stands based on terrain features, glassing visuals, and buck sign.

This old buck was very nocturnal, but once or twice a week he would show up at last light, using a specific mountain saddle to enter a clearcut for feeding. This saddle would be my ambush point.

On the third afternoon of early archery season, I settled into my stand. As the sun faded in the western skies, I began to scan the area, considering all the possible approaches the big buck might use to exit his bedding area. I drew my bow a few times, making sure my stand and bow were silent.

Nightfall neared and I began to doubt that he'd show up. Then, like an apparition, a massively wide whitetail buck materialized from the stand of Douglas-fir. He walked cautiously, angling his way at 45 degrees. I took my eyes off of his headgear and focused on the task at hand.

Slowly, I stood and readied my bow. Scanning ahead of the big boy's path, I located a stump I had ranged at 35 yards. When the buck reached the stump, I let out a grunt and he jerked his head my way.

I rested the 35-yard pin dead center on his lungs and tripped the release. The buck gathered and dropped slightly, but it was too late, the arrow hit home. I had just downed the buck of a lifetime! All of the hard work had paid off. My big 8x7 archery buck officially scored 177-5/8 net P&Y non-typical.

# Elton Ankney
## Nez Perce County, Mid 1960s

**E**lton Ankney killed this giant typical around 1965 in Nez Perce County, back when he was in his early 40s. At the time, he was working for Lenore Grain & Seed.

He was feeding cows on his home property when he heard a buck grunt up on the hill. He looked up and saw a big buck chasing a doe, so he ran into the house and grabbed a .30-30 he had borrowed from a neighbor.

He walked up on the hill and jumped a doe out of the brush and took a shot. He missed, and that's when the big buck jumped up and started running away. He readjusted his aim and was able to make his next shot count, dropping the buck within his view.

This buck has never been officially measured, but if it ever is, it should be one of the top typicals in the state. It was unofficially scored at approximately 175-3/8, which means it could potentially be a top 15 typical in the state of Idaho.

*Special thanks to Tracy Bennett for providing the photos and legwork on this buck and the one on the next page.*

# Les Ankney
## Nez Perce County, 1969

**N**ot to be outdone by his dad, Elton, Les Ankney took this huge buck just a few years later, in 1969. He was only 12 years old, and this was the first deer he had ever shot.

Les and his dad were hunting in the same general area where Elton had taken his big buck. He walked up on the buck in its bed, and shot it at close range.

His dad told him to gut the deer and that he was going to walk around the edge of the hill and then come back. Elton says that when he came back, Les was still standing over the deer with his knife in his hand, shaking from buck fever, and hadn't even started gutting the deer yet.

This buck unofficially scores 176 net typical, making Elton and Les Ankney's giant bucks from the 1960s among the best father/son tandems around.

# Rod Wolfe
## Shoshone County, 1989

ROD WOLFE

s I stood on a logging road watching my dad drive away, I felt apprehensive about my decision. Three weeks earlier, I was still in the hospital with a smashed leg and ankle I had received from a buckskin tamarack wood tree.

Dad had called and asked if I was up for a hunt. I told him I'd try, so there I was. I had my pack, my rifle, some rattling horns, my crutches, and a foot of snow. I had a couple hundred yards to get to the spot I wanted to be.

It was just getting daylight when I got there. There was no way I could get down to where I wanted to be except to slide on my rear, so down I went.

When I got to my spot, I looked over and saw a big buck standing broadside 300 yards away and looking at me. I had my Ruger .243 still slung over my head, so I took my eyes off of the deer and got all of my gear off of me. While standing on one leg and doing this on a steep ridge, it was all I could do not to look at the deer.

Finally, I had my rifle in my hands. I rested my elbows on my leg and knee and fired. Down he went, and since he had been standing on a steep glade covered in snow, he slid down the hill out of sight.

I couldn't make it back to the road, so I had to wait for Dad. After an hour, he showed up and helped me to the road. I stayed in the truck while Dad went down the ridge to find the deer.

It took him quite a while, but he managed to drag the big 5x5 up to the truck. We took it to The Blue Goose sporting goods store in St. Maries for the big buck contest. As it turned out, I won a Browning Silent Stalker .30-06 for the biggest buck. He green scored 169-3/8 net typical.

***Big buck winner*** Rod Wolfe, left, receives a Browning "Silent Stalker" .30-06 rifle from John Ragan, owner of Blue Goose Sporting Goods, after winning the store's third annual Big Buck contest. Mr. Wolfe bagged a whitetail with a rack of 169 and 3/8 points in the typical class under Boone and Crockett regulations. The rifle is made of stainless steel with a weatherproof stock. Photo by Al Voge

# Larry Knight
## Idaho County, 1969

**S**eventeen years before Donna Knight took her big 177-5/8 B&C typical, her husband, Larry Knight, took this big old buck only half a mile away. It was fall of 1969, and Larry was on an afternoon hunt near his home in northern Idaho County. The buck came up a ridge, and when Larry saw the rack, his first instinct was that it was an elk. Quickly recognizing his mistake, he fired his .308 Winchester and dropped the buck from a mere 50 yards. There were not a lot of field photos being taken in 1969, making this great natural and vintage photograph a real treat.

It turns out that taking that photo was a real fortunate deal for Larry, as it's all he has left. This buck was stolen from him that fall.

He had taken it to the Les Schwab Tires store in Lewiston for the big buck contest. When he came back to get it after the contest, it wasn't there, and no one had a good explanation why. It was just gone.

Please take a good, hard look and see if you might recognize this rack. It would mean a lot to Larry if it could be returned to him.

The Perl DeFord Family from the Twin Falls area provided this photo. Perl (above left) was in our book *Idaho's Greatest Elk* with a crazy-antlered elk. Here he is posing with an unbelievable non-typical whitetail. Currently, there isn't a story to go with the photo, but the deer is believed to have been taken in Idaho. What happened to the rack is unknown. Regardless, what an amazing buck!

This giant deer was found winterkilled in Latah County way back in 1945. It was found by a farmer, and was sold many years later. It was unofficially scored at 210 B&C, but has never been officially documented. It's a shame that a buck this significant faded into obscurity.

Denny Diaz submitted a photo of this Idaho buck, which he owned at one time. Unfortunately, he no longer has it, and doesn't remember who killed it. Perhaps someone will recognize it in this book and be able to put some history back into it. The buck looks as though it would gross score 210-220.

Dana Hollinger and Bob Howard, who own many of Idaho's top ranking mule deer, also have a few giant whitetails that were reportedly taken in Idaho. Unfortunately, the trophy above, as well as the next two non-typicals, were all taken by unknown hunters. This awesome 6x6 scores 179-1/8 net.

Another buck from Dana Hollinger and Bob Howard's antler collection. This huge non-typical scores 214-3/8. While it's believed this buck is also from Idaho, it currently has no history.

Yet another giant non-typical from Dana Hollinger and Bob Howard's antler collection. This buck was supposedly taken by a hunter, with name unknown. There was no information on this buck's score, but it looks to be in that 220 range. If you look at the uncanny resemblance of this buck to Kip Manfull's 219-7/8 non-typical, you'd have to believe that this was either its twin brother or even more likely that this is actually the mounted shed antlers from Kip's deer.

Gilbert Smith killed this low and wide 9x7 non-typical in Bonner County in 1973. It scores 192-2/8, with main beams of 25 and 27 inches. It's not a great photo, but it's at least a chance to see it. We'd like to have more information on this buck for a future edition.

Randy Clemenhagen found this winterkill in Latah County in 2001. He unofficially taped it at 200 gross. If the clean typical side had been mirrored on the deer's right side, this buck might have made 180 typical. What a great deer.

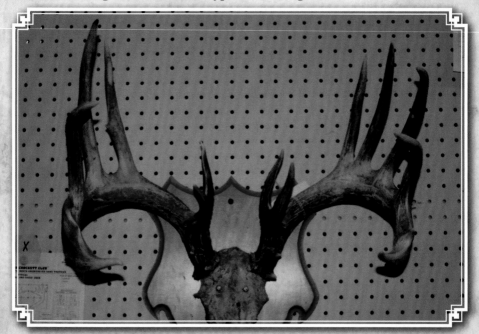

This buck was found dead by Clint Krasselt in Latah County in 1987. It scores 189-2/8 gross and 177-4/8 net non-typical. It's just another example of the many huge bucks that die by a multitude of reasons not involving hunters.

Guy Olson found this buck dead in Nez Perce County in November 2008. He was walking along hunting and stumbled onto it while pushing the brush on a drive. It was just 100 yards away from a small lake in an open area between thick lodgepole. He believes it was a wolf or cougar kill, but can't be sure since the buck had been out for a year. The buck grosses right around 170.

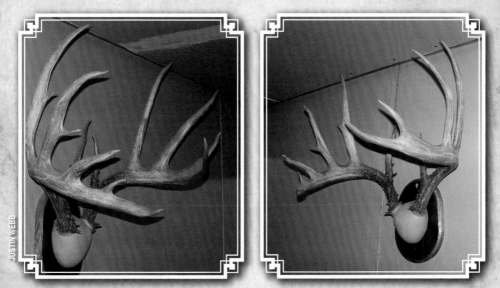

Ken Downard took this big-framed typical in Bonner County in 1978. He had been hunting with Bill Kohal all morning but hadn't had much luck, in part because of fog. They were passing through an area where they could see up in some rocky, cliffy areas and spotted this giant buck. The antlers looked so big that Ken thought it was an elk. Bill took a long shot and missed, and Ken followed up and hit it with his .25-06. The buck grosses in the high 170s, and nets in the lower 160s.

John Spenler killed this big 171-5/8 typical in 1966 in northern Idaho. The eyeguards on this buck are truly impressive. This photo was taken at the Big Horn Show in Spokane in 2004, where the buck was on display.

Denny Diaz, who was into hunting and collecting big whitetails in Idaho long before it became more commonplace, provided this photo of a buck he found dead while shed hunting in Nez Perce County in 1985. It is reported to score 176 net, but Denny no longer has the buck.

Denny Diaz killed this big typical (above) in Lewis County around 1990. It has been scored at 171 net typical, but has never been entered in the record book. The two different sets of shed antlers (below) can be seen side by side. This buck had a very distinctive rack, with beam tips that nearly touch, and tines as long as any buck anywhere. It was taken on Monty Ewing's place (Monty has a 201-3/8 non-typical of his own), before Monty sold it. The property changed hands again and is now owned by the Nez Perce Tribe.

August Barfuss killed this great whitetail in Bonner County in 1968. If you look very closely, you'll see that it actually has four separate antlers. The extra two come in the form of two small points at the base of the main left antler, each of which has its own pedicle and would have shed separately. When including these in the score, the buck nets 181 B&C non-typical.

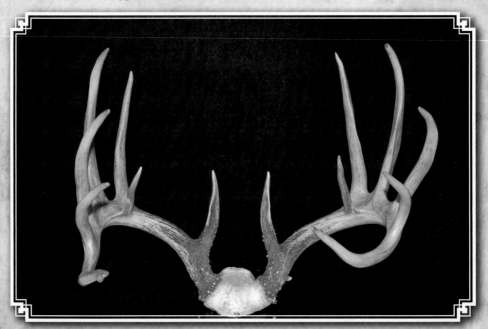

Larry Beeler had been given a tip about two big bucks in the Cocolalla area. He went up there in mid November with his dad, Ralph, hoping to run into one of them. The split up near a gas line right-of-way and hunted the afternoon in an inch of snow. Larry had hunted for an hour when he jumped this big

Neil DeWitt took this big 7x7 buck in the Little Salmon River drainage in Idaho County in 1982. It grosses 185-6/8 and nets 173-6/8 non-typical. The buck was spotted from a road, and after he shot it, the buck ran down and died only a few yards from his pickup. Neil's wife, Evelyn, was there to witness his great luck.

Bob Stone shot this tall, long-tined 8x9 non-typical in Idaho County on the South Fork of the Clearwater. It net scores 179-7/8.

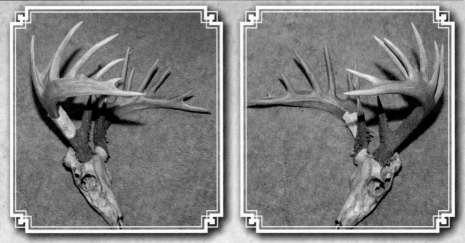

Jack Sheppard was hunting with Jeff Miller in the Little Salmon River drainage in 2007 when he shot this compact non-typical. It has not been scored, but looks to be in the 180 range or better, with at least nine points on each side.

Curtis Deming had the privilege of taking this great palmated monster buck. The following photo and caption appeared in the Coeur d'Alene Press. The title isn't accurate – while being an amazing trophy, the buck was not a state record. To his recollection, the buck scored around 168 non-typical. Still, it's a dandy.

*State-record white tail*
*Curtis Deming, 24, Hayden Lake, displays a record-setting white tail buck he shot in Unit 3 on Thanksgiving morning. The buck's eight-point rack set an all-time record for size in the non-typical category. The deer, which is the only one Deming has seen this year, dressed out at 200 pounds of hanging meat.*

—Press Photo By RIC CL

## State-record white tail

Curtis Deming, 24, Hayden Lake, displays a record-setting white tail buck he shot in Unit 3 on Thanksgiving morning. The buck's eight-point rack set an all-time Idaho record for size

in the non-typical category. The deer, wh the only one Deming has seen this dressed out at 200 pounds of hanging m

Bob Clemenhagen took this giant typical in north-central Idaho back in the 1980s. It hasn't been scored officially, but is believed to go in the mid 170s as a typical. The frame and mass on this buck is outstanding.

Darrell Tonn took this wide Latah County buck in 1969. He was parked and waiting for a friend, and first light was already coming. He saw this buck walking across a field half a mile away, and made a play but wasn't lucky. He then ran into his friend, and while they talked, the buck unexpectedly appeared. Darrell made a long shot with his .25-06 and anchored the buck. Darrell reports the deer to score 168.

Steve Johnson and his friend, Mike Archer, were on a 1983 hunt in Clearwater County when they crossed paths with this jawdropper. It was the first week of season, and an hour into first light they were walking down a logging road. Steve looked up into a clearcut and saw a small bachelor group of bucks browsing in the brush as they walked along. Steve could tell there was something different about the biggest buck, but at 200 yards, he wasn't sure what. He used a stump for a rest and hit the buck in the neck with his Browning BAR 7mm Rem.-mag. Both hunters were pretty amazed when they got to see Steve's trophy up close. This buck grosses 181-4/8 and nets 158-5/8. Those long, turned-down main beams measure 26 inches.

This balanced double-dropline beauty was reportedly found dead in northern Idaho. It was sold to an antler dealer and is now owned by Bill Lancaster. It net scores 183-1/8 B&C non-typical, and has droptines of 7-1/8 and 6-3/8 inches.

Mike Winslow was hunting alone in 18 inches of snow on the last day of the season in 1988. He was sneaking down the hill, his steps muffled by the snow, when he walked up on this buck bedded only 30 yards away. He could see its back, but couldn't see which end was which until the buck finally moved. He then shot the buck in the neck. He was pretty surprised when he saw what kind of buck he had just taken. His reward? Dragging the trophy through deep snow by himself for nearly a mile, with much difficulty. This Bonner County buck grosses in the 180s, and might have made the book if not for a broken point. The buck was exceptionally old, and fairly gaunt. Mike says its teeth were gone and it was fairly small-bodied.

Ed Mattson was hunting on the South Fork of the Clearwater with a friend in 1997. They were headed back toward the pickup and took different routes, and Ed's route took him straight to this great buck. A doe helped give him away and Ed took the shot without knowing exactly what kind of headgear this great buck was wearing, which he says was a good thing. This great double droptine buck, with the added bonus of two turned down main beams, is a stunning trophy. The pack out, which was two miles, somehow seemed easy, according to Ed.

Bill Adams was out for a spring walk with his dog and looking for shed antlers when he came across the remains of this amazing double droptine buck. It scores right around 158 and was found in Clearwater County back in 1980. It's easy to forget while being mesmerized by those droptines that this buck has some very impressive eyeguards as well.

BILL ADAMS

Paul Snider, Jr. found this buck in Nez Perce County in 2004. He was out "horn huntin'" with Lee Gruell. Paul had found three fresh brown antlers and Lee had only found one white one, so Paul gave Lee choice of sides as they headed into a new draw. Lee took "the good side", and Paul promptly hiked 200 yards and walked right up to this great find.

LARS EIDNES

This terrific quadruple-drop buck was reportedly taken in northern Idaho, but unfortunately, neither of the two photographers who submitted photos of this buck could remember the name of the hunter who killed it. It was taken around 1990, and was in Lars Eidnes' taxidermy shop in St. Maries. Hopefully we'll have more information later if and when a 2nd edition of this book is compiled.

RANDY HIGLEY

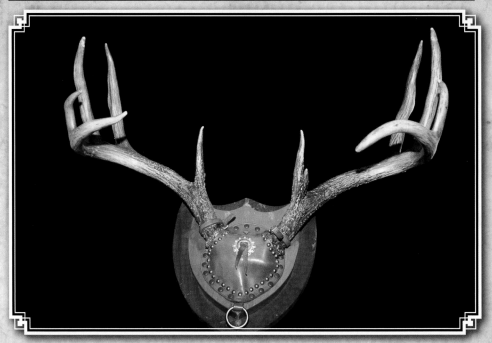

Chet Glauner took this buck in Boundary County in 1956. With a length of 30-5/8 inches, this buck has one of the longest main beams of any whitetail in Idaho. As is, it scores 167-4/8, but an abnormal point was cut off of the back of the rack so that it could be hung on a wall. As such, it can't be officially scored.

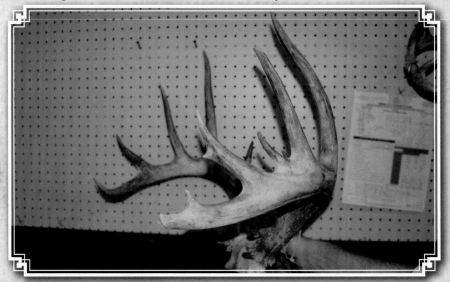

Jake Hamilton was elk hunting in Latah County in 2003 when he encountered this big whitetail. He was sitting on a bluff watching some bulls, and spotted a big buck nestled right into the middle of a patch of thorny wild rose. The buck had purposefully jumped right into the middle of them to be hidden and undisturbed. Jake had a good vantage point and saw an antler glisten. A 250-yard shot was enough to turn Jake from an elk hunter that day into a successful deer hunter. The buck scores 155-5/8 net.

LARS EIDNES

"Dennis Teal's big buck was taken in Benewah County in 1992 on the Farmington side of what we call Skyline Drive. It was a late season, middle of the rut hunt. My dad had jumped this buck early and had caught glimpses of him all morning, but could never get a shot. He was rutting does hard and had his head to the ground the entire time.

"A friend of my dad's, Steve Smith, was driving up the back side of Skyline from Farmington when the truck he was in backfired. It was loud enough to stop the buck in his tracks and he raised his head. This was proved to be a fatal move. When the buck raised up, my dad took a step to the side and shot. He was using a Remington Model 7600 pump action .30-06, and shot from about 200 yards. The bullet hit a twig and tumbled, which helped to make a large hole in the buck. Needless to say, he didn't go far. Steve didn't even know what had happened until he heard the story a few days later. To this day, he says it's really his buck!" ~ Derek Teal. Dennis has since passed away, but his son, Derek, was kind enough to write the story of what happened on Dennis Teal's big buck.

Lars Eidnes, of Eidnes Furs in St. Maries, is a taxidermist and has had a ton of big whitetails go through his shop over the years. He was a great help in providing material for this book, and sent the two photos on this page, along with many others.

Lars snapped this photo of a buck he mounted in the early 1990s. This buck was taken by Susie Milliken in northern Idaho, probably right around that same time. This buck, with good balance, heavy mass, and great eye-guards, looks as though it would score very well.

LARS EIDNES

This pretty typical was on display at the Lewis-Clark Trader Gun & Horn Show in Lewiston in approximately 2005. Aaron Smith killed the buck, which net scores 161-4/8 B&C, in Nez Perce County.

Jay Brady took this beautiful, long-tined typical on a hunt with Denny Diaz in 1986. They were hunting the Lochsa River drainage in Idaho County. The buck is reported to net score in the 167-168 range, and has some great tine length.

# Out in the Mountains

DALLEN LAMBSON

# Kyle Greene
## Nez Perce County, 2009

KYLE GREENE

I left my pickup that morning half an hour before daylight. My plan was to head for a rock bluff I frequently glass from at first light. After a bit of stumbling and cursing, I reached my rock perch just as light started to creep into the canyon.

After 45 minutes of glassing, I looked up from my binoculars to let my eyes rest. The sun was now hitting the south slope, so I shifted my position to spot whatever might be glowing in the morning sun.

Within 30 seconds, I spotted this buck feeding on an open hillside. I watched him mill around for 15 minutes until he bedded in a tall patch of thistle. He was over half a mile away, so I spent another 15 minutes figuring the wind and my approach.

In another half-hour, I was above and behind him 240 yards away and watching his antler tips. I lay watching and waiting for him to stand for probably an hour and a half. He was only a couple of steps from cresting over the ridgeline below me, so I didn't dare lift my head from the scope.

When he did finally stand, I was ready and shot him just a step before he went out of sight. The deer officially scored 181 gross and 177-5/8 net non-typical.

# BiJay Adams
## Benewah County, 2008

In spring of 2008, three shed antlers were picked up in an area where my family and I hunt. Two of these sheds were a very large matched set. The other shed was a large single four-point that displayed the very same genetics. This got my attention, and I really focused on this area for scouting.

My instinct told me that "Curly" lived there year-round and that I needed to change my hunting tactics in order to see him. I scouted game trails and funnels that deer could travel both pre-rut and during the rut. I guessed that this buck found his home in a dark brushy draw below where I hunted. I hung trail cameras and kept a journal. Once I determined the optimum locations, I hung two tree stands. In mid August, my tactics paid off when I captured the buck on a trail camera.

Even though I was diligent, I had no luck, and by the end of November I had not seen nor caught Curly on trail camera again. I began to worry that he might have already been taken by another hunter. By this point, I had passed up a number of mature bucks from my tree stand just for the slightest opportunity at Curly.

On the evening of November 28, all my anxiety, hard work, and patience paid off. I was in my tree stand in the rain when I saw a deer 180 yards below me. I put my binos up and saw it was a mature buck. I took a steady rest off of my shooting stick and squeezed the trigger. The "thwack" echoed through the draw.

After further observation, I could see what appeared to be a white blotch on the ground. I quickly scurried out of my tree stand and down to where the deer had been standing. When I arrived, there lay Curly, the buck I had spent 30 trips and 102 hours in the tree stand to harvest. He was much bigger than I imagined, and I was crazy with excitement. His total gross score was 179-3/8.

# Martin Goffin
## Craigmont, 2000

I n 2000, I shot the buck of a lifetime. I had only taken one deer in 18 years of hunting (and I hunted a lot). It started as an elk hunt with my friend, who told me not to shoot a deer unless it was a monster. He didn't want to spook the elk. Not having shot anything in ten years, discerning a monster would really test my mettle.

As I still-hunted across the rolling country, I crested a rise and there stood two deer, both does. I watched them and then a new deer came into the scene, a perfect ten-point basket-racked deer, nicer than I had ever seen. Boy! I had a tag, the season was open, and I had a loaded .300 Savage pointing right at him. The decision was ultimately made for me; as soon as I hesitated, the deer disappeared into thin air.

Just as I was kicking myself, I heard a shot, then two more. Sure that someone had just shot my deer, I went to investigate. To my surprise, one of our group had shot a nice six-point bull. If I had shot the deer, I surely would have scared the elk away. My good karma allowed me to fill my tag with a raghorn bull the next day.

On the final day, a friend and I left for a hunt. We made a plan for me to go around to a ridge and hunt up, and Jerry would sidehill, hoping to push deer to one another.

I had just started the hike when I spotted a deer's body with its head down behind a downed tree. As he lifted his head, I saw antlers, put my scope on him and pulled the trigger, and the deer dropped. I ran up to see the deer and was shocked. He was huge, but he wasn't finished. He was struggling to keep going downhill. I sprinted ahead of him and intercepted him, finishing the job with another shot. This great buck, with 26-inch beams and 18 points, gross scores 173-2/8.

My rifle is a .300 Savage my dad bought in the '50s from Benny's Pawn Shop in Boise. It has served me well, but I have now turned my attention to archery hunting.

# Justin Webb
## Bonner County, 2009

**T**he 2009 deer season is one I'll never forget. Having spent the past five years chasing high country mule deer, I decided to switch gears and pursue the large whitetail bucks I had been seeing on my hikes up the mountain.

Monday came with an inch of snow. My hunting gear was in my truck, so when I got off work I slipped into my hunting clothes and raced up the mountain.

Knowing the "chase phase" of the rut was peaking, and that daylight was fading, I leapt from my truck on a dead run up the mountain. My pack on my back and rifle in hand, I quickly "hopscotched" clearcuts and climbing the ridgeline to the timbered benches where I'd seen some bucks dogging does in the past.

After pausing to cool down and get a drink, I slipped over the rock ledges and onto a bench I had chosen as my destination. Moments later, I heard the sound of buck grunts and antlers raking brush uphill from me. It seemed abnormally loud and aggressive, so much so that I began to wonder if it was another hunter with rattling horns. A closer investigation revealed at least four sets of deer tracks in the snow, and one very large buck track.

I raced to circle downwind while gaining elevation. I could now hear the sound of deer moving through the steep, rocky ravine below me, and then the sound of antlers tapping against brush. The buck finally cleared the top of the draw, headed out of sight. At the last moment, I remembered to grunt. He paused briefly and then began a stiff-legged march in my direction. At 40 yards, I could see clearly; he was a tremendous buck. I grunted once more to stop him and then I pulled the trigger.

Some great friends helped me trail him and bone him out in the dark. The hike out was spent reminiscing about the day's events and basking all that goes into a successful hunt. The 6x7 buck scored 172-1/8, with a great amount of character.

# Levi Hunt
## Bonner County, 2008

LEVI HUNT

I t was the third week of deer season during the whitetail rut in November of 2008. That morning I had slept in, and I had to scramble to avoid missing the hunt altogether. I didn't get on the mountain until 8:30.

I started walking up a skid trail, and 30 minutes into the hunt, I heard something moving. Two whitetails flashed through the brush, so I gave a grunt call to stop them. When I did, a buck came out of the brush following the same path. The buck was unaware of my presence, so I raised my rifle, took aim, and shot. It was a clean miss!

The buck stopped and looked up toward me, so I quickly chambered another round and shot again. This time I hit my mark. After waiting for what seemed like hours, I made my way over to where I shot the deer to recover it. I followed the blood trail for 30 yards until I saw the buck lying on the ground. As I walked closer, the antlers just kept growing and growing.

# Todd Palmer

## Kootenai County, 2006

TODD FELTON

T odd Palmer was hunting with Mike Rust in Kootenai County in late fall of 2006. They had hunted hard all day, and were in their second hunt area for the evening hunt.

They split up to cover a large clearcut, with plans to meet back up closer to the pickup. Todd saw a small buck, but elected to pass.

He moved on, and was on an old skid trail when he saw this long-tined buck. It was snowing hard and visibility was slim, and even though the buck was only 75 yards away, he could barely see it. The rack looked a little narrow, so he was actually going to pass on it. That's when the buck took a step forward and turned his head, revealing its true size. The buck should net over the 160 minimum, but has not yet been officially scored.

# Scott Baldwin
## Nez Perce County, 2001

 n November 10, 2001, my brothers, my dad, and I hunted a large canyon in north-central Idaho that had great potential for quality bucks. We hunted and glassed hard, but only found a small buck.

We came back in two days hoping the rut might have started and a few bucks would be more visible. From the moment it got light, I knew we were in for a treat. By 9 a.m., I had seen over a dozen bucks, and several of them were good four and five-points. They were everywhere, and all of them were chasing does.

I had been glassing from the top of a bluff for close to an hour, and had been glassing a nice 5x5 for some time. I watched him make scrapes and chase does, and ultimately decided to try and get closer to make the shot.

I had only taken two steps when I instantly heard a crash below the bluff, not 40 yards away! It was a big whitetail buck that looked as big as a bull elk crashing through the trees and brush. I shouldered my rifle and shot, more like shotgunning a flushed pheasant than a typical whitetail shot.

I could no longer see the deer; he had disappeared into thick brush. I rushed to a log in anticipation of shooting the deer again on the other side of the canyon.

After several minutes of hearing nothing, I walked down to where I had last seen him. He hadn't gone ten feet after my shot, piling up in the brush immediately.

As I approached him, I could hardly believe the width of his rack. He had an outside spread of 28 inches and an inside spread of 26-1/2 inches. He grossed 173 and netted 162. He was the buck of a lifetime for me on an unbelievable day.

# "Jackson's Buck"
## In Memory of Jackson Baldwin

SCOTT BALDWIN

**Wyatt, Matt, and Jackson Baldwin (right) pose with a great find, just three weeks before Jackson passed away from cancer.**

This 2006 springtime adventure actually started out as a family turkey hunt. We had my father, my brother Tim and his son, Matt, and me and my two sons, Wyatt and Jackson.

We were walking down a canyon where we frequently deer hunt and have taken several nice deer and turkeys over the years. We were having a tough morning with the turkeys, partly because we sounded like a small army walking through the woods.

We followed a trail that led to the bottom of the canyon and hadn't been walking long when we found this buck lying in the creek bottom. We presume it was shot in the fall, and it must have been late in the season due to the location of the deer by a popular trail. We were simply amazed at how nice of a buck it was - a monster by our standards. He grossed over 176 B & C.

The reason we refer to it as Jackson's Buck is that this was one of my son Jackson's last hunts. He fought a courageous battle with cancer, but passed away only three weeks later at the age of ten. We will always remember that precious day with Jackson. He absolutely loved hunting, fishing, the outdoors, and people. He was a true inspiration to all of us, and all who knew Jackson were better from it. ~ *Scott Baldwin*

# Ken Preston
## Latah County, 2001

KEN PRESTON

I had found a big buck's rubs just before the 2001 season opener. To me, they were like finding uncut diamonds on top of the ground. He was clearly making a conscious selection with his choice of rub trees, choosing only mountain maples 4-6 inches in diameter. I knew from the size of the rubs - and the deep impressions his hooves left in the forest duff - that this was indeed a special buck.

I decided to leave him alone until at least mid November, when he might be more exploitable. However, on October 11, while on what was supposed to be a relaxed scouting excursion, a case of wanderlust led me too far into the deep timber. In order to be out of the woods by an hour after nightfall, I had to take a more direct route home. It was a route that would take me across the big buck's home ridge.

Light was fading quickly when I reached the area of his rubs. I paused briefly and admired his latest graffiti. The rain was a steady drizzle, and smoke from some burning slash piles nearly a mile away was drifting low through the woods. It was a serendipitous reminder of one of my favorite sayings, which is "move like smoke".

I worked my eyes through the timber, probing each open crevice until it dead-ended. Then I gingerly stalked forward a few steps at a time.

I had just taken a step around a large red fir when I caught a big buck doing the same. It was one of those breathless moments where time stops, a hunter's heart stops, and there is a very brief period of disbelief. We were facing each other, and I had beaten the odds by seeing him first. He raised his nose upward to search the air, showing me the underside of his beams, exposing the magnificence of a 26-inch-wide rack. A slight skiff of smoke glided between us, and I used that moment to ease down to one knee and lay the crosshairs on his chest. He dropped where he stood, no more than 20 feet from another of his freshly rubbed maples.

# Ken Preston
## Latah County, 2007

KEN PRESTON

hat November 2007 morning was perfectly scripted for a still-hunter. I had begun walking behind a gated Forest Service road in Latah County an hour before daylight. The wet snow had turned into a rain/snow mix when I turned off the logging road and began to stealth my way into the big timber.

The first deer I saw was a small 5x4. His neck was bulged, and he slashed his front hooves until he had carved out a black hole. He then proceeded to thrash his antlers in the cedar branch that hung above his fresh scrape. After a couple of minutes, he lifted his tail and trotted away, never knowing that I had been watching him. He felt the excitement that was in the air, as did I.

By 9 a.m. it was a full-on rain. I was able to glide so silently that I had to remind myself to slow down. I was soaked, but nevertheless, I was in heaven.

By 1:30 p.m., the rain had eased to a light mist. I walked up on a doe and fawn as they fed. I let them serve as scented decoys for 15 minutes before they browsed themselves into dark timber, where all things disappear as if by magic.

The first scrape I found was black and fresh, and the aroma of newly disturbed earth was overpowering. A few feet away were two fresh rubs, like white bone with shreds of orange flesh lying at the base of the saplings. I then found a larger scrape, made with such aggression as to be beyond exciting - almost intimidating.

I found another rub and two more fresh scrapes. I was now placing each step as cautiously as if each boot were filled with nitroglycerin rather than rainwater.

Light was beginning to play out when the buck stepped from behind a large cedar with an air of authority. His rack was elegant and tall. His peripheral vision caught the raising of my rifle, but it was too late. He leaped only once, clearing the final log of his life, and dropped on the other side.

When I reached him, I was even more pleased than I had first imagined. His eye-guards were 10 and 12 inches long, on a 5x6 rack of beautiful color, and just for character, a two-inch kicker point stuck out of the back near the base.

It was the kind of day from which hunting dreams are made. I didn't get out of the woods with him until hours after dark. I was exhausted, soaked, cold, hungry, and smiling as wide as I could possibly smile.

Ken Preston took this massive 4x5 (above) and the big 5x5 (below) in 2009, one with a resident tag and one with an extra nonresident tag. These are just two more examples of Ken's exceptional success. Of his thoughts on hunting, Ken wrote, "I hunt all my bucks the same way-- the old fashioned "still-hunting" method. I just sneak and peek through the woods, staying stealthy and moving like smoke, as I always say. I like the romantic ambiance of years gone by, and pride myself on still retaining some of the old time values of woodsmanship, instinctual prowess, and relying on a well-honed game-eye. I guess you could say I'm an endangered species, because so few hunt that way anymore. I find it very challenging and rewarding, and I have no desire to do it any other way."

David Monger was hunting an old, logged over area with his dad and brother-in-law Thanksgiving week of 2007. They split up and took different routes around a large clearcut. David had just started up the far side when he saw what he thought was a bush with yellow leaves. He lifted his binoculars and was amazed to see a big buck bedded under some trees 400 yards away. He used a small ridge to screen his approach, and after 45 minutes, he topped the ridge less than 100 yards away. One shot through the neck anchored the buck instantly. David's great trophy buck field dressed 225 lbs. and scored in the high 150s.

Tristan Stacy was on a 2006 late-season bowhunt in Unit 15 with his friend Dean Mc-Clellan when this heavy buck came strolling by his tree stand. It had been a long day, and he had been struggling to stay warm and keep focused. Seeing a big buck is just what he needed, and he arrowed him at 20 yards.

BUCK STAAB

Buck Staab took this awesome 5x4 in Lewis County in 2003. Mark Whitman had asked him to "brush dog" on a cow elk hunt, and toward the end of the day, Mark said, "I'll beat the brush for you this time. I'm gonna chase a big buck out to you." Mark went into the timber and promptly did just that. The buck gross scores 170-2/8.

BUCK STAAB

Buck's son, Justin, is following in his dad's footsteps. This Lewis County buck is a whopper, net scoring 158-1/8. Buck sent Justin down a strip of timber while he went another way. He jumped a buck and later heard a shot. He didn't think it was Justin because of the direction, but it was. Justin saw the buck, took off running, and was able to make the most important shot he's ever taken.

DAN MCCLURE

Cindy Moffis says that hunting with her brothers, Gary, Bob, Dan, and Mike Mc-Clure is a blessing. In November 2001 she harvested this beautiful buck, but gives credit to Bob and Dan. She shot him and then stalked toward him with Dan. They came in 100 yards above him with the wind blowing hard. She shot again and the buck rolled downhill. Luckily, after 75 yards, he stopped. On Christmas, Gary and Bob gave her the buck's previous year's shed antlers - her most treasured gift. This Idaho County buck grosses 157-3/8 and nets 150-1/8.

JOE SPARKS

In 1994, Jack McLaughlin (right) was hunting with Joe Sparks, who has a 175-7/8 typical. It was the last day of the season, and they rattled this 150-class buck in very slowly after a long cat-and-mouse session. Jack was able to put him down, ending the season on a high note.

Randy Clemenhagen killed this handsome 170 gross typical in 1994, just a year before his giant 222-1/8 non-typical. He had picked up some sheds from this buck, and knew he frequented the area. He shot at him in 1993 but missed, so the next year, on Thanksgiving, he staked out some does and waited. He was rewarded for his patience when the buck came to court Randy's "live decoys."

Only one year after taking his great 198-1/8 B&C non-typical, 17-year-old Luke Finney was back at it. It was fall of 1999, and he was hunting with his uncle, Gary Finney (left) and his dad, Jack (middle). Gary drove this buck out of the brush, and Luke says it sounded like elk coming at him. A 4x4 came out first, followed by this big 8x10 buck, which scored around 172.

Jack Palmer and Bob McClure, with a couple of big bucks from southern Idaho County on one amazingly productive day.

Mike Marek poses with his majestic Benewah County buck from 2007. It was a late November afternoon and Mike thought he'd try his hand at rattling. Fifteen minutes after he first clashed antlers, two bucks came to investigate at the same time. He shot the bigger one. The body mass on this huge buck is stunning.

Craig Knott shot this beautiful 160-class typical in Latah County in 2006. He had spent the first part of the day helping a friend get a cow elk packed out. Now tired and sore, he decided to take the afternoon whitetail hunt a bit easier. He left walking right from his house and eventually laid eyes on a deer in dark timber. He raised and lowered his rifle several times before he could verify what it was. His shot was true, and the buck died with his antlers in the ground. Craig actually videoed this buck from his kitchen window the previous winter.

This uniquely palmated double-droptine buck was taken by Jon Clough in Kootenai County in 2006. It was raining when he jumped him, but he never got a good look. Jon then circled down below and sat for five hours in the rain and wind watching a clearcut. His instinct told him to go back, and it worked. Jon saw this buck chasing a doe. Two shots resulted in the buck crashing into a tree. The buck gross scored 157-6/8. As Jon said, "What a thrill to walk up to."

Nathan Collins (left) poses with his big, handsome Latah County buck, taken in 2005 while hunting with Sean Watkins. A good friend of the author's, Gary Lester, shot at this buck and spooked it to Nathan, who made his shot count. Nathan saw the buck out of his peripheral vision and thought it was a rabbit, and nearly ignored it. After an intense five-minute stalk, he had his buck.

Denny Diaz is one happy hunter after taking this big buck late in the 1988 season. He was hunting in the Waha area.

In 2008, Tracy Bennett had found a couple of good bucks using a large stubble field. On the second day of the season, he was in position before daylight. When it started to get light, he saw deer moving, heading for their bedding area. When he thought they had all left, this buck showed up. One shot off of his bipod and the buck was down. He grosses 158-1/8 as a 7x7.

Tracy bought an extra nonresident tag that same fall, and waited for the rut. He had nine vacation days, and he and Lance Uppendahl hunted every day. They had seen too many bucks to count when this buck finally showed up chasing a doe in a field. They got permission to hunt there, but the buck was too far away that night. The next morning they spotted him chasing a doe and Tracy was able to take him. He's a 7x6 that grosses 162-7/8.

318

Tracy was rattling on a hunt in 2007 when this buck came out of the thick brush across the canyon from him. After getting set up, he touched off his .300 RUM and made a great one-shot kill. The buck ended up gross scoring 157-6/8.

Lester McDonald took this unique corkscrew droptine buck in Adams County in 2008. Northern Adams County represents the extreme southwest range (of any significance) of whitetails in Idaho.

Nik Galloway, who took a 185-4/8 non-typical when he was just 13, has taken as many big whitetails as anyone in the state. He took this great buck in 2009. He was hunting a new area and spotted this buck at dusk while glassing. He came back the next day and was able to find the great buck again.

In 2007, Nik had been watching this buck all summer and has video of the buck from scouting trips. He had last seen the buck in early September, and spent nearly 20 days hunting him, but never laid eyes on him again until November 20. It was close to a county road, with significant pressure, and he began to think it just wasn't going to happen. The buck net scores approximately 163.

Nik Galloway (right) had seen this big typical in a bean field while scouting in 2006. On November 18, he and Drew Mossman went out together, and found this buck across a canyon when the fog lifted. They watched for 15 minutes as he chased a doe, finally getting a great shot after being patient. The buck nets in the 168 range, and was aged at 8-1/2 by Fish and Game.

Back on November 23, 1996, only four years after killing his 185-4/8 non-typical, Nik was back at it again. He was supposed to go to school that day, but classes got canceled, so he went hunting close to home. He caught this buck trailing a doe and grunting. He passed on the shot once, but got a better view and reconsidered. This Clearwater County buck nets right around 163.

The author, Ryan Hatfield (left), and Paul Snider, Jr. pose with two nice 4x4s from 2005. Ryan's buck grossed 144 and Paul's went 153. Paul's buck was old and he probably did it a favor. This hunt took place on the Clearwater River.

Jack Snider took this handsome 150-class 5x5 while on a hunt with the author in 2006. They split up early and Jack assured Ryan that he was "giving him the good side." Jack caught this buck at first light when the buck was sneaking back to the timber after feeding in an opening.

Deb Taylor was hunting with her husband, Roger, when she took this great 7x7 in southern Idaho County. She had seen this buck earlier in the season, and held out for him for quite some time, much to the consternation of her husband. On the last day and at the last minute, she crossed paths with the buck near camp. The big 7x7 grosses in the mid 170s.

Ron Redmond, Bill Woltering, and Will Woltering show the results of a successful hunt in Benewah County around 1995. Will's big buck had exceptionally long main beams, each reported to measure over 29 inches.

Allen Burril poses with his wide, handsome trophy buck from the 2007 season. The big-bodied, wide-racked buck was taken in Clearwater County.

Cecil Cameron, whose 195-7/8 B&C Latah County buck is featured earlier in this book, took this photo of three unknown hunters posing with his trophy. They were out from Minnesota on a guided hunt with the same outfitter.

# Freak Antlers
## &
# Rare Occurrences

DALLEN LAMBSON

Kyle Bates was hunting in Unit 2 in 1987 when he happened upon what looked like two big bucks doing battle. Kyle shot at the one that was standing up, killing it right on the spot. When he approached, he noticed that neither buck was moving. Upon closer inspection, Kyle discovered the other buck was dead already, the victim of a broken back. The bucks weren't fighting; they had been locked together and the buck Kyle shot was trying to get away. Mostly out of curiosity, he took the locked set to Jack McNeel at the IDFG Regional Office in Coeur d'Alene. The rack has one G-2 that was broken off, likely in the fight. After Jack scored it, and unofficially figured in the broken G-2 the same size as the other side, it was determined that the buck would have scored 183-4/8. In other words, at that time, it would have been the Idaho state record typical. Also, take a look at the main beams on the bigger buck. They come completely back together, which is an amazingly rare trait.

H-87 White-tail bucks after a three-day fight near Farragut, Idaho

Bucks with locked up antlers are not uncommon. It's a slow and agonizing death if they can't "sort it out". This photo was taken in the early 1900s. The inscribed caption says, "White-tail bucks after a three-day fight near Farragut, Idaho."

Dana Daily and his son had been hunting elk all morning and were on their way back to the pickup when Dana saw this buck about 80 yards away. Deer season was open as well, so Dana took a closer look. The buck was still out feeding and had no idea they were there. Dana thought it was a nice 4x4, so he pulled up and took a shot with his .30-06. It hit the buck behind the shoulder and rolled it 70 yards downhill to the bottom of a creek. Dana had quite the surprise when he grabbed the antlers and had his first look. This three-antlered, uniquely built buck was taken in Benewah County.

DANA DAILY

Pat Mackey was hunting with Bob Stilson in Latah County in 1985 shortly after Pat graduated. They were doing a drive, with Pat on stand and Bob pushing. Bob saw a buck and shot, but it ran off. There was enough distance between the hunters that neither knew what the other was doing. When Pat saw a buck coming toward him, he shot and killed it. Only later would he find out that Bob had also shot at the buck. After talking it over, it was decided Pat would tag it. Neither hunter knew the buck had a "unicorn" point until they walked up to it.

Ben Brandt was the lucky hunter who took this exceptionally rare trophy. If you look closely, you'll see that this deer actually has four separate antlers.

For most hunters, taking a three-antlered or "unicorn" buck would be a once-in-a-lifetime treat. Not so for Ken Downard. He has taken two, both of which are pictured above. The buck on the left was taken in Boundary County in the late '80s. His other three-antlered buck was taken in Bonner County just a couple of years prior.

Here are a couple of very unique trophies, both with damage to the left antler and both with exceptionally massive bases. The left antler on the buck pictured above left actually has a nine-inch base circumference – among the biggest ever from Idaho. Both of these bucks were supposedly picked up dead and are now part of a private collection.

Harold Smith took this buck in northern Idaho. With split beams on both sides to go with great mass and a big frame, this buck is truly a unique trophy.

The author photographed this buck at the Lewiston Gun & Horn show around 2007. The buck has a huge five-point frame on one side and a triple split beam on the other. The hunter was J. Curtis Blum.

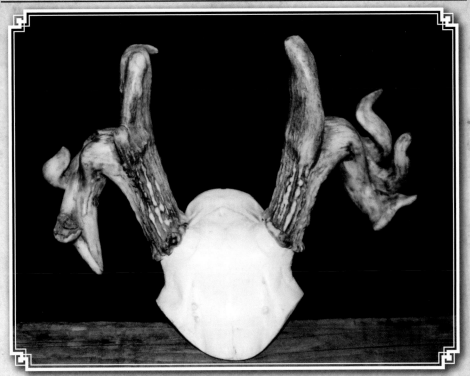

Steve Hornbeck shot this crazy-looking buck in Nez Perce County in 1983. The buck had been shot in his shoulder by a small-caliber weapon in early summer, and Steve feels that's likely responsible for the altered antler growth. The buck was severely infected, and the meat was not salvageable.

Denny Diaz killed this wild trophy buck in the lower Clearwater country in 2008. It was the last day of the season, and the weather was miserable. He was stuck at the tire shop for several hours and made it up to a spot fairly late. He encountered a young hunter and helped him get a doe, and then went on his way. Shortly after, he saw this buck and was able to bring it down. The pack out ended up being as miserable as the weather.

331

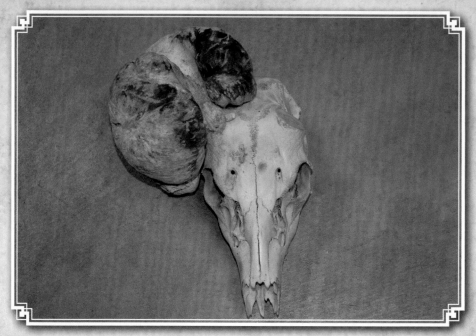

Frank Loughran, who took a 176-6/8 typical in Idaho County in 1987, also owns this amazing oddity. This buck's right antler had a major tumor, which at over 21 inches around, is as big as you'll ever find. It was found by a hunter after someone else had found it, cut off the good antler, and left the real treasure behind.

Casey Marek thought the buck on the left was a small one until he walked up on it and saw points going everywhere. The 11x11 deer was taken in Benewah County in 2005. He and his cousin, Mike Marek, were watching a doe, and just before dark, the buck came calling. The buck on the right is his grandpa's. This amazingly palmated buck was taken by Edward Miller in the late 1950s. It was taken with a bow in Shoshone County.

Russ Brisboy killed this big whitetail around 1990 in Bonner County. It was Thanksgiving morning, and he encountered this buck nearly instantly that morning. He used a .30-30 to take his trophy. Judging from the way the base of the right antler grew, this buck had to have been fairly miserable.

Denny Diaz found this wild-looking cactus buck alongside the Lochsa River in Idaho County in 1981. The buck had winterkilled and died right at the river's edge. He says that the buck's body and skull were both enormous. Cactus bucks are the result of physical, chemical, or hormonal castration and lack the necessary testosterone to grow and shed their antlers in a normal manner. Regardless, the uniqueness makes this one amazing trophy.

# Spectacular
# Shed
# Antlers

DALLEN LAMBSON

These are three sets of shed antlers from Steve Hornbeck's 220-2/8 non-typical, which was taken in Lewis County in 2000. The front set is from when the buck was four years old. The middle set is from the buck's fifth year, when he really blossomed, scoring in the 200-plus range as a non-typical and 170 as a typical. The set in the back is from the buck's sixth year, which shows a slight regression – 180s non-typical and 150s typical. The next year, he was back in a big way, with a 220-inch rack – the same year that ultimately ended with his encounter with Steve Hornbeck. Steve found some of these sheds, and was able to acquire the others.

A close-up of the buck as a five-year-old (left) and as a six-year-old (right). The buck's characteristic low sweeping beams and heavy mass are spectacular.

# Steve Hornbeck
## North-Central Idaho, 1990s

**Steve Hornbeck spent thousands of hours over several years trying to find the antlers of this buck, in hunting season when attached to its skull, and after the buck shed them each year. It's remarkable in several ways. First, the buck was not just any ordinary buck. It was a prime specimen that was pushing state record status. Secondly, to see this deer's antlers over such an incredible period of time, from an unbelievable three-year-old to when he died as an 11-year-old, is just phenomenal. Below is what Steve wrote about a buck simply known as "Big José."**

W hat you see on the staircase is the one thing that drives all obsessed whitetail hunters to lengths even we cannot truly imagine until viewed in retrospect. The pursuit of the elite is what drags us out from under warm blankets into a realm that is often cold, wet, windy, and dark in the predawn hours, so we can be in the precise position we feel will allow us to fulfill lifelong dreams. The buck that grew all these antlers will forever be an unfulfilled dream, but my relationship with him yields ongoing rewards to this day.

My antler hunting Lab (Louis) found the first shed off of him in spring of '91 (rack of '90), which we were quick to mate up. I knew then that if allowed to mature, this buck could easily surpass the B&C minimum of 170 in a year or two, as he was only 3-1/2 years old and would net in the 150s with a 15-inch inside spread. I hunted him in '91 and '92 without laying eyes on him in summer, fall, or winter.

I came to own his '92 sheds (rack of '91) through some heavy negotiating after I heard that an acquaintance of mine had found them. He had exploded into a net 160s typical at 4-1/2 years old.

In December of '92, I finally laid eyes on him alive under an apple tree. The antlers he carried that year would elude me for many years, and even now I'm not sure I have them paired correctly.

I got serious in '93 about hunting this buck, and hunted him with a dedicated trigger in '94, '95, and '96. If it wasn't him, the trigger went untouched. A lot of deer walked on his behalf. I did have a few shot opportunities at him, but they were always low-percentage shots and he seemed to have a force field around him.

The set of antlers fourth down from the top is from when he was 6-1/2 years old (rack of '93). This set grossed in the 190s and would net in the low to mid 180s. Louis (my Lab) again helped me collect this set from the field, and it is this "version" of him that I have on video. To this day, the video is one of my most prized outdoor-related possessions.

"Big José", as I came to call him, died in 1998 under the fang of a cat, after being wounded in the left front leg by a hunting partner of mine on the last evening of the '98 season. His skull is on the bottom step, and a tooth section confirmed my long-held suspicion that he was 11-1/2 years old at the time of his death. His skull is next to his 10-1/2-year antler that I picked up in January of '98, after having watched him from a distance of over 400 yards in the middle of a vicious sleet/snowstorm. I thought he had been dead for a couple of years, but I was wrong.

I hunted this deer for not less than 1,000 hours, and spent well in excess of 3,000 hours in an attempt to gain his antlers and a greater understanding of where, when, and how he survived in spite of my dedicated efforts.

It is him and others like him that we who are obsessed imagine and conjure up to keep us motivated as we climb that next ridge in pursuit of a dream. From 1991 until 1998, he was my dream.

**The 1993 antlers carried by Big José, as a six-year-old. The buck grossed in the low 190s and netted in the low to mid 180s, and could possibly have been the state record typical if the buck had been taken by a hunter.**

# Chris Bier
## Bonner County, Late 2000s

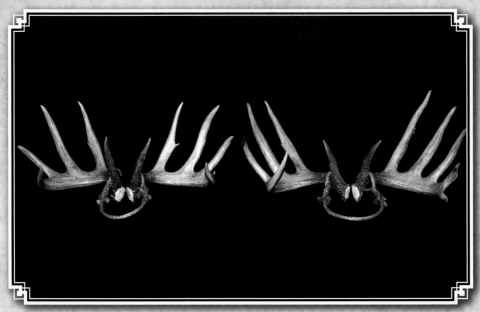

During the mid to late 2000s, Chris Bier developed a "relationship" with a big north-ern Idaho whitetail – one that was pushing state record status. He knew where the buck wintered and was lucky enough to pick up multiple sets of shed antlers from the buck. Above are the best two sets. The set on the left, found in March of 2007, scores 159-2/8 (178-180 gross after adding an inside spread). The biggest set, shown on the right, was found in January 2008 and scores 171-6/8 (190- 193 gross; 183-185 net typical). As of this writing, the buck was still alive, albeit on the downhill slide. Here's what Chris wrote about one of Idaho's greatest whitetails.

L ike many hunters, I love to be in the mountains. January is typically a slow work time for me, so I often find myself out looking for antlers. I'll grab my snow-shoes and my "antler hound" black lab, Ruby, and we hit the game trails.

Over the years, I have learned where the deer go every winter, and they like to come back to the same wintering places year after year. Several times I have found shed antlers from the same buck over different years from the exact same hillside. They are creatures of habit and pattern.

Several years ago, I went out on one of my trails in March after the snows had melted off. I had just stepped into a small alder patch when I saw the biggest whitetail ant-ler I had ever seen, lying right in front of me. I had probably walked over that antler half a dozen times that winter. Two weeks later, after crawling through every fir thicket, poking through every leftover snowbank and everything in between, I found the other side. Those antlers, as sheds, scored 79-5/8 each side!

Word spread and trail cameras sprouted like knapweed in the "neighborhood", which is nothing but woods until you get to Montana. Nobody got a picture of him. Come hunting season, I was sure I'd tag that buck (plenty of other hunters thought they would, as well). Nobody saw him. Hunting season came and went.

Around Christmastime, the same buck showed up in my camera again! Snow was deep by then, and the thought was that he's been up high in the mountains and had been driven down by snow. I looked every day and once again, I found both his antlers – this time in January. It was unbelievable. The second year scored 82-2/8 and 89-4/8. Add a decent spread in there and you're talking record-breaking buck.

More trail cameras went out, but again, nobody saw him. That hunting season I watched some nice bucks go by, wanting and hoping badly that my monster buck would step out in front of me. No such luck.

This buck became the subject of many campfire talks. Everyone who knew deer all came to the same conclusion; he didn't get that big by being stupid.

After the snow got deep, he came back to the same wintering ground, this time with a big herd. The winter of 2008-09 was deep in the Panhandle. My camera caught more images of him, and showed that he had sprouted a kicker at the base of one antler, and lost a point. He's getting old now. That set scores 84-2/8 and 77-7/8.

Summer of 2009 came, and again no trail cameras took any pictures of him. He's an elusive creature.

I get asked by lots of folks if I hunt that buck. Yes and no. I look up the creek where he most likely comes from, and I see square mile upon square mile of prime whitetail habitat. He could be anywhere. I just hunt like I usually do and whatever happens, happens. I do get around and poke into different spots, always in the back of my mind hoping to get a crack at him.

My common sense says he is too smart to get caught in the daylight exposed. Maybe he'll die of old age, or get taken down by predators; or maybe some lucky hunter will stumble onto the buck of a lifetime.

I can't help but wonder if one of those deer I've jumped out of thick brush - the ones where all you see is a tail flip and maybe a shiny brown tine as it rockets out of sight - could have been the monster?

I'll just wait again until the snows get deep and see if he comes back to spend Christmas in the same place again. If he does, I'll be ready.

CHRIS BIER

Chris Bier's trail camera picked up these images of the buck during its best year. If a hunter had taken this buck, it likely would have been in the top five typical ever taken in Idaho. These are some of the most significant live photos ever taken of a whitetail in Idaho.

STEVE HORNBECK

Steve Hornbeck has a penchant for finding antlers. A story about Steve and his ant-ler-seeking dogs was even featured in *North American Whitetail* magazine. Steve found this awesome set of sheds on a property he would later buy and currently lives. The deer's left antler scores 106-7/8 and was found back in 1984.

This shed antler, scoring 122-1/8, is currently the state record in the non-typical shed antler category. It is listed as having been found in Bonner County in 1950.

This magnificent buck was reportedly living clear down in Long Valley near Cascade in the early 2000s. No story was available, and it's not believed that anyone ever killed this buck. It is by far one of the more significant whitetails to ever come from "non-traditional" whitetail country in Idaho.

This set of matched shed antlers was reportedly found in northern Idaho, possibly around the Coeur d'Alene area. Not much information was available, nor is it known if anyone ever killed this tremendous double-drop-tine non-typical. Still, what an incredible find.

Steve Alie and Bill Woltering were hunting together near Potlatch around 1990. While they were hunting, Steve found this amazing set of matched sheds and gave them to Bill. Bill proceeded to hunt for him every day that fall, passing up 14 bucks and never shooting one. This double-droptine beauty is 31 inches wide, making it one of the widest bucks in Idaho history.

This huge set of shed antlers was found by loggers in Latah County in the early '80s. They had seen the buck, along with some other deer, coming in to feed on the moss of the downed trees, and eventually came across where the big buck had dropped both antlers. It looks as though it would score right around 200.

Denny Diaz has quite a collection of shed antlers, many of which he found himself. These thin but amazingly long-tined antlers were found on the lower Clearwater in a driveway outside of Kendrick in 1989. Given an inside spread, they reportedly would have scored near 177 net typical.

Denny also has these massive sheds, which were found in Clearwater County in 1985. The estimated score is 195.

343

These massive and somewhat palmated sheds were found north of Bonners Ferry, near the junction of Highways 1 and 95. The buck dropped his impressive headgear down on farm ground in the early 1980s. On the hoof, the buck would have scored approximately 176 net.

Another set from Denny's collection, this fantastic buck would have scored around 182 net. They were found in the Post Falls area in 1990. Photos don't do justice to how impressive this buck is, particularly in regard to the main beams.

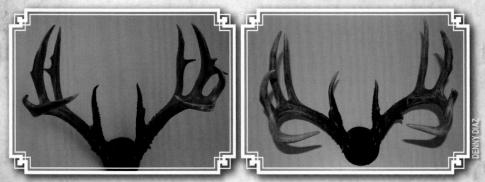

The buck above right was taken by Brian Dunlap in Nez Perce County around 2005. The buck had been hit poorly by another hunter, and Brian found it much later, wounded, and finished it off, according to Denny Diaz. The left photo is the sheds from the same buck. Both sets appear to break the 170 mark.

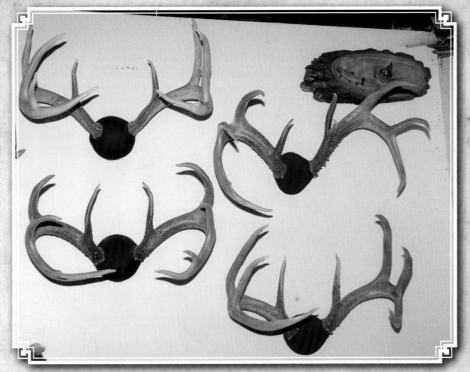

Denny Diaz found most of these sheds, all of which are from the same buck, in the early 1980s. He spent over 100 days trying to find the buck, but it never happened. The buck was pushing the 180 mark as a 4x4 in its largest set.

This set of sheds was found in the same area as the sheds above, at nearly the same time. Denny thinks the bucks were related, maybe even brothers. To his knowledge, no one ever killed this big buck.

COURTESY OF RUSTY KIRTLEY

Bobby Jenkins found these shed antlers in the spring while harrowing his property in Lemhi County a few years ago. They were less than five feet apart, and he almost ran them over with the tractor. The buck was never killed, at least to anyone's knowledge, but likely would have made the all-time record book. Ron Thompson had the sheds mounted after acquiring a cape.

# Index

**Kyle Kilborn snapped this great photo of a curious whitetail fawn high in the mountains in the Cuprum/Bear area near the Snake River Breaks. Far out of their historic element, whitetails are surviving and expanding in fringe areas due to changes in predator balances and habituation to humans.**

Mike Duplan, a good friend of the author's, took this breathtaking photo near Lake Pend Oreille in 2000. The buck is huge, and likely would have qualified for the record book. Perhaps even more impressive, though, is the pose. It's extremely original, and leaves no doubt the buck knows the score. The way he looks at the camera, it's almost as if to say, "Alright, I'm here. What are you gonna do about it?" Looking right into his eyes is almost paralyzing.

## MENT UNIT DESCRIPTIONS

...lary County and that part of Bonner
...he Pend Oreille River, Pend Oreille
...River. (Myrtle Creek and David
...es—Closed).

...s of Bonner and Kootenai Counties
...ribed boundary: Beginning at the
...Oreille River and the Idaho-Wash-
...east along the Pend Oreille River
...ce east and south along the west-
...shoreline of Pend Oreille Lake to the south boundary
fence of the Farragut Game Management Area, thence west
along the south boundary fence of the Farragut Game Management Area to its intersection with State Highway 54
at Good Hope, thence west along State Highway 54 to
U.S. Highway 95, thence south along U.S. Highway 95...
Coeur d'Alene, thence west along U...
Idaho-Washington state line, thence...
line to Pend Oreille River, the point...
gut Wildlife Management Area and...
Closed).

Unit 3 — Those portions of Kootenai
ewah ... hin the f...
Begin... aries, ther...
95 (A... ... rsection...
Road)...
Highw...
th...

the Clearwa...
the Clearw...
River, the...

Unit 10 -
Idaho Cour...
Beginning a...
water River...
the Clearwa...
Old Camp...
of Swamp...
the Dent-Elk...
with Elk Cr...
River, thenc...
Road to Go...
ter-Roundtop...
Goat Mount...
Round...

...d R...
...ke ...de,
...rr ...eak...
...d ...e L...
...t ...out...
...g ... A...

...ay ... to

...western shoreline of ... ...olet,
...wah Lakes t... the St. Joe Riv... ...heast
...main chan...l of the St. Joe... ...ries,
...of begin...g. (Heyburn St...

...— Those ...rtions of Bon...
...wah ...unties within ...e...
...Be...ning at the ...

...west
...outh
...outh

Holly wood-B...
do... n Snake...
C...ek to its...
...ater River,...

Unit 10-A
Counties y...
...ning at...
River, ...nce...
to ... mout...
...on with...